More
Than a Trial

More Than a Trial

The Struggle Over Captain Dreyfus

ROBERT L. HOFFMAN

THE FREE PRESS
A Division of Macmillan Publishing Co., Inc.
NEW YORK

Collier Macmillan Publishers
LONDON

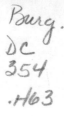

Copyright © 1980 by The Free Press
A Division of Macmillan Publishing Co., Inc.

The Free Press
A Division of Macmillan Publishing Co., Inc.
866 Third Avenue, New York, N.Y. 10022

Collier Macmillan Canada, Ltd.

Library of Congress Catalog Card Number: 80–642

Printed in the United States of America

printing number

1 2 3 4 5 6 7 8 9 10

Library of Congress Cataloging in Publication Data

Hoffman, Robert Louis
  More than a trial.

  Bibliography: p.
  Includes index.
  1. Dreyfus, Alfred, 1859-1935. I. Title.
DC354.H63   944.081'092'4 [B]   80-642
ISBN 0-02-914770-0

Except for the cartoon, "Rothschild," all illustrations in this book are reproduced by permission of the Houghton Library, Harvard University.

Contents

Preface

The story of the Dreyfus Affair has often been told before. But new knowledge now helps put the Affair in a rather different perspective, and for that reason I have thought it worth examining again.

In Chapters One and Two can be found the familiar story—accusations of espionage against a French captain, his trial, conviction and imprisonment on Devil's Island, then later the endless argument over evidence and other crimes alleged. Here this part of the story is radically simplified and shorn of most of the complicated and mystifying details that have fascinated many others. In the rest of the book I try to show how and why the Dreyfus Affair became very much "more than a trial," how it was indeed a virtual civil war.

I have concentrated in writing this book not on the evidence of alleged crime but on what I call the artifacts of the struggle: the polemical tracts, newspaper articles, speeches, broadsides, and manifestos; the recollections of combatants and bystanders; the cartoons, posters, photographs, poetry and doggerel, novels, plays, and even toys and games that were produced by the Affair. The artifacts show us, I think, the best part of the story, the part most worth telling. This book cannot reproduce or describe more than a small portion of them, but it can synthesize what examining them has enabled me to see of the age in which they were created.

Much of my work was made possible by Lee M. Friedman, a Boston attorney who graduated from Harvard College in 1893, just before the Dreyfus Affair began. Throughout his life he collected the artifacts of the struggle. In 1957 he bequeathed this collection to Harvard, together with an important Judaica collection and a substantial fund to maintain and improve both. In 1964 Harvard used part of this fund to purchase another major Dreyfus Affair collection, that of Léon Lipschutz of Paris. The Friedman bequest with this addition is housed in the Houghton Library of Harvard. It is augmented by substantial material in this and other Harvard University libraries.

The riches included in all this are astonishing. The only collection of comparable worth is that of the Bibliothèque Historique de la Ville de Paris. At Harvard is just about everything that might be thought important, plus innumerable items of less significance when taken individually, but priceless in combination for rediscovering the living spirit of the struggle. There are, for example, three huge scrapbooks assembled by admirers for the anti-Semite leader Edouard Drumont. His and anti-Semitism's political successes are commemorated here, with such items as photographs, posters, clippings, cartoons—and even "anti-Jewish confetti": bits of paper with anti-Semitic ditties, each verse on a different piece.

Writing the book has put me in debt to many people who have stimulated and helped me. Especially important have been those who read and criticized parts or all of the manuscript—Paul and Liliana Vogt, Warren Roberts, Dan White, Thomas Beck, Donald Birn, and Valerie Hoffman—as well as Marte Shaw, formerly Curator of the Houghton Library Reading Room.

The Dreyfus Affair is the kind of story that makes people wish for a cast of characters with identifying labels. This requirement is met here by providing such labels along with each name entered in the index.

1

Crimes and Cover-up

Struggle in the Dreyfus Affair whirled around court trials. There were so many trials that it is scarcely possible to count them all. Evidence and legal issues became the principal material of controversy.

Judicial proceedings in the case of Alfred Dreyfus himself extended over a period of nearly twelve years. A number of Army officers involved in these proceedings were themselves charged with criminal misconduct, and a few were prosecuted. Other Frenchmen were brought to court by the State or individuals for libel and slander. There were trials for espionage, attempted murder, bribery, rioting, seeking to overthrow the government, and assaulting the President with a walking stick, all of them part of the Affair.

After nearly five years Dreyfus was freed in 1899, and later amnesty legislation quashed nearly all the prosecutions and lawsuits still in process. However, the main issues of the Dreyfus case remained unresolved. Their examination by the Army and the courts continued until 1906, when a way was found to exonerate him. Even then many believed the court's action illegal.

Evidence in all of this had rapidly grown to proportions almost beyond the powers of intellect to encompass. Most of this growth was a matter of grasping for anything that might damn Dreyfus. The bulk of the documents and testimony brought forth to prove him guilty was actually irrelevant. Of the relevant material, none withstood critical scrutiny of its evidential worth. The most damning evidence proved to be spurious: forged documents, perjured testimony, and even documents that never existed, although many readily believed that they did. Throughout the Affair, the prosecution relied on forceful, repeated assertion of its allegations, however ill-founded, and the defense upon reasoned criticism. For a long time the former proved more persuasive.

Simply put, there was no substantial evidence that Alfred Dreyfus was guilty of any crime. It has, however, been very difficult to put the case simply. With the struggle having been fought over evidence, histories of the Affair have concentrated on this evidence, the concomitant drama of the major trials, and the heroism of those determined to fight against all odds on the behalf of Dreyfus.

Many aspects of the case do remain cloaked in uncertainty, including matters that were thought most important at the time. Production of novel and ingenious explanations of these mysteries is almost a minor industry in France.

Now, after so much time has passed, the old controversies over evidence need not be fought any longer, and the remaining mysteries have value only as puzzles for idle curiosity. Most of what so exercised the minds of Frenchmen fighting over Alfred Dreyfus need no longer concern us. There never was an adequate basis for *suspecting* him of a crime, much less for convicting him. That much was not plain at first, because the supposed proofs of his guilt were kept secret. Once they became known, it was indeed plain that Dreyfus was not guilty. The struggle, the mountains of useless and fraudulent evidence, and the confusion that suffused the Affair all resulted from the persistent reluctance of most people to admit what should have been obvious, even though veiled by a screen of lies and nonsense. The persistence and passion with which both sides maintained their arguments now matter more than the arguments themselves.

Exactly how the Dreyfus Affair began is among the not quite resolved mysteries. In the General Staff of the French Army was a small counterintelligence unit known as the Statistical Section; it consisted of a few officers and some lower-level staff in Paris, plus some agents in the field. Like all officers on the General Staff, those in this unit were a highly select group, supposedly the best in the nation. Brave fighting men they probably were, but they made terrible counterspies.

Sometime in September 1894, the Statistical Section obtained a *bordereau*, or memorandum of goods to be delivered, announcing that information about the French Army was being sent. With typical inefficiency, the date of receipt by the Section was not recorded, and the manner of its transmission has been much disputed. Ostensibly it had been stolen by a French agent from the German military attaché in Paris, who it appeared was receiving information regularly from the document's author.[1]

General Staff officers studying the *bordereau* assumed that the information it listed was very important and secret. They concluded that it could only have been written by a French artilleryman among the officers being rotated through the various General Staff sections for training purposes. Later, critical examination proved these beliefs to be wrong: The information was less significant and more easily come by than the investigators supposed, and the document was unlikely to have been written by anyone trained in artillery or among the rotating officers. Both the invalid conclusions and their refutation came primarily from evidence internal to the *bordereau* itself.

Working with their incorrect inferences, the investigators soon found that Captain Alfred Dreyfus fitted their requirements for a suspect. They thought they detected a resemblance between the handwriting of the *bordereau* and that of Dreyfus; the resemblance was not at all close, but this was explained by the supposition that he had attempted to disguise his hand.

Suspicion thus quickly fell on the unfortunate Dreyfus. He was arrested on October 15, imprisoned, and interrogated at length. Later the reasons for suspecting him seemed so insubstantial to his defenders that they generally believed he had been picked out mainly or solely because he was a Jew. Anti-Semitism certainly colored the whole Affair, and irrational behavior came easily to be understood as a matter of prejudice. Sometimes it was just stupidity and stubbornness, and that seems to have been the case here.

The investigating officers later amply demonstrated that they were neither adept nor practiced at reasoning based on the discriminating use of evidence. Here they seem to have leapt hastily to foolish conclusions, then stubbornly refused to consider alternatives. They may also have been anti-Semites, but there is insufficient reason to believe prejudice determined the identification of Dreyfus as a suspected spy and traitor.

However, believing him a traitor was not enough to convict him of the crime, even in a military court. The case against Dreyfus seemed weak even to those on the General Staff who were handling it. Had the investigation remained secret, as it was supposed to be, the case might well have been dropped for want of evidence.

Two weeks after the captain's arrest, though, word leaked out that someone had been arrested for espionage, and shortly after that Dreyfus was identified as the presumed culprit. The news appeared first in *La Libre Parole*, a popular daily paper whose stated primary purpose was anti-Semitic propaganda, expressed in the most violent terms. Presumably the secret investigation was disclosed by a General Staff officer who wanted the predictably resulting public clamor to force the Army to prosecute Dreyfus.[2] If so, the stratagem succeeded.

General Auguste Mercier, the Minister of War, was already in an extremely precarious political position. Through mistakes and character defects he had aroused wide animosity in the officer corps, the press, and the chambers of the French parliament. He was in danger of being removed from his office at any moment. Now the Dreyfus case created an enormous uproar, with the many anti-Semitic newspapers and politicians screaming about Jewish treason. Even those who did not scream much about Jews were generally still strident about the treason and its irresolute prosecution. They knew neither the charges nor the evidence, but this did not matter: Newspapers daily published further details of supposed evidence and horrendous crimes attributed to Dreyfus, retailing as factual the rumors then current. When rumor did not suffice, fresh stories of crimes and evidence were invented by the ever imaginative press.

Mercier was endlessly and viciously damned for having permitted the Jew to be placed in a sensitive post in the first place, and still more for not rushing forward with his prosecution and condemnation. "Jewry" was supposed to have made a tool of Mercier, inducing him through influence or money to suppress the case against a Jewish officer.

Under such pressure, Mercier succumbed and decided to court-martial Dreyfus. The other Government ministers went along with him, for they were subject to much the same pressure and, besides, he assured them that the evidence was indeed substantial. While they knew him to be a blundering incompetent, they took him at his word. As so often happened later in the Affair, customarily cynical people assumed that a man of honor would not lie about or misrepresent the facts—and Army officers were surely all honorable men.

For Mercier to elude political ruin, Dreyfus had to be convicted. To other officers, conviction was essential to redeem the Army's honor after discovery of this traitor in their midst. The officers involved in the case easily convinced themselves that Dreyfus really was guilty. Once certain of this, they were most unlikely to consider any alternative, for theirs is a profession where decisions are rarely subject to challenge or change.

The public was also universally convinced that Dreyfus was an especially vile traitor. Many accepted the anti-Semites' claims that French Jews were "cosmopolitan" aliens, ready to betray France through ties to their brethren in Germany. Even people ordinarily skeptical about political provocation and polemical excesses allowed themselves to be deceived. Frequent wide repetition of unfounded allegations eventually produced belief. The most outrageous and strident of the papers, La Libre Parole and L'Intransigeant, thrived on the public's susceptibility to lies; the skeptical might discount what they said, but much of it could also be read elsewhere. Mass circulation newspapers might be comparatively honest much of the time, but on this case they had to make the most of so sensational a story, if only for the sake of circulation. Even newspapers that ordinarily avoided sensationalism could not afford to leave such unverified stories alone.

Moreover, the government had examined the case for a month before the news leaked out, and after that more than a month passed before completion of the pretrial investigation and the ordering of a court-martial. Such deliberate review of the case before decisive action seemed to demonstrate that the government had crushing proofs. General Mercier claimed just that in an interview published in the newspaper *Le Figaro* on November 28.

This case would have caused a huge sensation even had Dreyfus not been Jewish. He was a captain on the General Staff ot the French Army and a graduate of two citadels of elitism, the Ecole Polytechnique and the Ecole Supérieure de Guerre. That made him a most important person, with high social rank despite his being a Jew, and with the presumption that he was a paladin of patriotism. That Dreyfus had supposedly violated these high expectations outraged most people so much that they were all the more likely to accept his guilt as definitely proved.

And all this made people far less likely to believe, years later, the "troublemakers" who dredged up the case again, claiming that Dreyfus was innocent after all.

The court-martial was held in Paris on December 19–22, 1894. Press and public were excluded, because it was alleged that facts to be disclosed in the trial were diplomatically and militarily sensitive. When the court unanimously found the defendant guilty of espionage, the verdict was generally accepted, just as it had been expected. The public still did not even know just what criminal acts actually had been imputed to Dreyfus. In addition to having been persuaded by the prior publicity, few could suppose that seven officer judges, all honorable men, might have found Dreyfus guilty if there were any doubt.[3]

In fact the prosecution never made a genuine case against the accused. It relied especially upon unfounded allegations given credence because authoritatively asserted by confident officers, men widely assumed incapable of testifying to anything but the truth. Documents said to incriminate Dreyfus appeared to do so only if one first accepted the proposition that the defendant was guilty. Handwriting experts concluded that the *bordereau* was written in his hand because they had first been told that other evidence amply proved his guilt. Eventually their testimony was effectively impeached.

Typical of the kind of thought involved was a supposedly crucial document that spoke of someone identified only by the initial, "D." That *could* be "D" for Dreyfus, hence it *was*. Incredibly, no real effort was made to consider alternative suspects with the same initial, although there was actually at least one possibility ready at hand. Besides, "D" could well have been a code identification rather than the initial letter of a real name.

If there had been enough of such dubious evidence, when regarded as an ensemble it might really have made Dreyfus look suspicious, but at the time there were only a few scraps. All the additions of later years failed to make a significant ensemble, and no single item of substantial evidential value ever was turned up. The only evidence that might have incriminated Dreyfus seriously was exposed as forged or perjured.

The evidence found decisive by the court-martial judges had even been kept secret from the defense. Under French law this procedure was completely impermissible and ultimately contributed to the annulment of the conviction in June 1899, and the ordering of a new court-martial. But it took the most bitter and protracted struggle to get any but "troublemakers" to admit either that the illegal action had occurred or that if it had, this was reason to reconsider the conviction.

In December 1894 it mattered only that the traitor be sufficiently punished. French law barred capital punishment for political crimes, and the Dreyfus case was adjudged political. Thus the only possible sentence was public degradation and life imprisonment "in a fortified place."

On all sides there was intense outrage that Dreyfus could not be executed. Anti-Semites consoled themselves, however, with the thought that because he was Jewish the traitor at least was not a true Frenchman. On the other hand, socialist leader Jean Jaurès, who eventually became the most eloquent defender of Dreyfus, insisted at this time that the traitor could in fact be legally executed but was getting favored treatment because he was a rich bourgeois officer. A private had recently been executed for much less, a trifle judged mutinous. In speaking of this to the Chamber of Deputies, Jaurès became so passionately abusive that the Chamber censured and temporarily excluded him from entry there.

Originally scheduled for January 4, 1894, the ritual degradation of Alfred Dreyfus was postponed until the next day, Saturday, the Jewish Sabbath. (The degradation is described in Chapter Three.) A law was hurriedly passed, making a desolate little tropical island off the South American coast into a prison just for him—Devil's Island. It had been a leper colony and was used for other prisoners only after Dreyfus left it. He spent more than four years there, alone except for jailers who would not speak to him. He had no recreation, no visitors, no news, and his mail was heavily censored. Until the end he did not know of the struggle being waged to free him.

For most of his defenders Dreyfus was always less a real person than a symbol for their crusade. Nevertheless, the conditions of his imprisonment were so severe that many defenders were all the more stirred to outrage. The selection of Devil's Island and the imposition of solitary confinement were penalties gratuitously added by General Mercier, and the prisoner's later confinement to irons and other mistreatment were also thought cruel and unwarranted. Indeed, the island was one of a group previously used as a prison colony but abandoned because most of the prisoners quickly died. The letters from Dreyfus in prison to his wife were published during the struggle;[4] the stoical fortitude and dignity reflected in them excited additional support for his liberation.

Dreyfus's family never ceased the effort to prove him innocent. His brother Mathieu gave up his work in the family textile firm and devoted himself for long years to exonerating Alfred and caring for his wife and children. At first there were very few sympathizers, just a handful whom the trial and its irregularities had left doubtful or who had been positively impressed by Alfred's protestations of innocence at his public degradation.

Many of those who remained convinced of Dreyfus's guilt really believed that there was a conspiracy organized by Jews to free the traitor. Consequently, throughout the Affair they spoke of "the Syndicate of Treason," "the Jewish Syndicate," "the Judaeo-Masonic Syndicate," and, most often, just "the Syndicate." The Syndicate was supposed to be orchestrating the campaign to free Dreyfus and marshaling huge sums to finance it and bribe journalists, witnesses, officials, and judges. It was thought that the Syndicate conspired to advance German as well as Jewish interests. Gentiles in league with it were "sellouts" to the German foe.

Instead of a syndicate there was just Mathieu acting alone at first and later with a few allies. He was a rich man and spent much in the Affair, but the fabled treasure chests were as unreal as the Syndicate itself. The French Jewish community and its leadership were committed to assimilation into the French nation. In an era of increasingly virulent anti-Semitism, Alfred

Dreyfus was a very dangerous embarrassment. They wanted no part of him or of any effort on his behalf, for that would keep people from forgetting that a Jew had been condemned for treason. Although Jews did give some support in the Affair's later stages, only two Jews besides Mathieu Dreyfus were to be important in Alfred's defense: Joseph Reinach and Bernard-Lazare. In his memoirs Mathieu wrote:

> We had been able to form a few convictions for ourselves, but what were these convictions in the face of hostile masses, in the face of a whole people who saw my brother as a disloyal soldier, a traitor to his country?
>
> On the one side, a family and a few friends; on the other, all the forces of society, the whole world that it was necessary to arouse.
>
> We were in the depths of an abyss, powerless to get out.
>
> However, I tried everything, I neglected not one piece of information, not one trail, however unlikely it might appear.[5]

Mathieu quietly visited many influential people seeking support and, sometimes, information—usually in vain. He tried many devices to obtain information, employing private detectives while he himself was kept under surveillance by police detectives. Swindlers tried to sell him counterfeit evidence. The police and Army became alarmed that his search for the real traitor was a potentially dangerous attempt to set up a straw man who would assume brother Alfred's guilt. They even sent agents who tried to trap him into the criminal purchase of supposed confidential government information or documents. Mathieu carefully avoided entrapment.

In early February 1895 Mathieu had consulted a clairvoyant called Léonie, and from her heard for the first time that evidence unknown to the defense had illegally been shown to the court-martial judges. Shortly afterward, on February 21, this was confirmed by the President of the Republic, Félix Faure, during an interview with an intermediary representing Mathieu, and Faure agreed to the latter's being told of this. Even though the President had admitted an illegal act, which alone was sufficient to overturn the conviction, few would concede that this illegality had occurred or that if it had, it was significant.

Gradually Mathieu learned other important fragments of what really had happened in the supposed espionage and the court-martial. He needed to expose what he had uncovered if Alfred's case were to be reconsidered. Still, he was quite circumspect, knowing that hostility to his brother was so great that untimely or incomplete exposure of the truth would bring rejection of their pleas. He worked with a talented young writer, Bernard-Lazare, to produce a tract presenting their case, but withheld publication until the moment was opportune.

Finally, in September 1896, a Paris newspaper, *L'Eclair*, published distorted revelations about the secret evidence at the Dreyfus court-martial. The articles' author and the informant for them are another mystery. Mathieu thought the time had finally come, and Lazare's pamphlet, "A Judicial Error: The Truth About the Dreyfus Affair," was published on November 6. The tract was mailed to 3,500 politicians, officials, journalists, and other molders of opinion. It was a well-done, persuasive piece, but the audience was too unreceptive for it to have much immediate effect. However, both the campaign for Alfred Dreyfus and reaction against it were mounting in intensity and attracting public attention. In a year they exploded into the gravest crisis the French Third Republic had seen.

At the same time, more important developments were going on unknown either to the public or the partisans of Alfred Dreyfus. Major Georges Picquart had assumed command of the Statistical Section a few months after its misdirected efforts had sent Dreyfus to Devil's Island. The new counterintelligence chief was to play the leading role in the drama of the Dreyfus Affair and become a hero admired all over the world, though despised by many of his countrymen. Picquart, an extremely capable officer, at forty-one became the Army's youngest lieutenant colonel. He was highly intelligent and cultivated, an intensely rational man who took evidence seriously and knew how best to use it. Few of his brother officers shared these qualities or his commitment to a republican constitution and ideology.

The Statistical Section had found indications that important Army secrets continued to be transmitted to Germany. In March 1896 the Section obtained a document (always referred to afterward as the *petit bleu*) which pointed to a French Army major, Ferdinand Walsin-Esterhazy, as the person responsible for the suspected espionage. He seemed to be an agent of the German military attaché in Paris, Colonel Max von Schwartzkoppen, to whom Dreyfus was supposed to have sent the *bordereau*.

Picquart investigated Esterhazy and found that he wá thoroughly corrupt and dissolute scoundrel, who had long since deserved dismissal from the Army. He was a stock market speculator badly in need of money and had evinced a suspiciously eager interest in confidential military information. An agent of Picquart twice saw Esterhazy visit the German embassy. Another agent's report from Germany further incriminated him.

When Picquart obtained examples of Esterhazy's handwriting in late August of 1896, he saw that it was identical to that of the *bordereau*. Picquart had been an observer at Dreyfus's trial and degradation; sure that the Jew was a traitor, he had made biting anti-Semitic remarks about him at the degradation. Now for the first time he examined the secret file containing the evidence shown to the Dreyfus court-martial judges but not the defense. Picquart saw with astonishment that this evidence did little if anything to prove Dreyfus's guilt. The conclusion seemed to him inescapable: Dreyfus was innocent, and there had been just one spy all along, Esterhazy.

Later there was additional evidence damning Esterhazy, and in 1898 he fled to England, where he confessed to having written the *bordereau* as a double agent acting for France to deceive the Germans. Many Frenchmen long refused to believe any accusations against him or his confession and came only to concede that he might also have been a spy, while Dreyfus remained guilty as charged.

There does still remain some not quite resolved mystery about who was communicating what information to whom, and for what reason. However, it is clear that Dreyfus was not guilty and highly probable that Esterhazy was the sole spy throughout, acting treasonably and for his own sake only. During the Affair this conclusion was the only reasonable one. Later the German military attaché, von Schwartzkoppen, confirmed it in recollections published posthumously in 1930, and this assessment has also been strengthened by more recent research, including electronic spectral analysis.[6]

Picquart brought the fruits of his investigations to Generals Boisdeffre, Billot, and Gonse—the Chief of Staff, War Minister, and Deputy Chief of Staff, respectively. They began by being skeptical about the new evidence and apprehensive about damage to the Army if its errors were made public. It was hard enough for generals ever to admit being mistaken, and from the beginning the Dreyfus case had been handled so badly that the potential harm to the Army's reputation and authority was very great.

By stages these and other generals as well as other officers became entangled in an ever more complex and bizarre cover-up, trying at any cost to preserve the fiction of Dreyfus's guilt. As events progressed, evidence was suppressed, obligatory action avoided, and court testimony perjured. There was illicit, even comical intrigue.

And there was Major Hubert Henry, second in command to Picquart at the Statistical Section. From Dreyfus's initial arrest until exposure of his own crimes in August 1898, Henry did all he could to obtain Dreyfus's conviction and prevent its reversal. Like other officers implicated, he seems to have been driven primarily by a desire to serve the Army's interests, but, as his crimes multiplied, self-protection must also have become important to him. Before the Dreyfus trial he had probably leaked confidential information to the press, and at the trial his perjured testimony had done much to determine the verdict. Thus, like the Army that he served, Henry was vulnerable to gravely damaging exposure through the simultaneous though independent probing by Picquart and Mathieu Dreyfus.

In response to this threat Henry employed the stratagem of "enriching" the evidence with forgeries. He may have done this before, and certainly did it later, but the critical piece was fashioned on November 1, 1896, All Saint's Day. At that time he created two documents, the first designed only to authenticate the other. The second forgery, known later as the *faux Henry* ("Henry forgery"), was clever enough to seem clear and credible proof of Dreyfus's guilt. Henry kept the document from his immediate superior, Picquart, who might well have recognized that it was fraudulent. The forgery probably was accepted as genuine by War Minister Billot, who was relieved thus to find cause for rejecting Picquart's claims. However, there is substantial reason to think that the document's fraudulence was known or suspected by Deputy Chief of Staff Gonse, two subordinates of Henry, and possibly Chief of Staff Boisdeffre. Together they helped Henry to establish the forgery as genuine.[7]

Previously Generals Billot, Boisdeffre, and Gonse had strongly discouraged Picquart without actually ordering him to cease his probe into these dangerous matters. He did continue, driven by his conviction that the dictates of reasoning based on evidence had to be followed. Moreover, he was concerned lest Mathieu Dreyfus discover and disclose the truth. In vain Picquart tried to persuade his superiors that the gravest damage from exposure would result if the Army did not reveal its errors in the Dreyfus case before others did.

Not only had Picquart been digging up things better left buried, but he had been annoyingly independent in his investigations, despite the evident skepticism and displeasure of his superiors. Moreover, confidential information was leaking somehow to the press, to Mathieu Dreyfus, and to Bernard-Lazare. Though not actually responsible for the leaks, Picquart was a plausible suspect, and the generals thought that he had been indiscreet in other ways. Unable to tolerate Picquart's troublesome conduct any longer, on November 14 the three generals confronted him, denounced his actions, and ordered him away on a mission whose only real purpose was to keep him far from Paris.

In Picquart's absence, Henry schemed to destroy him. By a variety of means, including additional forgeries, Henry made it look as if Picquart had committed a number of serious transgressions. Critical among these were Picquart's supposedly having forged the *petit bleu* (the first document incriminating Esterhazy) and having showed Louis Leblois, Picquart's lawyer, the secret file of Dreyfus case evidence. Henry drew others into his intrigues, including some of his subordinates, Esterhazy, and Major Mercier Du Paty de Clam, a General Staff officer who had played a central role in the conviction of Dreyfus. The intrigues led in time to Picquart's removal from command of the Statistical Section, his forced retirement from the Army, and his imprisonment. Henry replaced Picquart in the command.

Before any definite official action had been taken against him, Picquart realized that his Army career was in jeopardy. In vain he sought help from his patron, General Ferdinand Millet, the Director of Infantry. Picquart's subsequent actions have been regarded as nobly heroic, but his motivations appear to have been more those of self-interest and, eventually, revenge.

In late June 1897 Picquart obtained leave from his North African assignment and returned to Paris, where he consulted with Louis Leblois, an old friend as well as an able lawyer. Picquart told Leblois most of the story of his investigation of Esterhazy and Dreyfus, and of consequent intrigues against himself. Though seeking Leblois's aid, Picquart required that he make no contact with the Dreyfus family and not disclose publicly the information confided in him. Picquart told his friend that he acted now only to protect himself, and not for Dreyfus at all. The lawyer made Picquart see that he was doomed unless his conduct could be justified and redeemed by the exoneration of Dreyfus.

Needing an influential ally, Leblois went to Auguste Scheurer-Kestner, who he had learned was concerned about the Dreyfus case. Scheurer-Kestner was one of France's most respected statesmen, a founder of the Republic, Senator for life, Vice-President of the Senate, and a likely choice for the next President of France. Long interested in the case, in recent months he had become obsessed with it, for the seeming miscarriage of justice gravely disturbed him. He had been in touch with Mathieu Dreyfus and others working on Alfred's behalf and had been conducting an independent and intensive investigation, without solid results.

On July 13, 1897, Leblois repeated to Scheurer-Kestner what Picquart had told him. Thoroughly shocked by the revelations, the Senator determined to obtain justice for Dreyfus and Picquart, but he was hobbled by the latter's insistence that neither his identity nor his confidential information be revealed.

Scheurer-Kestner at once let it be known among political associates that he was now convinced of Dreyfus's innocence. He hoped to resolve the affair by using his influence privately, and he explored possibilities with the President, the Premier, and the War and Justice Ministers. These efforts got him nowhere.

The leaders approached were sure of Dreyfus's guilt, and Scheurer-Kestner could not disclose Picquart's confidences. More important, nationalist and anti-Semitic sentiments were extremely powerful political forces. The Ministry might well be forced from office if it allowed any opening to the campaign for Dreyfus. With Cabinet support Premier Méline determined not to allow parliamentary or any other official review of the case, relying on the legal principle that the court-martial's decision was final. When Justice Minister Darlan began to think Dreyfus's conviction illegal and possibly unfounded, Méline replaced him with a nonentity.

While Scheurer-Kestner's overtures to government leaders were thus frustrated, his intervention served as the catalyst that transformed a comparatively minor dispute into a major strugg... From late October 1897 onward, the affair was what the French have known since simply as the Affair. The number who believed Dreyfus was a victim of injustice was rapidly augmented. These were the "Dreyfusards," most of them drawn into the fray initially through personal contacts with friends already involved and stimulated by the clamor over Scheurer-Kestner's intervention and the events following from it.

Beginning on October 31, much of what Scheurer-Kestner knew leaked out in several newspaper articles; neither Esterhazy nor Picquart was named at first. The articles provoked a torrent of invective directed at the elder statesman by the patriotic press. Lines of battle were being drawn between Dreyfusards and those immovably convinced of Dreyfus's guilt—the anti-Dreyfusards.

On November 6 Bernard-Lazare reissued a revised, expanded version of his tract. Also printed was a facsimile of the *bordereau*, which had first appeared in a newspaper a year before. This time a banker named de Castro saw the facsimile and recognized the handwriting to be that of a client: Esterhazy. He told Mathieu Dreyfus, who immediately went to Scheurer-Kestner and asked him if Esterhazy were the unnamed officer whom, reports said, the Senator suspected as the actual spy. Scheurer-Kestner admitted that he was; on November 14 a newspaper identified a different officer as the suspect and to avoid more harmful speculation the Senator had Mathieu denounce Esterhazy to War Minister Billot.

Thus Esterhazy stood formally accused as a spy, with the denunciation made public. Billot was compelled to initiate an official inquiry about him. Esterhazy had been frantically but cunningly trying to save himself from exposure. He had even threatened President Félix Faure, using a fraudulent document that he claimed would be diplomatically embarrassing. Though his maneuvers were ineffective and his generally villainous character was recognized, Army leaders sought to protect Esterhazy, for his fall would be a disaster for them, and they genuinely thought him victimized by the Dreyfusard conspiracy.

The determination of Esterhazy's fate would soon bring the conflict to a climax. In the meantime the combatants were engaged, through impassioned debate in the parliament on December 4 and 7, and in the press.

Newspapers, which were always widely read and influential, now were the public's chief source of information, misinformation, and polemic in the Affair, especially because of the secrecy or obscurity of many of the relevant facts. Acrimony and invective were commonplace, as was the wide repetition of tales based on gossip, invention, and both calculated and careless leaks by nearly everyone with access to genuine information. The newspapers were very numerous, and all repeated and commented on each other extensively, so that every interesting story, wild or wise, was bound to circulate very widely.

Two successive Army inquiries cleared Esterhazy. However, both he and the Army leaders believed that his court-martial would be desirable, since his acquittal there should more decisively squelch the accusations against him and thus do more damage to the Dreyfusard cause. Esterhazy's court-martial was ordered on January 2, 1898, and held on January 10 and 11, its verdict a foregone conclusion. From their chiefs the officer judges knew that Esterhazy was innocent and Dreyfus guilty, and that at stake were the Army's strength and the esprit de corps of its officers. Acquittal was quickly and unanimously decided.

Having accomplished that, the Army arrested Picquart, with the allegations against him supported only by Henry's fabrications and suborned testimony by the latter's subordinates. On the same day, January 13, the Senate refused to re-elect Scheurer-Kestner as its vice-president.

While anti-Dreyfusards exulted, the Dreyfusard position had coalesced. United by common outrage over the treatment of Esterhazy and Picquart, for the first time the Dreyfusards now had a whole picture of the pertinent facts. After more than two months of revelations, the last, crucial bits they needed had been made public as evidence in the Esterhazy trial. In the months that followed, Dreyfusards conducted a highly organized and determined campaign. What they lacked in numbers they made up in energy, talent, and unstinting dedication.

2

The Affair Explodes

At this juncture there appeared what must be the most celebrated piece ever published in a newspaper, Emile Zola's "J'Accuse!" Zola had already published five Dreyfusard newspaper articles and pamphlets in recent weeks. Now, inspired by indignation and a zealot's sense of mission, he addressed an open letter to the President of France. On January 13 it appeared in the newspaper *L'Aurore*, with the headline "I Accuse!" across the top of page one. Parisians fought over possession of the 300,000 copies printed, and anti-Dreyfusards burned the paper in the streets.

When striking rhetorical brilliance, Zola reduced the complexity and obscurity of the Affair to simple terms. He attacked General Staff officers for having conspired from the beginning to condemn a man they knew to be innocent and clear one they knew guilty. His accusations were exaggerated much beyond what could be justified by the evidence, which he scarcely discussed. Near the end came the refrain from which *L'Aurore's*

17

editors took their headline: each repetition of "I accuse . . ." was followed by grave charges against a succession of generals and others, indicting them for crimes even more reprehensible than those truly chargeable to them.

Zola openly invited prosecution for defaming those he accused. Since the government had refused to reconsider the Dreyfus conviction, Zola hoped to obtain its review through evidence offered in his own libel trial. Fearing just this, the government did not want to charge him at all. However, it was heavily attacked in the parliamentary chambers and the press for allowing Dreyfusards to do their vicious and dastardly deeds with impunity. The Ministry and even the President might well be forced from office over this issue. Consequently Zola was prosecuted, but with an indictment so narrowly drawn, by excluding most of "J'Accuse!", that the court would be able to reject as irrelevant a review of the Dreyfus case by the Zola defense.

Although only one of many developments which together stimulated rapid intensification of the struggle, Zola's "J'Accuse!" probably did more than any other single act to arouse interest and passions. Its provocation came at a most opportune moment, and Zola's subsequent trials for libel provided occasion for especially sharp conflict—even more outside the courtroom than within it.

Argument over Dreyfus often led the participants to blows, with fist fights even forcing suspension of parliamentary debates. Beginning in Paris on January 14, the day after "J'Accuse!" appeared, a wave of rioting spread all across France and Algeria. Although they have not usually drawn much attention, these riots were quite serious in number, size, and intensity.[1] Some sixty-six occurred in January and February, and they continued sporadically throughout the Affair. Rioters in this first wave demonstrated against Zola and for the Army. Violence in the riots was directed primarily at Jews, with especially serious anti-Semitic violence in Algeria. In addition, there were many violent clashes between anti-Dreyfusards and Dreyfusards, occuring especially outside court and legislative chambers and at public meetings and demonstrations organized by one side and interfered with by the other.

Zola was tried on February 7–23, 1989, with excited crowds filling the court and the streets outside. They numbered in the tens of thousands. Disorder verging on riot prevailed outside, with police intervention needed for Zola to come and go safely. His friends were frequently insulted, threatened, and assaulted. The police believed the Dreyfusards were the seditious ones and did not often try hard to protect them or restore order.

To shout "Long live the Republic!" was sure to provoke assault: Most people in the crowd had little liking for the Republic, though they loved France, and they knew the slogan was intended as an affront to the Army. When a young lawyer named Courot called out, "Long live the Republic! Down with the [Army] chiefs!", he was assaulted by an Army major and a gentleman wearing Legion of Honor insignia. Then Courot was faced with prosecution for insulting the Army! He escaped prosecution only because the major had accepted his apology and refused to make a formal complaint.

Zola and his defense counsel had only partial success in getting the Dreyfus case reviewed at the trial. It scarcely mattered, for people did not want to change their minds then anyway. The trial was quite dramatic enough to deserve the attention given it in subsequent cinema and stage plays. It was the combat of enemies who would give no quarter. Zola was convicted and given the maximum sentence, a year's imprisonment and a fine. The conviction was overturned on technical grounds, and in July he was again condemned with the same sentence. The next night he reluctantly fled to exile in England.

With Zola's original conviction, retaliation against Dreyfusards began. Picquart, who had earlier been condemned for indiscipline by an Army court of inquiry, was retired from the service with reduced pension. His lawyer, Louis Leblois, and the lawyer who had "insulted" the Army, Courot, were suspended by the Paris bar. Leblois was also removed from his post as an assistant mayor. A distinguished scientist, Edouard Grimaux, was dismissed from his professorial chairs at two very important national institutions, the Ecole Polytechnique and the Institut Agronomique; he had signed a protest petition and testified for Zola. The most intensely hated Dreyfusard, Joseph Reinach, lost his officer's commission in the Army reserve, although this action was suspended until June, after he was defeated for reelection to the Chamber of Deputies. Other Dreyfusards were also victimized by government, military, and Catholic Church authorities.

Duels between antagonists in the Affair became frequent,

with some serious injuries and at least one death, when a Jewish officer was killed by a comrade.[2] Among the better-known duelists was Picquart, who fought a duel with Henry and refused one with Esterhazy because the latter was not a man of honor. (Henry at first refused the duel with Picquart for the same reason.) Georges Clemenceau, an editor of *L'Aurore* and later the Premier of France, fought a duel with Edouard Drumont, *La Libre parole* editor and chief leader of French anti-Semitism.

Before the Affair was over, many figures prominent in it had died, some of them in circumstances believed suspicious. Although probably not justified in any instance, suspicion of murder added ominous undertones to the struggle. With the atmosphere highly charged by hatred, and physical violence breaking out frequently, hysteria about assassination came easily. Especially disturbing were the deaths of Emile Zola and a petty criminal known as Lemercier-Picard. Zola died of asphyxiation in 1902 when his bedroom chimney flue was blocked; his death was ruled an accident. On March 3, 1898, just after the violence of the Zola trial and nationwide rioting, police found Lemercier-Picard's body hanging from a window frame in a dingy Paris hotel room; the death was ruled a suicide. Shortly before then the man had tried to sell faked evidence to Joseph Reinach, in what seemed an effort to incriminate the Dreyfusard leader for having bought official secrets. Dreyfusards believed the would-be swindler to be an agent of Army counterintelligence and later became convinced that Henry's forgeries had actually been manufactured by Lemercier-Picard, working under Henry's direction. While the Dreyfusards probably were wrong about Lemercier-Picard's role, to them it seemed plausible that the criminal had been killed to ensure his silence.

At the first Zola trial there had been testimony that paraphrased the *faux Henry*, although the document itself was not produced. Elsewhere it had been said that a record existed of a supposed oral partial confession made by Dreyfus just after his degradation in 1895; the record of the alleged confession had surfaced only much later, and in very dubious circumstances. Eventually both documents would be produced officially; the authenticity of the *faux Henry* was immediately suspected, although not disproved until later, and the "confession" could never pass serious critical examination. There were also often

repeated press reports that the Army possessed documents w
ten by the German Kaiser, including his annotations on a c
of the *bordereau*, that spoke quite explicitly of Dreyfus as a German spy. There was wide belief in the existence of these mythical products of the Kaiser's indiscretion.

At first credulity about these supposed proofs may have been possible for well-informed, reasonable people, especially given the aura of authority of government spokesmen and the frequent rhetorical skill of anti-Dreyfusard polemicists. However, by the spring of 1898 revelations and arguments of the prolonged intense controversy had made quite clear how inadequate the "proofs" against Dreyfus were. Only minds resolutely closed to reasoned assessment of evidence could continue to deny the principal Dreyfusard claims.

Nevertheless, at this point comparatively few people believed the Dreyfusards, and most Frenchmen who knew of the Affair abhorred them. Admitting that the Dreyfusards were right seemed to have implications which reached far beyond this one judicial dispute. Issues of both practical politics and fundamental ideology were involved, and reasoning about evidence did little to determine decisions against the crusade for the prisoner of Devil's Island. With respect to practical politics, perceptions of anticipated consequences of Dreyfusard victory could and did change. Ideologically based views were far less flexible.

With parliamentary general elections due in May 1898, few members of the parliament wanted to risk voter hostility by supporting the Dreyfusard claims. The Affair at first seemed too hazardous politically for members to care much about evidence and injustice, until it began to appear to them that the continued existence of the Republic itself depended on the outcome of the mounting conflict. It required fear of this, discovery of political advantage to be gained, and an even stronger legal case for Dreyfus to get many republican politicians to commit themselves to revision of his conviction.

In the elections some important Dreyfusards lost their seats; the Affair seems to have been only a secondary issue in most of these defeats, but too little really is known to determine this. About nineteen of the Deputies elected based their campaigns on anti-Semitism, and clearly the Affair's agitation contributed to their successes. Joseph Reinach's defeat did result from his notoriety as a Dreyfusard leader; it had been impossible for him to speak in public, so intense was the hostility, and he received only 17 percent of the votes he had won five years before.

In the Chamber of Deputies, the principal legislative body, 196 of 581 members were newly elected in May. Premier Méline's handling of the Affair was increasingly unpopular, and with the changed membership in the Chamber he could not keep his shaky majority any longer. He resigned, and on June 28 Henri Brisson formed a new Ministry, all but one of whose members were Radicals. The so-called Radical party, while not radical in most respects, was less conservative than most of Méline's coalition; in due course most Radicals recognized that since their conservative opponents were anti-Dreyfusard, they themselves had to take the opposite tack.

However, the new War Minister, Godefroy Cavaignac, was an immovable anti-Dreyfusard. An ambitious man seeking political gains, he determined to settle the Dreyfus uproar quickly by bringing forth undeniable evidence of guilt. After reviewing the Army's files, on July 7 he addressed the Chamber of Deputies, insisting that Dreyfus was guilty. Cavaignac read to the Chamber what he said was the best evidence: the forged document that would become known as the *faux Henry,* two items (one of them another Henry forgery) speaking of someone identified only as "D," and the supposed Dreyfus confession. He explained at length why these pieces should be judged authentic and conclusive, especially the *faux Henry* and the confession.

The whole Chamber rose to cheer the War Minister and voted almost unanimously to post his speech on each of some thirty-five thousand city and town halls in France. It was the greatest moment of the anti-Dreyfusards, and it soon led to their worst.

The Dreyfusards also exulted, for now Cavaignac had exposed the most damaging evidence the Army had, and they were confident none of it would survive close critical scrutiny. Moreover, he had conceded to them many of their contentions. Cavaignac was furious when they continued their propaganda more vigorously than ever. On August 11 he sought to arrest all the leading Dreyfusards, charging them with sedition, but Premier Brisson squelched this effort.

Two days later Captain Louis Cuignet discovered that the *faux Henry* was a forgery.

Cuignet was examining the Dreyfus files for Cavaignac's aide, General Roget. The document was written on faintly lined paper that had been torn and pieced together, as was common with documents removed by agents from wastebaskets. Under a bright lamp Cuignet noticed that the barely visible printed lines on the top and bottom of the paper were colored differently from those in the middle section. Henry had added to and combined parts of two genuine documents. (Then other defects in the forgery could also be recognized.) Cuignet took the *faux Henry* to Roget, and the two officers, both anti-Dreyfusard but honest, went to Cavaignac, who also was honest, and now the most horrified man in a France papered with thirty-five thousand copies of his speech.

Cavaignac told no one until he could interrogate Henry upon the latter's return from leave on August 30. The War Minister questioned him in the presence of Roget and the Chief of Staff, General Boisdeffre. After almost an hour Cavaignac pressured Henry into admitting that he had fabricated the document. Boisdeffre resigned on the spot; at Zola's first trial he had testified that the piece was genuine and that he was ready to resign if not believed.

Henry was placed in a cell under arrest. The next evening he was found there dead, his throat cut in an apparent suicide, although murder was suspected. When Esterhazy heard the news that night, he immediately fled the country, going to England and permanent exile.

It should have been as decisive a moment as the final disclosure of Watergate tape recordings in August 1974. With the most important evidence discredited and a presumption of Esterhazy's guilt established by his flight, the case against Dreyfus was demolished. The remaining evidence had been rendered suspect, for Henry might also have fabricated most of it. Dreyfusards thrilled at the victory of Reason and Truth, the twin deities for which they fought. Among their enemies, strong men wept.

For a brief time Reason and Truth did prevail. On September 1 and 2 most newspapers came out for "Revision," official review of the Dreyfus case. Until then nearly all of the press had been anti-Dreyfusard or neutral, mostly the former. The only Dreyfusard paper with a large circulation had been the socialist *La Petite République* (about 100,000 copies daily). This was also the decisive moment for many politicians who previously had been unable to espouse Revision, yet had not been led to oppose it through ideological antagonism toward the Dreyfusards.

By September 3 the sometime opponents of Revision had begun to recover from the first shock. Unable to endure the consequences of their recent concessions, many reversed themselves again. Within days the anti-Dreyfusards had regathered their forces, including a major but reduced portion of the press.

The rationalizations of "anti-Revisionism" were monuments of illogic and sophistry. It was insisted that the one forgery did not diminish the value of the remaining evidence, which was ample to prove Dreyfus guilty. Moreover, the *faux Henry* somehow authenticated the other evidence, and Henry had created it for that purpose, sacrificing himself in the end to serve the Army and the Nation. He was thus a great hero. . . . His forgery was a substitute for a genuine document with the same message that somehow was not available. . . . He had fabricated evidence in order to avoid revealing the Kaiser's compromising letters and the *bordereau* copy the Kaiser had annotated—for such revelations would be dangerous to French national security. . . . In any event, Revision would surely mean war with Germany, and with the Army disorganized by the Affair, there would be another debacle, like France's 1870 humiliation by Germany. . . . Picquart had forged the *petit bleu* to incriminate Esterhazy, and that demonstrated Dreyfus's guilt. . . .

Most of all, anti-Dreyfusards relied on continued uncritical acceptance of all evidence said to incriminate Dreyfus, while automatically rejecting all argument to the contrary. Any discomfort caused by the Henry and Esterhazy disasters was quickly shoved aside, its place taken by the fantasies repeated above, and even more by the comforting assurance that those inclined to Revision were traitors, to be reviled and not believed.

Exposure of the *faux Henry* converted Premier Brisson to Revision, but his political position was too weak for him to act before carefully preparing the way. War Minister Cavaignac insisted that he was more convinced than ever of Dreyfus's guilt, and he renewed his demand for the arrest of the leading Dreyfusards. Some of his Cabinet colleagues thought him quite mad. Brisson's determined Revisionism caused Cavaignac to resign; he then became a leading spokesman of the anti-Dreyfusards. General Zurlinden was named to succeed Cavaignac and was himself succeeded two weeks later by General Chanoine. Each first time since before Henry's exposure. The opposition in the Chamber was eager to force Brisson from office for the way he had been handling Revision and the Army. The Ligue des Patriotes, the Ligue Antisémitique, some socialist leaders, and anarchists had called for demonstrations outside the Chamber that day. The police were out in great force, and Army cavalry units were ready close by in the Tuileries Gardens.

When the Chamber session began, the General Chanoine astonished the assembly by announcing his resignation as War Minister. His action came without prior warning to Brisson and may well have been planned with Déroulède to promote the latter's efforts against the Republic. In the subsequent tumult the Brisson Ministry was forced to resign.

Outside, police controlled the mob. Guérin and his Ligue Antisémitique sought to invade the Chamber and seize control of the government. The attempt was clumsy and swiftly crushed.

Four days later the Cour de Cassation announced its decision that there were ample grounds for appeal of the Dreyfus conviction, and the court would give the case a full reconsideration. L'Aurore proclaimed "Victory!" in a banner headline, just as it had proclaimed "I Accuse!" nine months before.

The combatants did not draw back to await completion of the high court's deliberations. If anything, the struggle was more frenzied than ever. Each side continued its efforts to build support while attacking its opponents. Polemical newspaper articles, pamphlets, and books poured forth in a flood, and frequent public rallies with large audiences were held around the country. Since February 1898 the well-organized Ligue des Droits de l'Homme et du Citoyen had conducted much of the Dreyfusard rally campaign. To counter this league with similar activities and to provide an organizing vehicle less extreme in its antigovernment politics than the Ligue des Patriotes, at the end of December anti-Dreyfusards formed the Ligue de la Patrie Française. Many of its more prominent figures were men of letters, who at last had found a bastion from which to sally forth against the many Dreyfusard intellectuals.

Much of the anti-Dreyfusard invective was now directed at the Cour de Cassation's criminal chamber, which was handling the Dreyfus appeal. The criminal chamber's president, Louis Loew, was said to have sold out to the Jews and Germany, or

was thought ready to preside over Revision, and e
ferred to resign.

Nevertheless, on September 26, the Cabinet d
a divided vote to initiate Revision. It sent the Dre
France's highest court, the Cour de Cassation, whicl
liminary examination of the case.

At the same time France was engaged in an ii
crisis. Conflict with Britain over rival African territ
reached a climax on September 19, 1898, when French
forces confronted each other at Fashoda on the upper
Tension between the two countries remained high
and they seemed dangerously close to war. France fina
down on November 3. Simultaneously, civil war als
dangerously close.

In Paris there was a disorderly strike by some twe
sand construction workers, those working on preparati
huge 1900 Exposition and their allies. This agitation se
have been aggravated by intervention of the ruffians of t
Antisémitique, an especially nasty, violent organizati
trolled by an adventurer and swindler named Jules Gu
was secretly subsidized by the Duc d'Orléans, the exilec
ant to the French throne. Also coming onto the stage at tl
was Paul Déroulède's reconstituted Ligue des Patriotes,
aimed at the imposition of an authoritarian regime.

Agitation over the Affair was more intense than ev
multuous public meetings and demonstrations organiz
other groups were frequent, the level of public excitemer
very high, and the violence of clashes between oppc
mounted. An imminent coup d'état was widely rumored. \
a rail strike also threatened, Premier Brisson brought into
more than sixty thousand troops, in addition to the city's
mally large garrison.

With troops marching and bivouacked all over Paris, t
was little chance of the government's being overwhelmed by
or coup. Nevertheless, among leftists fear of a royalist or mili
seizure of power reached the level of panic, especially during
second week of October. Many leftists prepared for civil war
defense of the Republic. At the same time there was wide an
ety, even panic, over the apparent danger of war with Gre
Britain.

On October 25 the Chamber of Deputies reconvened for tl

even to be a German Jew himself. Anti-Dreyfusards made wild, baseless charges of grave judicial misconduct in the inquiry itself, so that findings that favored Dreyfus would be discredited in advance.

In addition to all that had already been exposed, the criminal appeal chamber examined new and still more convincing evidence that Esterhazy had written the *bordereau*. The court's inquiries tore the Dreyfus confession story to shreds and found abundant reason to regard the rest of the evidence as worthless. Correctly fearing that the court was nearing a decision to overturn the Dreyfus conviction, opponents of Revision pressed for legislation to take the case away from the criminal appeal chamber and have it heard by all three chambers of the Cour de Cassation, meeting together. The new premier, Charles Dupuy, sought this and met especially sharp parliamentary resistance, because it would clearly be a travesty against basic principles of criminal justice. After protracted debate the transfer was enacted on March 1, 1899.

Two weeks earlier President Faure had died suddenly, having suffered a stroke while in his office amorously enjoying the company of a woman. Some anti-Dreyfusards said it was murder. His successor, Emile Loubet, a known Revisionist, was immediately the object of furious abuse. Faure's funeral was the occasion for a comically inept attempt to seize power by Déroulède's extremists and some of Guérin's. They tried to divert troops in the funeral procession into an insurrection. General Roget, in command, simply refused to take Déroulède and company seriously, and their effort dissolved into a farce. There would be other coups planned, none of them serious threats either, but they were symptoms of deep public antagonism against parliamentary, republican government. This antagonism was far more serious than were the farces of Déroulède, Guérin, and their fellow conspirators.

Dreyfusards had an additional crusade to wage. Picquart had been in prison since August 12, awaiting disposition of criminal charges placed by the Army against him on the basis of the evidence fabricated and suborned by Henry. The generals were not willing to recognize that, since Henry had forged one key document, he might well be responsible for forgery charged to Picquart. Civilian authorities were unable or unwilling to compel the Army to release its prisoner, and Dreyfusards helped arouse sympathy in much of the world for Picquart as well as Dreyfus.

Resplendent in their number and their dignities of office—scarlet and ermine robes—the forty-six judges of the Cour de Cassation's united chambers heard the entire case all over again. Once the evidence had been examined, it was clear to the judges that the Dreyfus conviction had to be annulled. They differed on questions of law, evidence, and political judgment, and consequently could not agree at first on whether the case should be quashed without possibility of retrial or sent back to the Army for a new court-martial. To achieve a unanimous verdict the latter course was chosen.

The Cour de Cassation announced the verdict on June 3, 1899. *L'Aurore* once more printed a huge headline, this time in one word: "Justice!"

At the Auteuil horse races the next day, Baron Fernand Chevreau de Christiani struck at President Loubet with a walking stick, hitting his hat. Elegant bystanders cheered the baron, then battled the police in a sizable melee. There followed a counter-demonstration for Loubet at Longchamp, in the Bois de Boulogne park. Even non-Dreyfusards were outraged by the *lèse majesté* against the President. One hundred thousand republicans marched with cudgels, canes, and red rose boutonnieres, singing the *Marseillaise*. Police in force attacked the peaceful crowd.

On June 12, the day after the Longchamp demonstration, Dupuy was forced to resign for having failed to defend the Republic adequately in the face of the Affair's disorders. He was succeeded by René Waldeck-Rousseau, a skilled and forceful leader. The new Premier was determined to bring to an end both the Affair and the threat to the Republic posed by some of the anti-Dreyfusard elements.

On June 9 Alfred Dreyfus left Devil's Island on the Navy cruiser *Sfax*, and Georges Picquart was released from prison. Four days later a civilian court dismissed the charges against Picquart and Louis Leblois. While on board the *Sfax* Dreyfus learned for the first time of the struggles fought to free him.

The Cour de Cassation had pointed to General Mercier's crime of forcing Dreyfus's convinction by illegal means in the 1894 court-martial. The government now had to prosecute Mercier, but proceedings soon were suspended until after Dreyfus's retrial. This meant that the officers of the new court-martial could not find the Jew innocent without effectively declaring the general guilty. Mercier himself said this in an interview published by the newspaper *L'Intransigeant* on August 3, just before the court-martial began.

The second Dreyfus court-martial was held from August 7 to September 9, 1899, in Rennes. The Breton city was crowded with a multitude of journalists from all over the world, prominent participants in the past two years' struggle, and celebrities of all sorts. Even the Lord Chief Justice of England came as a fascinated spectator.

And spectacle it was, with both witnesses and attorneys posturing endlessly and outrageously, often with no visible attempt to make their words germane to the case. To many it seemed like just another theatrical performance when an unidentified assailant shot Dreyfus's histrionic attorney, Fernand Labori, without hurting him seriously or getting caught. But some Dreyfusards feared this was the first stroke in an organized assassination conspiracy against them.

Much additional evidence against Dreyfus was presented, none of it worth more than the old material. One honorable officer after another indulged in fantasies, distortions, and even lies with reckless abandon. The Cour de Cassation had ruled that this trial could only consider certain questions, the rest having been finally decided in favor of Dreyfus by the high court. At Rennes this was ignored. General Mercier, perhaps rather mad and with his own fate at stake, acted as if he were himself the prosecutor. He dominated much of the trial as a witness and as a spectator freely intervening in the proceedings. His lies were the most reckless and extensive of all.

The court found Dreyfus guilty by a five-to-two vote of the officer judges. Although many people were shocked at the conviction, they should instead have been surprised that even two officers had voted for acquittal. The judges sentenced Dreyfus to only ten years in prison plus degradation, because there were "extenuating circumstances"—in a case of treason!

Abroad, the verdict occasioned anti-French demonstrations in many cities, including New York, with attacks on French consulates and citizens. In France, civilian combatants apparently were ready to fight on endlessly, but Alfred Dreyfus was not.

Devil's Island had broken his physical and emotional health, and his brother felt sure he could not survive more imprisonment or yet another trial. It seemed likely that no military court would ever clear him. An agreement was made with Premier Waldeck-Rousseau for Presidential clemency.

On September 19, 1899, President Loubet commuted the sentence of Alfred Dreyfus to the time he had already served and canceled the new degradation ritual. Dreyfus was immediately released from confinement, for the first time in nearly five years.

When Loubet signed the commutation, Joseph Reinach's first thought was to inform Auguste Scheurer-Kestner, who had given so much of himself to their crusade and now was very sick. Just as Reinach finished writing the message, he learned that Scheurer-Kestner had died that morning.[3]

Two days later the War Minister, General Galliffet, distributed a general order throughout the Army: All soldiers should defer to both the court-martial and the clemency, with no "reprisals." "This incident is closed! . . . Long live the Army!"

But it was not closed. Dreyfus and Picquart were free but still disgraced.

For many months the more active Dreyfusards had been fully absorbed by the Affair. Their crusading momentum and their animosity toward their opponents were too great for them to stop without first accomplishing the full rehabilitation of the two innocent men. Moreover, they saw France as afflicted by a sickness of intolerance and political atavism, which could be cured only by complete justice and final political as well as judicial defeat of the anti-Dreyfusards.

On the other hand, Premier Waldeck-Rousseau and many among the Revisionists believed that the goal of full justice had to be set aside in order to achieve civil peace in France once more. Dreyfus had been released for that reason, to avoid further appeal proceedings and the attendant conflict. Waldeck-Rousseau next sought amnesty legislation to terminate the prosecution, imprisonment, and civil suits of others involved in the Affair, notably General Mercier.

Other pressing business and disagreement over who should be included delayed the amnesty for a year. With a few exclusions it was enacted on Christmas Eve, 1900.

In fact, the struggles of the Affair had diminished to a comparatively minor level with the release of Dreyfus, which deflated the ballooning passions of both sides. Subsequent legal maneuvers and polemical interchanges occurred in a far cooler climate than that prevailing from October 1897 through September 1899.

Nevertheless, there were scattered occasions for intense conflict, including campaigns in some constituencies in elections of 1900 and 1902. Repeated quarrels over the Affair in the Chamber of Deputies at times threatened the government's tenure in office. Antagonism between sometime opponents in the Affair receded from prominence without fundamental alteration.

The Dreyfus Affair could never be altogether liquidated, but the canker of unredeemed injustice had to be excised if the pretense of civil peace and that of republican righteousness were to be maintained. Obtaining a new legal review of the Dreyfus conviction required new evidence. Official and private investigations went on fitfully, but neither turned up much. The situation changed when, on April 6 and 7, 1903, the socialist leader Jean Jaurès managed to make a real issue in the Chamber of Deputies about the mythical notes by the Kaiser.

That led the War Minister of the day, General André, to order the first thorough search of Army files for any evidence on the Affair. This took six months and turned up much evidence that previously had been either suppressed or ignored. The new evidence gave more weight still to the case for Dreyfus and to the cases against Esterhazy for espionage and Henry for fouling the entire affair with his machinations.

The whole elaborate procedure of review and reconsideration began yet again, this time with little of the frenzied uproar attendant upon the deliberations of the Cour de Cassation in 1898–99. Legal, political, and incidental practical matters much delayed the proceedings, which required almost three years to complete.

Again the judges of the Cour de Cassation's united chambers could readily agree to overturn the Dreyfus conviction but found difficult the decision whether to send the case back for another court-martial, which was the normal procedure. The crucial law, Article 445 of the Criminal Code, lacked clear definition on this point and was subject to variant interpretations. In its final verdict the court concluded that it could find in the evidence no basis whatever for suspecting Alfred Dreyfus of any crime, and hence Article 445 prohibited remission of the case for a new trial.[4]

On July 12, 1906, the Court de Cassation announced its decision to reverse the Dreyfus conviction once and for all. Legislation was immediately enacted restoring Dreyfus and Picquart
to the Army, with the rank that the passage of time would normally have brought them—major and brigadier general, respectively. Dreyfus was made an Officer of the Legion of Honor. He
refused to have the Legion award ceremony in the same court-
yard at the Ecole Militaire as his degradation eleven and a half
years before. On July 22 it was held discreetly in a smaller court-
yard nearby, without prior public notice and with all but a few
people excluded.

Picquart was soon promoted again and then, in October 1906
he was named War Minister! As a stroke of revenge he had been
selected by the Dreyfusard leader, Georges Clemenceau, who
had moved quickly from political outsider to Premier. Picquart
was a bitter and vindictive man. Much of the Army officer corps
and he confronted each other with mutual hostility. He accomplished little as War Minister and eventually moved on to command the Second Army Corps. In January 1914 he died of injuries
sustained in a fall from a horse. As world war began later that
year, Jean Jaurès also died, shot by a patriotic assassin.

Esterhazy remained in England to avoid imprisonment in a
matter not connected to the Dreyfus Affair: In 1899 he had been
convicted for swindling money from his cousin. He lived in obscurity using assumed names and in 1923 was buried in England
under one of them, Comte Jean-Marie de Violement.

Major Dreyfus soon retired from the Army, returning for
active duty during World War I. He survived until 1935, remaining quietly in the background and refusing to have anything to
do with the sorts of people and politics that had liberated him.
In his outlook on life and politics he always remained very much
like the Army officers who had victimized him. Their prejudice
not withstanding, the religion of Alfred Dreyfus did not keep
him from being one of them.

As for others, some were ruined by the Affair, some survived despite injuries suffered in it, and some prospered because
or in spite of it. French political anti-Semitism soon declined
sharply, but the underlying causes did not; anti-Semitism remained a symptom of the discontent and antagonism that divided France and had given force to the anti-Dreyfusard cause.
Rehabilitating Dreyfus and Picquart really did not terminate

the Affair, even though one may draw the curtain for the drama with the ceremony awarding Alfred Dreyfus the Legion of Honor. Too many people had had their political views profoundly shaped or reshaped by the Affair. Anti-Dreyfusards would not change their minds about Dreyfus's guilt, and on both sides there were many who remained permanently embittered by the opportunistic ways some winners in the conflict used the victory.

The Affair gave birth to the Action Française, a radical neo-monarchist organization, which remained the intellectual center of political reaction in France for four decades. Continuing fury over the Affair had been demonstrated in 1908, when Emile Zola's ashes were ceremonially transferred to the Panthéon. On that occasion a well-known right wing journalist named Grégori shot Alfred Dreyfus, wounding him in the arm, and a jury quickly acquitted the would-be assassin. The Action Française made his trial the occasion to advance a campaign of propaganda and attention-getting, scandalous acts (such as courtroom interruptions) that attacked the Cour de Cassation's use of Article 445 to quash action against Dreyfus. Thus "445" became the "talisman," as they called it, of rightist agitation for years, appearing in graffiti and on page one of Action Française's newspaper every day.

Veterans of both sides in the Affair continued in significant political roles for decades afterward, their perspectives indelibly imprinted by their experiences in that struggle. They continued to be directed by attitudes and ideas whose importance for them the Affair had established. Like the Action Française, though perhaps with less substantial effect, the Dreyfusards' Ligue des Droits de l'Homme et du Citoyen lived on as an embodiment of the ideology precious to the struggle's participants. France next suffered near civil war during the mid-1930s. Then the specific issues differed, but many of the characters and underlying causes came from the Dreyfus Affair, including a Dreyfusard, Léon Blum, as Premier of the period's Popular Front government.

It has been said with justice that the authoritarian Vichy regime in France, 1940–1944, was the "revenge of the anti-Dreyfusards," because it embodied so much of the anti-Dreyfusard spirit and overall view of the world, and it drove out the heirs of the Dreyfusards. The Action Française had done much to make the continuity possible. After the collapse of the Vichy government, political conditions and personalities were enough different for that continuity to be broken. Thus is can also be said that the Dreyfus affair finally ended with the fall of the Vichy regime, half a century after that *bordereau* turned up at the Statistical Section of the French Army General Staff.

3

Dreyfus, the Man

At the time of his arrest Alfred Dreyfus was not quite thirty-five years old, married, with two children. He had been born in Mulhouse, in Alsace, where his family had a flourishing textile manufacturing business. When Germany annexed Alsace from France in 1871, the family preferred to remain French and moved to Paris. Two older brothers, Jacques and Mathieu, remained in Mulhouse to operate the factory. Captain Dreyfus was wealthy, with a large income from this business and a rich wife. That made it unlikely that he had transmitted secrets for the sake of money, and at first it made socialists and anarchists indifferent to his suffering. Anti-Semites thought Dreyfus was an alien because he was Jewish, although he was a lifelong resident and citizen of France. Their belief was reinforced by his having two brothers whom annexation had made German nationals and an income from a business on German territory.

Dreyfus had been among the best students at the Ecole

Polytechnique and the Ecole Supérieure de Guerre. As an officer he was efficient, extremely hard-working, ambitious, and eager to master his profession. Dreyfus was a very proper, upright officer and husband, wholly dedicated to the Army and his family but with no other known interests. Many of the clever people who later struggled in his defense would have thought him very dull, had they had a chance to know him.

Until his arrest Dreyfus had enjoyed a successful career, culminating in his appointment to the General Staff almost two years earlier. His commanders and military instructors usually recorded excellent evaluations of his performance, although there were some negative remarks about his personality. Negative reaction may have been inspired in part by anti-Semitism, but he received the favorable ratings nevertheless.

Other officers did not much like Dreyfus. Many of them were aristocrats, many were anti-Semites, some like Henry were modest in both social background and individual ability. For any of these types, it would have been difficult to like this bourgeois Jew with his wealth, intelligence, and ambition. He was, moreover, a very reserved, seemingly cold man who could not share the camaraderie of his brother officers, court their favor, or make amends for being Jewish. He simply was not sociable in these or any other ways important for acceptance into the brotherhood.

Dreyfus had no physical presence either. He was just average in size, with an ordinary face marked by the pince-nez he habitually wore. His voice was toneless, with a pitch and timbre some found annoying. In an age and an officer corps where it was important to have style, he had none.

When this apparently flat and unappealing man was accused of espionage, many of the officers who had known him came forward to testify to how obnoxious and dubious a character he was. They exaggerated his shortcomings and misconstrued his unusually active interest in military information. The officers found it easy to imagine that such a man was a traitor. Esterhazy, with his dash and personal magnetism, fitted their image of a traitor much less readily, despite his longtime ill-concealed pattern of misconduct. Alfred Dreyfus was the perfect scapegoat.

To others besides officers and family, Dreyfus remained an invisible man during nearly all the Affair. Unknown before his arrest, then confined away from public view, court-martialed in a secret proceeding, and afterward shipped to Devil's Island, he simply was not present for the struggle fought over him. On a few key occasions during the Affair he emerged into view: on January 5, 1895, when he was degraded in a public ritual as part of his sentence; three years later, when his letters to his wife were published; at his second trial in August–September 1899; and, after the crisis was largely over, with the publication in 1901 of his *Five Years of My Life*, a selection of letters, diary entries, and recollections.

After the degradation, newspapers competed to produce the most vivid description of that remarkably dramatic event. Of many graphic reports, probably the most striking was one that appeared as the leading front-page article the next day in *Le Figaro*, a highly respected daily newspaper with a select audience of cultivated readers. Its author was Léon Daudet, the twenty-six-year-old son of a great writer, Alphonse Daudet. Léon would later become the leading polemicist of the Action Française.

Headline: The Punishment   *Dateline:* With the French army

"Eight o'clock. It is a raw and rainy Paris morning. The sun is fat. Gross livid clouds float under the dull sky. Passersby hasten toward the Ecole Militaire. The Place Fontenoy is already invaded by a surging crowd, kept under control by police. Smocks and jackets, caps and hats make a moving pedestal for the commemorative column of 1870–71, the hard testimony of heroism. The streets nearby are rivers of restless figures.

"Behind the great iron gate, in the vast solemn square of the Cour Morland, the troops begin to mass. The companies file past. I hear that unique step formed by hundreds of steps, the brief commands, the clatter of guns, leather gear, and sabers. I see the setting: on the sides, the squat buildings which will enclose the drama, ochre and chalky, their windows full of faces. In the background, the Ecole de Guerre, its central clock, its columns, a deserted grassy court closed by a second iron gate, and military and civilian spectators on the side pillars in various poses, living caryatids already overexcited by anticipation.

"Minute by minute, the regular enclosure is fenced in by soldiers from all units, who take their places methodically, as their stamping dries the sodden turf. Trumpets resound quite near, with others distant and still others which seem to respond to them. Now the spectacle is ready. The court is encircled by a long geometric ribbon of cloth, of bodies, and of steel, the infantry, cavalry, artillery, and quartermaster corps, in fine, strict order; but despite the varieties of uniforms, all are blended in a blue-grey mass interrupted here and there by reflections from helmets with spotless silver bands and from sparkling musical instruments, like instruments of torture. The central space remains empty, immense and shiny with mud. It is here that destiny must be fulfilled.

"The universal gaze is fixed on the great clock which slowly chews up the time. Below in the corner is the gloomy, guarded door through which *he* will have to come out. How does *he* bear the approach of the punishment? In a side street between two buildings shine armor breast-plates, close by a black van which will be the conclusion of the disgrace. Five cavaliers arrive, a general, two officers, and two dragoons; they do half-turns in the space between and give to it a terrible significance. They face the Ecole Militaire. Only a few minutes . . . Only two . . . Nine o'clock sounds. The general draws his sabre. The drums roll. Their dull rumble translates the restrained shudder of this entire mute assembly. The fatal door opens and lets out the frightful cortège: four artillerymen, the guilty man between them; close at hand the executioner, a sergeant-major of the Republican guard. This bleak little group arrives in military step, slanted diagonally. It stops a few meters in front of the general. All hearts shiver. He rules a tumultuous silence. The clouds part: a ray of sunlight, brief and bloody, pours a bit of life on this dead man who is worse than dead.

"The clerk of the court comes forward. He reads the judgment. But his voice is lost in the space, as is that of the general. At once the executioner, a sort of helmeted giant, approaches the condemned man, his silhouette rigid and somber, the one on whom all attention is concentrated. He does not hesitate and applies himself to the képi: he tears off the insignia, the fine gold strands, the facings of the coat front and sleeves. The mannequin lends himself to the atrocious task; he even raises his arms. He cries out a few words—'Innocent! . . . -nocent! . . . Long live France!'—which go ill through this atmosphere so heavy with strain.

"Outside on the square and the pedestals, the crowd really is agitated and shouting. They howl. They whistle. It is a hurricane of intersecting and strident outrage. Anger prevails over dejection and stupor.

"But no one falters inside among the soldier witnesses and judges. I take my opera-glasses. They dance in my hands and, through a kind of steamy blur, I am close to this symbolic decortication, the fall of buttons and epaulettes. The condemned man neither draws back nor flinches. He submits like a stiffened puppet. I catch a glimpse of his pinched, sly, pallid face, this discredited, mendacious body which has been pulled to pieces by those who gave him his social status, his rank, and his usurped dignity.

"Now the executioner is completely bent over. Briskly, thoroughly he grasps, tears, and removes the red bands on the pants. Are these objects which fall, or pieces of life, these scraps of honor?

"The general and his retinue remain steady on their horses. The military enclosure is impassive and tense. A single breath, which gives rhythm to a single horror. It is the end of material torment. The giant draws the saber of the one who had been captain and with a sharp blow, the final lightning stroke, breaks it on his knee. Those remains are on the ground, lamentable old rags, punished for their infamous bearer, dead in his place and shriveled up with him.

"How can more be done to this little automaton, black and skinned of everything, to this hideous beast of treason who remains upright on his stiff legs, surviving in his catastrophe, boogieman for the weak and desolation for the strong? They are going to expose him to the scorn of those who were his companions and for whom he prepared defeat, of all these gallant officers, of all these humble, immobile soldiers, in whom fury struggles with disgust and the debris of pity which subsists in their noble souls, even in the presence of the worst forfeits. He is going to march off before these worthy people, before the rectitude, before the discipline, before the duty, before all this heroism in strength, all feelings deprived of sensibility for him, the traitor, who is obscured behind monstrous moral deviation, and incomprehensible and greedy perversity.

"The funeral cortège resumes its march. It makes the tour of this military wall, of these inflated chests in which all exterior show of feeling is prohibited, so that their contraction is all the more atrocious. Now, one who is part of the crowd feels in the chaos the impressions from all around him. I am in each man, in each officer. I associate myself with their revolt, with their indignation. 'This is the distress of a fellow man.'—'Yes, but he patiently, coldly sought everyone's ruin.'—'He was born a traitor.' —'No, each one makes and unmakes his soul. He could rely on the example.'—'He suffers martyrdom.'—'For this scoundrel, moral suffering is nothing. He is beyond that; we are more tortured than he.'

"However, he draws near between his guardians, the moving corpse, with an unconscious parade step, thin to look at but grown large through shame, so that hatred seizes and dominates his evident tumult. Close to us he finds once more the strength to cry, 'Innocent!', in a toneless, precipitate voice. Here he is before me, at the instant of passing, eyes dry, his gaze lost in the past, no doubt, since his future is dead along with his honor. He no longer has any name. He no longer has any hue. He is colored *traitor*. His face is ashen, deflated, and sunken, without appearance of remorse, assuredly a foreigner, a stray from the ghetto. A steadiness of obstinate audacity persists, and banishes all compassion. It is his last promenade among humans, and one might say he profits from it, so much does he keep himself under control and brave the ignominy. It is a terrible sign that this will of his had not foundered in the mud, that there was neither collapse nor weakness. In this tragic circumstance, tears would not have seemed cowardly.

"The shouts of the people have ceased. The bit of sun has disappeared. Our nerves are exhausted. It is time for the drama to end. The degradation and the marching off have lasted just ten minutes, but our emotions have made a full circuit of the clock. The end of this sinister march is the black van over there in the little avenue, where the cadaver finally arrives and is inserted, lifted up by the gendarmes. We are relieved of his presence.

"Life resumes. The troops break up. Beat, drums! sound, fanfares! Throw upon this vile burial your sonorous mantle. The guns bristle upward. The soldiers march steadfastly, and this spectacle is fixed forever in their eyes. For the idea of the fatherland is so deep-seated and proud that it draws from strengths in its antithesis, and is excited further by attempts directed against it. In the debris of so many beliefs, one faith alone remains real and sincere: that which safeguards our race, our language, the blood of our blood, and which brings us all together in solidarity.

These closed ranks, these are ours. The wretch was not French. We have all understood it through his act, through his carriage, through his face. He has plotted our disaster, but his crime has exalted us. And as, in the midst of the tumult, the commands, and the martial steps I go out from this accursed spectacle, I see rise up in front of me the haughty and simple column erected 'to the memory of the officers and soldiers of the armies of the land and sea fallen on the field of honor for defense of the fatherland.' "

—Léon Daudet

Thus was the news reported in the time of the Dreyfus Affair.

Dreyfus then disappeared from public view, isolated on Devil's Island as if he were one of the lepers who had occupied the place before him. He wrote copiously to his wife. Letters to him and printed materials were severely restricted in quantity and subject to rigorous censorship. On January 19, 1898, the Dreyfusard newspaper *Le Siècle* began publishing his letters to his wife. These soon appeared in a book, which was translated into several languages and read around the world. They showed Dreyfus to be a different man from the one imagined. The following excerpts convey something of their quality and may suggest how they were able to impress sympathetic readers.

December 5, 1894, from the first letter published. Dreyfus was then in prison awaiting trial:

My dear Lucie:

At last I can write a word to you; they have just told me that my trial is set for the 19th of this month. I am refused the right to see you.

I will not tell you all that I have suffered; there are not in the world words strong enough to express it. Do you remember when I used to tell you how happy we were? Everything in life smiled on us. Then all at once a fearful thunderbolt; my brain still is reeling with the shock. For me to be accused of the most monstrous crime that a soldier can commit! Even today I feel that I must be the victim of an awful nightmare.

But I hope in God and in justice. In the end the truth

must come to light. My conscience is calm and tranquil. It reproaches me with nothing. I have done my duty, never have I turned from it. . . .

December 7, 1894:

. . . At the bare thought that they could accuse me of a crime so frightful, so monstrous, my whole being trembles; my body revolts against it. To have worked all my life for one thing alone, to avenge my country, to struggle for her against the infamous ravisher who has snatched from us our dear Alsace, and then to be accused of treason against that country—no, my loved one, my mind refuses to comprehend it! Do you remember my telling you how, when I was in Mulhouse, ten years ago, in September, I heard a German band under our windows celebrating the anniversary of Sedan [surrender of the French Army, 1870]? My grief was such that I wept; I bit the sheets of my bed with rage, and I swore an oath to consecrate all my strength, all my intelligence, to the service of my country against those who thus offered insult to the grief of Alsace. . . .

December 12, 1894:

. . . my brain reels, and my thoughts are at times confused. My soul alone remains unshaken, as steadfast as on that awful day before the monstrous accusation was thrown in my face. My whole being still revolts at the thought of it.

But in the end the truth must be known in spite of everything. We are not living in a century when the light can be hidden. It must be that the whole truth will be known, that my voice will be heard throughout the length and breadth of our dear France—just as my accusation has been heard. It is not only my own honor which I have to defend; it is the honor of all the corps of officers of which I am a part, and a worthy part. . . .

December 14, 1894:

. . . I am happy over the good news you give me regarding the children. You were right to begin to give P[ierrot] cod-liver oil; the time is propitious. Kiss the little fellow for me. How I long to hold the dear children in my arms! . . .

January 5, 1895, from the first of four letters written after the degradation ritual earlier that day:

. . . I have asked myself why I was there; what I was doing there. I seemed the victim of an hallucination; but alas! my garments, torn, sullied, brought me back roughly to the truth. The looks of scorn they cast on me told me too well why I was there. Oh, why could not my heart have been opened by a surgeon's knife, so that they might have read the truth! All the brave, good people along my way could have read it: *"This is a man of honor!"* But how easy it is to understand them! In their place I could not have contained my contempt for an officer who I had been told was a traitor. . . .

January 11, 1895:

. . . Even now it seems sometimes that I must be the victim of a horrible nightmare.

I do not complain of physical sufferings, you know that I despise them; but to know that an accusation of infamy stains my name, when I am innocent—oh, no! no! This is why I have borne all my torment, all the anguish, all the insults. I am convinced that soon or late the truth will come to light, and then they will do me justice.

I can easily excuse this anger, this rage of all the people —the noble people, who have been taught to believe that there is a traitor; but I want to live so that they may know that the traitor is not I.

Upheld by your love, by the boundless love of all of ours, I shall overcome fatality. I do not say that I shall not still have moments of despondency, even of despair. Truly not to complain of an error so monstrous would require a grandeur of soul to which I cannot pretend. But my heart will remain strong and valiant. . . .

You know, moreover, my darling, that the only mercy I have ever asked for is the truth; I hope that my countrymen will not fail in the duty which they owe to a fellow-man, who asks one right only—that the search for the truth may be kept up.

And when the light shines in on my vindication; when they give me back my *galons* [insignia of rank] that I won, and that I am as worthy to wear now as when I won them by my own might; when I am once more in my own place, at the head of my troopers, oh, then, my darling, I shall forget everything—the sufferings, the torture, the insults, the bleeding wounds.

May God and human justice grant that the day break soon! . . .

October 26, 1895, from Devil's Island:

. . . When a man is subjected to a misfortune so undeserved he conquers it; and he does not conquer it by tears, or by recriminations, but by going straight forward. Our goal is our honor, and we should press forward with active, indefatigable energy, an energy that should be as great as the circumstances that exact our effort.

After all, there is a justice in this world, and it is not possible that the innocent should remain subjected to such martyrdom. . . .

May 7, 1896:

. . . Please do not send me any more provisions. The sentiment which inspires me to beg this favor may be puerile, but everything you send me is, by regulations, subjected to a most minute examination, and it seems to me each time that they give you a slap in the face, . . . and my heart bleeds and I tremble with pain of it. . . .

November 24, 1897. By this time, the furor of the Affair was well under way, without Alfred Dreyfus's knowing anything about it. (On this day La Dépêche *of Toulouse published a news article claiming as fact that there was a Dreyfus Syndicate with ten million francs, striving to free the traitor.* La Dépêche *was an important left republican newspaper, with Jean Jaurès a frequent contributor.)*
Dear Lucie:

All these months I have written you many long letters, in which my oppressed heart has unburdened itself of all our too long-endured common sorrow. It is impossible to disengage the mind from its *ego* at all times; to rise above the sufferings of every instant. It is impossible that all my being should not quiver, should not cry aloud with anguish at the thought of all you suffer, at that thought of our dear children; and if when I fall I again and again raise myself up, it is to send forth the thrilling appeal for you, for them.

Though my body, my brain, my heart, everything, is worn out, my soul remains intangible, ever ardent, its determination unshaken and strong in the right of every human being to have justice and truth for himself, for those who belong to him.

And the duty of every one is to co-operate in every effort, by every means, toward this single object—justice and reparation; to put an end at last to this appalling and too long-continued martyrdom of so many human creatures. . . .[1]

Throughout this correspondence Dreyfus maintained the belief that the error made in convicting him would be recognized at last, and he would be vindicated. He repeatedly sought to have his case reopened, trusting in the good will and rectitude of General Boisdeffre, the Chief of Staff, to accomplish this for him. Of course, Boisdeffre was determined that nothing whatever would cause the conviction to be re-examined.

On October 29, 1898, the Cour de Cassation decided that there should be a full-scale reconsideration of Dreyfus's case. More than two weeks later he was told of this decision, but only after the court ordered that he be informed. After that the legal proceedings required that he receive a little more information; otherwise he learned nothing until after the court overturned his conviction the following June. From that moment he was restored to the privileges of a captain, although he remained in confinement on board ship and back in France, pending his retrial two months later.

The second court-martial was held in Rennes rather than Paris, in order to keep the capital more calm than it had been during the trials of Emile Zola. The world's press described every detail of the court-martial. Nothing in that often bizarre display struck the journalists so forcibly as their seeing at last the occasion for all the furor, the prisoner from Devil's Island. The following was written by a young English journalist, George Warrington Steevens:

> Instantly the black, rippling hall is still as marble, silent as the grave. A sergeant usher went to a door—the tramp of his feet was almost startling—on the right hand of the top of the hall.

It opened and two officers stepped out. One of them was the greatest villain or the greatest victim in France—and for the moment men wondered which was he. It seemed almost improper that the most famous man in the world was walking in just as you or I might.

Then all saw him, and the whole hall broke into a gasp. There came in a little old man—an old, old man of thirty-nine. A middle-statured, thick-set old man in the black uniform of the artillery; over the red collar his hair was gone white as silver, and on the temples and at the back of the crown he was bald. As he turned to face the judges there was a glimpse of a face both burned and pale—a rather broad, large featured face with a thrusting jaw and chin. It was not Jewish in expression until you saw it in profile. The eyes under the glasses were set a trifle close together, and not wholly sympathetic either; you might guess him hard, stubborn, cunning. But this is only guessing: what we did see in the face was suffering and effort—a misery hardly to be borne, and a tense, agonized striving to bear and to hide it. Here is a man, you would say, who has endured things unendurable, and just lives through—maybe to endure more.

He walked up two steps to his seat with a gait full of resolve yet heavy, constrained, mechanical—such a gait as an Egyptian mummy might walk with if it came to life in its swathing grave-clothes. He saluted the President with a white-gloved hand, took off his *képi*, sat down.[2]

In his *Five Years of My Life,* Dreyfus said nothing of this trial and very little of other events after the June 1899 reversal of his original conviction. In recalling how he heard of this reversal, he wrote of his great joy, then went on to say:

Of my own story, I knew nothing. I had remained in 1894, with the *bordereau* as the sole document in the dossier, with the sentence of the court-martial, with the frightful execution parade, with the "Death!" cries of a deluded crowd; I believed in the rectitude of General de Boisdeffre, I believed in a Chief of State, Félix Faure, both of them anxious for justice and truth. A veil had been stretched in front of my eyes, rendered more inpenetrable each day; the few facts that I had learned in the last few months had remained incomprehensible to me. I had just learned the name of Esterhazy, about the forgery of Lieutenant-Colonel Henry, his suicide; with the heroic Lieutenant-Colonel Picquart I had only our past contacts in the service. The grandiose struggle set in motion by a few great spirits in love with light and truth, this was totally unknown to me.[3]

Although he would learn many of the facts, Alfred Dreyfus would never be in a position really to comprehend the struggle waged over him. In the pages that follow, we shall try to see what he could not.

4

A Country Divided

Twelve years. Twelve years required to dispose of treason charges that should never have been brought in the first place. Two years of the most intense factional struggle, in which the future of the nation seemed at stake. Fifty years before France could escape the shadow cast by the experience. And, after a time that now approaches a full century, the legacy of those twelve years still seems a heavy burden. Every year new books and articles try to comprehend the Affair's great and little mysteries.

All this could not have begun with the crime that was the occasion for it. We must look farther back to discover what developments conditioned the responses in battle of those who cared so much for how an alleged criminal was judged. Like contemporary observers in other countries, who watched the conflict in amazement, most of us can readily begin to grasp what motivated the Dreyfusards. Their values were very much in what we have understood to be the main current of modern Western culture. There may be riddles about them too, but they do not baffle us as may the stubbornness and fury of the anti-Dreyfusards. Because of this, inquiry into antecedents should concentrate mainly upon the origins of anti-Dreyfusard attitudes. It should also look for chronic conflict in the country that might have found expression in the struggle over Captain Dreyfus and help to explain its intensity.

At the end of the nineteenth century France was a severely divided country. Although long bound by a centralized and bureaucratic state system, it was nevertheless much fragmented by regional, social, and ideological differences which made its supposed unity an illusion. Each of these categories will be examined in turn, with emphasis upon the last, especially the disaffection of many from the government of the Third French Republic.

People in many parts of the country felt more reason for attachment to their own locales than they did to the claims of French nationalism. Before the mid-nineteenth century France was not an integral nation but a composite bound together by a succession of political regimes, none of which had won the general allegiance of the peoples governed. There was no general sense of community or commonality: Too few ties existed between different parts of the country. Abstract political visions of nationality did capture some people but could not readily transcend the actual divisions felt by the rest. By the nineteenth century's end a national identity had become better established but conflicted still with regional particularism, and with indifference or antagonism toward the metropolitan center, Paris, which often seemed alien.[1]

Locales very often had little contact with one another. With primitive inland transport and mostly localized economies, isolation was inevitable for most of the population. During the second half of the nineteenth century this changed, with rapid, comparatively cheap transport and wire communications making the breakdown of isolation possible, though not automatic. People in every corner of France were increasingly affected by what their fellow citizens elsewhere did.

France was divided also by lack of a common language. At mid-century French was a foreign tongue to half the citizens, and few were literate in it. Perhaps a fifth or more knew no French at all. Dialect differences were substantial, and patois speakers were not likely to be receptive to outlanders, especially when the latter so often brought sharp commercial practice, more government control, or other apparent harm. The unity of culture, language, and literature dear to nationalists was an ideal realized only for the well-educated, and even among them it was often countered by particularism in their native provinces.

Internal barriers were reduced in the 1850s and 1860s by economic development, especially railway construction. Much more effort at reduction of differences and nation building was undertaken with the establishment in 1875 of France's Third Republic.

After Napoleon III's imperial regime collapsed in 1870, Republicans eventually prevailed but for many years had to contend against a powerful royalist opposition. Insecure in their shaky claim to citizen allegiance, and endowed by their republican forebears with a nationalist ideology, the new regime's leaders were determined to make the people truly republican and French in their loyalties. This was to be accomplished above all by political education, which would indoctrinate the populace with the requisite political values. Education would also enlighten it, banishing superstition—especially that of Catholicism—raising moral levels, and preparing people to be useful, docile participants in modern progress.

Previously schooling had with a few exceptions been rudimentary and crude, and much of it had been conducted by priests and nuns. The Third Republic made major improvements in all aspects of education and did much to secularize it through limiting the role played by the Church's schools and teaching orders. Moreover, every effort was made to staff schools with committed republicans who would give political indoctrination a central place in their teaching. They made French language and history instruction their best instruments for the purpose of indoctrination, which was proudly proclaimed by the Republic's leading educators.

In time the desired effects were at least partly achieved, with ever more people able to speak and read French and with a sense of French national identity seeming to be ever better established. Republicanism's successes were less readily apparent, but election results indicated that indoctrination might be increasingly effective in this respect as well.

Nevertheless, such education could not end regionalism and distrust of the regime. Antagonisms dividing France remained, more transformed than transcended. In particular, the secularization of education was the most obvious and probably the most substantial action taken by the Third Republic to reduce the influence of the Catholic Church. This aroused intense hostility among the clergy and many of the Catholic faithful. Controversial measures implementing secularization policy were adopted over the course of decades, thus keeping this education issue one of the most important reasons for continuing severe antagonism toward the Republic.

Development of the French economy created strains that contributed fundamentally to conflict. While strain seems to have been limited in extent earlier, by the late nineteenth century industrialization and urbanization were finally making their impact felt throughout France. Geographic isolation had once insulated people in many places from change and all the dangers it might bring. Now this protective isolation was scarcely possible, as railroad branch lines and increasingly vigorous modern economic activity touched almost everywhere. Traditional crafts and agriculture became subject to the new forces of commerce and finance. Workers often were displaced from their jobs by the effects of industrial and commercial development and competition, and industrial centers drew labor from all over the country.

Modernity brought both real and illusory advantages to many of the French, and they often welcomed and rejoiced over the changes. Yet modernity brought harm as well, notably the widespread effects of recurrent economic slumps in the last quarter of the nineteenth century. Change also brought uncertainty and strangeness. Old, familiar forms often seemed more desirable, and stability promised security, while novelty could seem to threaten harm. Isolation's end introduced outside influences, which severely disrupted local folkways and led to the discarding of many customs. Even where the immediate practical harm of change was not great, people could be concerned about what might happen next.

Thus, dread of potential injuries and resentment of actual ones were powerful forces shaping a wide range of attitudes in late-nineteenth-century France. Inevitably many of these attitudes found political expression, especially through hostility against the Republic—which represented itself as the principal agency of change. It was indeed a major innovative force, both through such direct intervention as educational indoctrination and through its regular, energetic actions to protect and advance private business interests, especially those in the more aggressive segments of capitalist enterprise.

Urban workers had originally been receptive to the promise of universal benefits to be derived from republican politics and liberal economic development. The poor of Paris and other cities had risen for this cause in the Revolutions of 1789, 1830, and 1848. Then came bloody, brutal repression of additional worker rebellion later in 1848, and much more terrible repression of workers who revolted in 1871. In the cities the social distance between the middle and working classes had grown so great that they had little contact and often viewed each other with mutual enmity. The bourgeoisie by turns ignored the workers and feared them, anticipated revolt and prepared repression. Workers endured, but as their anger welled up they became more threatening still. And rural folk feared both the urban workers and the middle classes, who intruded into rural life by means of modernizing economic activity, increasing government intervention, and periodic political upheaval.

Workers disillusioned with the promise of republicanism and liberalism turned gradually to trade unionism and proletarian political movements, most of them leftist in orientation, though some were associated with the right. Strikes became more common, both with and without union organization, as did violent clashes between workers and either employers or, more often, the State's guardians of civil harmony and free enterprise. Indeed, strikers and bosses often did not negotiate with each other, and government officials intervened to maintain order by either resolving labor disputes or repressing them.[2]

The Republic's promise to proletarians remained effective enough to cause most of their political action to follow legal paths, especially those of electoral and parliamentary politics. Anarchists and other especially militant rebels also had influence, however, for they better expressed the anger and impatience that suffering people often felt. Still, development of all proletarian movements proceeded at a modest pace; workers belonging to unions or voting for socialist candidates remained minorities in the general population, and popular attitudes were not radically transformed by other movement activity, either. In retrospect proletarian revolution in France appears to have been most unlikely.

Nevertheless, the bourgeoisie took the threat of militant labor and the radical left to be very grave. Employers were loath to accede to any worker requests, and socialist intentions against private property were anathema. It was common to regard workers as little more than brutes whose human qualities existed mainly as potential for future evolution. Bourgeois observers supposed that a subhuman existence of poverty, ignorance, alcoholism, hereditary defects, and disease had left them degenerates who threatened the continued progress and even the survival of society. Memories and fantasies of riot and rebellion made more fortunate people fear any gathering of workers as a potentially dangerous mob.

Actual disturbances and attacks were magnified out of all proportion to their real frequency or import. One killing in a strike became the germ of widely believed fantasies about frequent murderous strike violence. Extremist rhetoric by radicals was taken as a serious indication of devilish plots afoot. Rhetorical excesses by anarchists were accompanied by by a rash of sensational bombings and other violence, which were concentrated in the two years just before the Dreyfus Affair began. While most of the assassins were deranged individuals with little connection to any actual movement, these attacks produced hysteria and anticipation of an Armageddon of class war. The fears did not vanish when the assaults subsided. Especially alarming was the rise in the late 1890s of revolutionary syndicalism, a seemingly potent movement directing organized labor toward anarchist social revolution.

The State security apparatus worked assiduously to counter these supposed threats, with the greatest effort directed against anarchism and revolutionary syndicalism. Much energy was expended upon collecting intelligence about supposedly subversive activity. Repressive laws were enacted, and criminal prosecution of radicals was employed as a political weapon. Preparation was made to contain or suppress trouble ranging from disorderly strikes to riots to full-fledged revolt. From 1898 on there were elaborate contingency plans to mobilize both police and Army in any strength needed for this purpose.

Anxiety over the threat of proletarian upheaval colored the outlook of many during the Dreyfus Affair, especially with a prominent part being played in it socialists and anarchists, and with the Dreyfusards organizing many large meetings and demonstrations, any of which might explode into riot, as some did. This helps to explain the acute crisis of October 1898, when there was a conjunction of hysterias, with strikes of construction and railroad workers occurring at the same time as the Fashoda confrontation and rumors of an imminent rightist coup. (See Chapter Two.) Security contingency plans then led to the massive Army intervention in the strikes.[3]

The French security apparatus was also obsessed with espionage by foreign powers, especially Germany. While a few instances of spying were uncovered, the actual danger was minor. Nevertheless, spy paranoia was fed by a combination of feelings —insecurity over the military situation and bellicosity with respect to Germany. France's humiliating defeat in the 1870 Franco-Prussian War and consequent loss of territory left many of the French with a passionate desire for revenge, and the assumption that Germany was reciprocally bellicose. By the end of the century the urge to revenge had diminished, but it had contributed to an altered, xenophobic nationalism. Yet France could not be sure of the adequacy of its Army, and this insecurity was much aggravated by a sense of isolation in international affairs. Germany had built anti-French alliances for which France could not compensate until the conclusion of the 1894 Franco-Russian alliance, and that was a relationship of uncertain value.

These factors then provided the context for the sensationalism of the Dreyfus espionage case, and the gravity attributed to the alleged crime. They also contributed powerfully to the urgency with which many rejected any challenge to the Army leaders and condemned their critics. Although *domestic* politics made the struggle over Dreyfus what it was, the *context* of military and foreign affairs was essential.

Actually neither the left nor espionage could really subvert the Third Republic, but danger from the right in France was another matter. There were, as we have indicated, many French conservatives who were in no way content with the country's system of government. A century of revolutions had left France with a republican constitution and a political tradition that most citizens regarded with ambivalence if not outright antipathy. The two-decade-old Republic did not function well enough to have engendered general respect or loyalty; many in France would not attach to this regime any national loyalties they had. Ideas of the French revolutionary tradition had widely potent evocative force, but it often was very negative. There were still many people who hated or feared what they thought revolution and republicanism had produced. Even where this tradition evoked positive response, it was mainly a matter of ill-defined symbolism and vague if passionate attitudes. There was no single coherent ideology upon which French republicans could stand firm against challenge or from which they could proceed to reconstitute the system.

One traditional republican passion was anticlericalism, which contributed greatly to deep-seated antirepublicanism among most of the Catholic clergy and a large part of the Catholic faithful. This conflict reflected the larger division between those whose outlooks were formed by Catholicism and the many others with primarily secular perspectives, or those shaped by other religions.

Most French citizens were nominally Catholic, but indifference and agnosticism were common, and irregular observance of rites still more so. Genuine devotion to Catholicism was much more general in some regions than in others. Protestants and Jews formed a significant presence, but more through their *supposed* weight in French life than through their actual numbers, which were not large.[4] Prejudice against both minorities was substantial, and connected to their imagined influence in the economy and politics. Both groups had been persecuted in the past but had benefited in the nineteenth century from liberal tolerance.

Toward the end of the century this tolerance was countered by growing, virulent antagonism toward Jews and Protestants. Rejection of them was premised upon the rightists' proposition that Catholicism was essential to French identity, and Jews and Protestants were thus unassimilable interlopers.

At the same time, the French right was renewing itself, assuming a vigorous, reshaped form on the basis of enmity toward the Republic, which was secular, and insistence upon a vital national being, which was Catholic. By no means all of those adopting such views were pious Catholics; some of those prominent on the right professed Catholic allegiance as a matter of political ideology only, or at least their religious beliefs were not profound. Likewise, very devout Catholics often allowed them-

selves to believe that a politics of rancor was consonant with
Christian faith and the God of Love. Catholicism thus was very
much embedded in political ideology.

When one looks at the daily practice of politics, the right
appears to have been endlessly varied and amorphous. France
did not at this time have a regular, stable array of organized
political parties. Alliances and voting blocs for electoral and parliamentary purposes were loose and frequently shifting. Nevertheless, elements of the right were linked through a common
antipathy to the Republic, and this remained the evident basis
of coherence for the right.

In the first years of the Third Republic the right had been
essentially monarchist, though divided by differences in ideology and by disagreement over which of several claimants to a
French throne should command loyalty. Many on the right were
deeply reactionary and unreconciled to the modern political institutions introduced since 1789. Others accepted different parts
of that legacy but remained conservative about its application.

Monarchists had firm bases of support in many sections of
the country and among influential groups: the clergy, the aristocracy, army officers, and some journalists and men of letters.
Nevertheless, after 1879 the electoral strength of republicans was
greater, and monarchists were repeatedly frustrated in attempts
to supplant them. Two of the three principal royal pretenders
died without direct heirs, leaving a poor residue of alternatives
upon whom to pin hopes of a revived monarchy.[5] Monarchism
suffered further setbacks through failed efforts at a restoration
and through Pope Leo XIII's 1892 encyclical, *Inter multiplices sol-
licitudines*, calling upon French Catholics to "rally" in support of
the Republic. Most royalists rejected this order, but it undermined their position nevertheless.

These developments helped make monarchism effectively a
lost cause, but the more general and profound changes occurring
during the same period did more to accomplish that. In a modernizing France, other forms and movements better suited evolv-
ing attitudes.

However, the political effects of modernization across the
country were highly varied, with minimal political change not
confined just to the most backward areas. The political inclinations of each area were shaped through the interaction of so
many variable factors that seemingly homogeneous populations

were in fact highly differentiated from one small district to the next. With the overall differentiation of individual districts went wide variation both in the weight and nature of modernization's impact and in political mutability.[6]

In many districts monarchism survived even after it had become a lost cause, although less through voter's love for kings than through their deference to local notables. Although the motivations of aristocracy and Catholic clergy differed, the bulk of each still refused to accept the consequences of the Revolution of 1789 and continued to keep faith for royalism. Other notables sometimes had similar views. With the right combinations of factors these reactionaries could regularly bring their districts along with them. At the national level this enduring base gave monarchists a political weight that was much reinforced by the sympathy of the elites mentioned earlier and by the personal prestige and the oratorical and writing skills of monarchist spokesmen.

Their politics was scarcely distinguishable from that of other traditionalist conservatives—many of them with similar backgrounds and support in home districts—who had tried to come to terms with the Republic. Leo XIII's command or lost hope in restoration had made onetime monarchists discard loyalty to a pretender but not change their basic attitudes.

Monarchism and such kindred conservatism were important in the Dreyfus Affair, but not primarily because agents of the pretender attempted coups to restore him. These still influential conservatives fought the Dreyfusards in defense of the Army and the Church, while seeking to transform the Republic in order to realize their vision of what France should be, even without a king.

Their role exemplifies a basic condition of the Affair's political struggle: Factions could be potent without either a very broad base of popular support or effective party organization. The highly differentiated population provided bases for a wide spectrum of disparate factions, which elicited support mainly through the personal prestige of leaders and the evoking in speech and print of vague but powerful symbols. There was too little room for the politics of compromise and pluralism, but much room for embittered struggle over issues and symbols that seemed vital.

The broad central segment of this spectrum was republican.

French republicanism had once led a continental movement for the radical transformation of civilization, through the reconstitution of government and law. The universal rights of all men, all citizens . . . equality before the law and liberty under its rule . . . popular sovereignty . . . science's mastery over nature and superstition . . . progress through freeing man's limitless energy and capacity from ancient bonds. Such beliefs belonged to an eighteenth-century legacy, one cherished fiercely in the nineteenth as primary faith by Europeans who fought to make republics an enduring reality. Critics on both the left and right often found such beliefs vague, simplistic, self-interested, and blind to the reality of poverty, but this criticism left most republicans virtually untouched and confident that political virtue was exclusively theirs.

From one generation to the next, French republicanism became ever less radical. Articles of faith that had served well in fighting for the cause lost their power as republican goals were realized, or seemed to be. More important, as the supremacy of the bourgeoisie was established in nearly every sphere, the class no longer needed to preoccupy itself with challenging the old elites. Instead, it felt its own position threatened from below, and the egalitarian premise of republican ideology assumed a different and distressing import. Bourgeois conviction about the actual equality of all men may never have run very deep, but a century after the Declaration of the Rights of Man in 1789 that idea seemed positively foolhardy.

For many republicans the legacy of radicalism was supplanted by a kind of conservatism, bent upon preventing any disruption of the existing social order. Government served to protect and promote private wealth more than universal human rights. The old formulas of republican ideology were retained, but its onetime fire was largely quenched and the reality of government seemed to be a matter of practical, defensively cautious pursuit of personal and class self-interest.

The radical elements in the republican tradition were not altogether discarded, and they were still cherished by some, but this "social conservatism" was characteristic of the way republicans governed France in the years before the Dreyfus Affair. The long-lasting refusal of so many republicans to entertain the possibility of a new trial for Dreyfus can be partly attributed to these shifts in their political values. Their conservatives' caution made them resistant to anything so likely to disrupt the unstable equilibrium in public affairs, especially when much of the impetus came from the left. And their much attentuated idealism made it difficult for them to be stirred by the injustice said to have been done to Dreyfus and others. Theirs was an anti-Dreyfusism of passive resistance.

Most anti-Dreyfusard activism, on the other hand, came from a "new right," which was reacting against the politics of the Third Republic and against modernity itself. Its reaction was quite different from but linked to the traditionalist conservatism already mentioned. This new right was heterogeneous, but its different segments had some common themes and purposes; in particular, there was a general urge to obtain substantial change in both the constitutional form and the animating spirit of France's government. In this sense and in its hostility to the republicanism of the dominant parties, this new right was anti-republican—and in 1898 "Long live the Republic!" was immediately understood as a provocative Dreyfusard slogan. However, most of its spokesmen affirmed their dedication to *a* republic, though not to this one as it stood.

Calling this current of opinion the "new right" and saying it was reactionary and antimodern suggests that it should also be regarded as conservative. So it should, yet it had radical, even revolutionary elements, involved a sort of demagogic populism, and included some who called themselves socialists (although they were not accepted as such by most socialists).

The new right's antipathy to the Third Republic involved a complex of reactions against current practice of both parliamentarism and democracy. By the late 1880s this reaction had begun to coalesce. There were concerted attacks upon the regime, especially in association with the Boulangist agitation of 1887–89 and uproar over the Wilson and Panama scandals in 1887 and 1892. Criticism of the Republic was given further definition during the 1890s in the discourse of politicians, journalists, and men of letters. As antipathy became more fully defined and frequently expressed, the way was prepared for a clash that would be much more severe than any before.

The Boulangist agitation involved an attempt to bring a popular general to power. General Boulanger had managed to appeal widely both to left republicans and to patriots who thought that national vitality had been sapped by a corrupt regime. The stink of alleged corruption was intensified by discovery that the President's son-in-law, Daniel Wilson, was conducting a busy trade in official decorations (like the Legion of Honor), and operating this commerce right in the Presidential Palace. The Republic was badly shaken by the ensuing crisis, then was threatened anew and more gravely by a vigorous campaign across the country to make Boulanger the national savior, if need be setting aside constitutional process to do it. Support for the general came from many quarters, inspired by hopes for a government genuinely responsive to the people, for national regeneration, or even for restoration of king or emperor.

When in fear of arrest Boulanger fled to Belgium on April Fool's Day, 1889, the movement soon dissolved, but the sentiments and personalities that had driven it lived on. (With no money or friends left, the general himself committed suicide in 1891, at the grave of his mistress.) In 1892 came a fresh shock: the collapse of the company formed to build a canal across Panama. Investors lost enormous sums, much of which had been obtained through government support of the venture. It was revealed that there had been massive bribery of large numbers of politicians and journalists, including some of the most prominent republican leaders. It was a perfect opportunity for those who thought this regime beyond redemption, and they made the most of it. Panama did not provide them a long enough lever to overturn the Republic, but from then on verbal attack upon it was increasingly strident and potentially dangerous.

The immediate focal point of opposition was the apparent corruption and ineffectuality of parliamentary government. Recent history seemed to prove that politicians were concerned with enriching themselves individually and with securing their party and class interests, without care for morality, law, or the interests of France as a whole. Limited government accomplishment and frequent changes of ministries appeared to demonstrate constitutional inability to act effectively, no matter how urgent the need. To many it seemed that the Republic had no firmly determined policy except the suppression of potential antirepublican sentiment, especially through persecution of the Catholic Church.

Behind this rightist perception of corruption and ineffectuality lay other attitudes and ideas, which varied with the opponents. Their objectives were nevertheless comparable. They would end corruption by substituting some higher morality for the egoism that had prevailed in the Third Republic until then. Ineffectuality would be ended by rendering political authority less diffuse and more firmly determined.

Many opponents had no definite program for accomplishing these purposes. Others prescribed constitutional change, transferring some power from governing ministries and the parliamentary Chambers to the President of the Republic. More drastic solutions involved instituting some basically authoritarian regime, with decisions of the national leadership confirmed by plebiscites, and with the new regime perhaps achieved through a popularly supported coup d'état. This was supposed to be democratic, since the people would speak through plebiscites, as well as through a more restricted use of voting to select officials. In addition, the Affair was to give birth to the neoroyalism of the Action Française. This sought rule by a hereditary monarch as the logical way to have authority centered in someone who would always remain above the self-interest and instability of partisan politics.

Among the attackers, typical bourgeois conservatives wanted only limited change, making the national leadership more undivided, authoritative, and stable in order to resist the threats of social upheaval and socialism or anarchism. Part of their charge against the Republic was its supposed vulnerability to the mob and to the rising parliamentary influence of the left, especially socialists. But at the same time there were others, radicals of the right, who thought the existing regime much too unresponsive to the will and needs of the people. The urge to plebiscitary "democracy" was felt by many onetime left republicans, as well as Bonapartists. For both the populism of the 1789 Revolution's Jacobin tradition remained important, but they sought to fulfill its promise through creating a popular authoritarian regime.

While some of these populists carried on the anticlericalism of the republican tradition, another strain of radical populism sought to make the Church once more the vital center of national life. In this vision, the Church drew all people to its bosom, rescued the unfortunate, and shaped the moral core of the community; it provided salvation in both this life and the next. The community was sustained by legions of simple priests and nuns selflessly devoting their lives to serving the ordinary people of

France, and Catholicism was the opposite of the Republic's un-caring inhumanity and rationalist amorality.

Some Catholic populists drew upon the tradition of Jacobin democracy, despite its anticlericalism. In the Church all were equal, as they had proved not to be in the bourgeois Republic. However, the counter-Revolutionary tradition of the century since 1789 also contributed to this populism, with long-nurtured hatred of the Republic giving it added force. Priests played a prominent part in this—especially those of the Assumption-ist order—and thereby reinforced loyal republicans in their view that clericalism was more than ever the archenemy of the Republic.

With all their variety, opponents of the Republic did find common ground, and they found it in nationalism, with a new twist. French nationalism had long been typically republican. This older nationalism sprang from belief in the fraternity and equality of all humanity, because all men are rational beings and thus fundamentally the same. France was simply the most ad-vanced civilization on a road all would travel; thus it was the leader on mankind's march to liberation. Although in practice less pure about its universalism than in this ideal, republican nationalism was not exclusive. Rather it aimed at spreading the virtue of French civilization to less fortunate peoples. Both in this and with its faith in liberalism, science, and progress, the republican tradition differed sharply from the nationalism devel-oping on the right.

The new nationalism stemmed to begin with from the hu-miliation of defeat in the 1870–71 war with Prussia. Compensat-ing for the disaster's shock led to exaltation of France as superior *by her very nature*—along with attribution of the defeat to moral and spirtual decline of the nation. Whatever one did not like about contemporary France could be identified as a cause of the degeneration. Even though not created until after the defeat, the Third Republic was often blamed, by accusing the republican opposition to the pre-1870 imperial government and by regard-ing France as corrupted by republicanism ever since 1789.

Military calamity and a desire for revenge had provided the occasion for an upsurge of nationalism, but not for its departure from the old republican form. As the decades passed, nationalist sentiment continued to intensify among much the same politi-cally engaged individuals who were so aggrieved by the Republic. Their dissatisfaction was not simply political in origin. Such characteristics of modern culture as rapacious and exploitative capitalism, the filth of urban industry, and new philosophical and literary modes repelled and even terrified them. They saw all this as corruption or loss of the virtue and spirit that had animated man.

Many of the people thus disturbed knew only from a distance much of what they so disliked and dreaded; its very unfamiliarity made distaste more likely. Often it was a matter of felt vulnerability to forces beyond ken or control, feelings probably common to much of the population. These forces were human ones, the agencies and creations of modernizing civilization.

For provincial farmers or small businessmen the alien powers might be simply wholesale markets in distant cities, railroads, or the Paris stock exchange. For the men of letters, journalists, and others articulating discontent, the trouble lay in rationalization of modern culture. Decadence resulted from substituting the artificial constructs of intellect for practices and ideas that grew naturally through man's experience.

Those who said this wanted in effect to replace machines with mystiques, the overarching mystique being that of the nation. *La Patrie*—the Fatherland—was the land, the earth itself, and the generations that had lived, died, and been buried there. It was one people united by the heritage of that land and those generations by common blood, common language, common culture, common history. Modern rationality cared little for that organic unity, and in the name of progress divided and corrupted the nation by forcing upon it innovations alien to its nature.

So went the mythology of the new nationalism. If there was actually little unity in France, any perception of this was submerged in passionate conviction or explained away. Social class divisions, for example, were symptoms of modern decadence. Regional differences were integral to traditional France, whose superior being incorporated all into the whole. Religious differences were the consequence of alien incursions (Genevan Protestantism and Oriental Judaism) and the sins of abstract intellect (freethinking). Political divisions could disappear if true patriotism became the basic determinant of politics.

The myth was complete, persuasive, and impervious to counterargument. It may not have gained the widest currency in a country where national sentiment of any kind was still not well established. Yet it could be a potent propaganda instrument, if nationalist spokesmen could get audiences to associate the unwanted effects of modern change they felt with the targets of attack.

And there stood the Third Republic, the self-proclaimed champion of modernity, the obvious target, one that seemed to represent all the others. In particular, the Republic embodied the impersonally rational approach to judgment and action supposed to be characteristic of modernity. Thus, liberal parliamentarism was obnoxious because of its ideal that disinterested, reasoned debate should make policy and because it was seen as responding much more to special interests than to national ones. Liberal individualism—the essence of republican philosophy—was still more opposed to organic nationalism in practice than in its basic idea: Individualist pursuit of self-interest was believed especially responsible for national division and decline. The republican dream of progress relied upon the fruits of scientific thought and would have science supplant religious faith; but science involved above all the unnatural constructs of intellect that nationalists found so abhorrent.

Above all, the nationalists sought spiritual and moral vitality, part of their metaphor of the nation as organism, and saw decadence as national enervation. They believed that the prevailing republicans could not appreciate how essential was this vitality, for there was little room in the republicans' rationalist tradition for such a mystique. Thus, however much the Republic pursued national purposes, like preparing recovery of territory lost to Germany, it could not fulfill the requirements of the new nationalists. Instead, it had to be made over, not *reformed* but *transcended* into a truly national regime—one that would be moral and animate instead of amoral and artificial.

Patriotism itself was a higher morality to rescue France from decadence, but patriotism needed institutional embodiment, and neither the contemporary State nor its chiefs could yet be that. Catholicism was the obvious answer: It provided moral and spiritual foundations, and it was regarded as a major part of France's traditional core. Many nationalists were devoted Catholics, though many others looked to the Church primarily for tactical reasons. Thus the new nationalism was usually clerical, but often not particularly religious.

However, the Church was not a sufficient vehicle with which to carry patriotism. For one thing, anticlericalism remained a passion for some nationalist militants and for many whose support the nationalists hoped to win. For another, there was the unacceptable Papal encyclical commanding cooperation with the Republic. More generally, it seemed to many nationalists that the Church had compromised itself and had failed to be a staunch enough champion of the nation. Even the Catholic populists thought the Church had departed from its vital role and had to be brought back.

The primary embodiment of the national ideal was the Army. Despite the frightful incompetence of its effort in the 1870 war, the Army came to be seen as the one major institution unsullied by its part in modern developments. One contemporary of the Affair called the Army "the age-old institution binding us to the past—not mingled with the nation but above it, . . . bearing the role, the lofty mission of the protector of society, once belonging to the Church, but which the Church can fulfill no longer."[7]

The nationalist mystique required an ethic of discipline, courage, readiness to act forcefully, honor, and devotion of self to nation. These antique virtues assumed fresh importance in their supposed opposition to the perceived vices of a decadent society. With yearning for renewal of these military qualities came nostalgia for a lost past in which they were thought to have prevailed. Added to this were still fierce desires for revenge against Germany and recovery of Alsace and Lorraine. The result was a cult of the soldier, which had taken form soon after the 1870 defeat and grew with the new nationalism. The soldier not only was bearer of the purified ethic, he was above factional struggle, for his sole cause was that of France. Only he could bring cohesion to the divided land.

This cult began with impassioned rhetoric and poetry. The greatest impact was due to the poetry of Paul Déroulède, who during the Affair was to lead quixotic attempts at a coup d'état. His verse, appearing in many editions from 1872 on, glorified the Army and created a legend of its heroism in 1870.

> *In France, which everything divides,*
> *What Frenchman takes for his device*
> *Each one for all, and all for France?*
> *The Soldier.*

In these our hours of indifference,
Who keeps deep in his heart a hope
Which everything strikes, but does not destroy?
    The Soldier.

Who makes the rounds when all do sleep?
When all in peril are, who keeps the watch?
Who suffers, who dies, who fights?
    The Soldier.

Oh role immense! Oh holy task!
On march without cries, falls without complaint
Who works for our redemption?
    The Soldier.

And on his tomb obscure and proud,
For recompense and for prayer
What would he want carved there?
    "A Soldier." [8]

Initially the cult of the soldier and Army lacked precise intellectual form but gained it as some of the most talented minds in France constructed a nationalist theory. In it they treated the Army as the essential foundation of national unity, because its disciplined and hierarchical structure made it immune to division and instability. Thus it was the necessary antithesis to the most despised characteristics of civilian politics.

Militarist cultism and a rationale of the Army as unifier made a very effective combined appeal. However, the Army was actually a major cause of political division, between champions and opponents of the military. Much opposition to the Army resulted from thinking it politically reactionary. Thus, antimilitarism intensified when reactionary civilians made so much of the military's importance for political salvation. Divisions deepened with reciprocal interaction of antimilitarists versus nationalists and soldiers.

As should be expected, the officers of the French Army were indeed conservative and nationalistic. By late in the century the officer corps had become a haven for aristocrats with few other opportunities in a bourgeois age, and they were still more conservative than their middle-class brethren. Many of them had monarchist sympathies. Some officers, including even senior ones, may have been at least nominal republicans, but their republicanism often was only grudging acceptance of the inevitable or opportunism for sake of careers. The officers were rather like cloistered monks, having limited contact with civilians and bound to a military society that molded their views and demanded conformity to its prevailing values.

Whatever their opinions, French officers generally kept themselves aloof from civilian politics, as indeed was required by the state. Despite almost universal hostility among officers toward the Dreyfusards, the fears of the latter that the Army would join or initiate a coup d'état had little basis. Any officer sentiment in that direction could not develop far enough to overcome long-established restraints.

However, the officer corps was accustomed to autonomy in conducting most aspects of their Army's affairs. Intervention by Dreyfusards demanding revision of a court-martial was quite intolerable. The officers' resistance was the reflex of a closed corporation affronted by the creatures they found most contemptible: politicians, intellectuals, hack journalists, Jews.

Contempt, distrust, and animosity were the common coinage of social intercourse in France. If war between states is an extension of international politics, French domestic politics was an extension of chronic civil war. Much of the time the warfare was covered by a façade of prosperity and conventional civility, but public debate often deteriorated into brawls, even in the national parliament. Political invective was a highly developed art form, much practiced in the press and on rostrums, with audiences actively expressing their outrage or delight. The open antagonism so often displayed in words suggests that there were acute and pervasive hostilities that otherwise were not readily exposed to view.

Nowhere was this violence more evident than in the rapid upsurge later in the century of hatred against Jews, Freemasons, and Protestants.

5

Diabolical Trinity: Jews, Masons, and Protestants

The Semite is money-grubbing, greedy, scheming, subtle, sly; the Aryan is enthusiastic, heroic, chivalrous, disinterested, frank, trustful to the point of naiveté. The Semite is an earth-dweller scarcely seeing beyond his present life; the Aryan is a son of the sky ceaselessly preoccupied with superior aspirations. The one lives in reality, the other in the ideal.

The Semite is by instinct a merchant. He has a vocation for trade, a genius for all matters of exchange, for everything giving an opportunity to deceive his fellow man. The Aryan is farmer, poet, monk, and especially soldier; war is his true element, he goes to meet danger joyously, he braves death.

The Semite has no creative faculty; on the contrary the Aryan invents—not even the slightest invention has been due to a Semite. In contrast the latter exploits, organizes and effects the production of the Aryan creator's invention, whose benefits he naturally keeps for himself. . . .

In sum, all which is for man an excursion into unknown

regions, an effort to enlarge the terrestrial domain, is absolutely beyond the Semite, and especially the Jewish Semite. He can live only as a parasite in the middle of a civilization that he has not made. [Edouard Drumont, *La France juive* (1886)].[1]

Thus goes one of the best-selling, most widely read books of nineteenth-century France, two volumes and more than twelve hundred pages of wide-ranging invective and spurious history. So long a book should not have been so popular, but its author was a propagandist of imposing genius, and readers were ready to be fascinated by him.

Public eagerness to consume anti-Semitic claptrap was something new, with nothing before Drumont's *La France juive* attracting comparable attention. Jews had in fact gained a remarkable degree of acceptance in France. Liberalism demanded religious toleration, and consequently Jews in France had been emancipated from all legal disabilities in 1791. Liberal values and active participation by Jews in a changing society had gone far to win them acceptance.

Before the 1880s anti-Semitism in politics was evident mainly among some, not all, socialists, who associated Jews with finance capital. Their anti-Semitism was selective but expressed in general terms, because liberal taboos against generic prejudice had not yet become established. The Affair would teach socialists the hazards for their own cause of anti-Semitism.

Social prejudice against Jews did continue throughout the nineteenth century. They were often caricatured in literature, with frequent derisive treatment of them reflecting a common aversion. Nevertheless, they were ever more freely accepted into society, especially its higher strata. Marriage of aristocrats with rich Jews was notorious, perhaps more widespread in gossip than in reality, but intermarriage in general was common enough, and an indicator of how well advanced assimilation was. Jews had gained admission to preserves still closed to them in other countries. For example, there were many Jewish officers in the Army, and even some generals. Alfred Dreyfus was supposedly the first Jew on the General Staff, but this is not clearly established; the uncertainty should be significant, for most of the French seem not to have paid close attention to who and where the Jews were.

Similarly, the actual numbers of Jews in France were unknown.[2] Anti-Semites claimed high numbers—a half-million or more—when saying the country was being overrun by them, and low numbers when ranting about secret conspiracies to subvert the nation. The best genuine estimate would be about 80,000 at the time of the Affair, with perhaps 45,000 more in Algeria. There were then nearly nine million Jews in Europe as a whole, and the total French population was about 38,350,000. French Jews lived mainly in urban centers, with about 50,000 in Paris (in a total population of 2,700,000) and much smaller numbers elsewhere; just four other cities had more than a thousand. Most of France had few or none.

There had been substantial recent immigration of Jews from Alsace and Lorraine and from Eastern Europe, many of the latter having fled persecution. Those from Alsace-Lorraine, like Alfred Dreyfus, cared enough for France to move rather than remain in what had become German territory; anti-Semites preferred to see them as German Jews, infiltrating for nefarious purposes.

Among French Jews religious observance was minimal; there were probably no more than five hundred serious practitioners of orthodox Judaism in France, most of them recent immigrants to Paris from Eastern Europe. Few Jews converted to Christianity either, with most acknowledging and valuing Jewish identity as a matter of traditional ties and custom rather than profound faith.

French Jews identified with the Gentile society around them to a much greater extent than did larger Jewish communities elsewhere in Europe. Liberal politics and modernization had yielded them places as Frenchmen, and they seized the opportunity. While Jews elsewhere were often in perilous positions, in France they thought they had found safety in assimilation. Since the values that made this possible were enshrined in the Third Republic, most of them embraced it. Most were likewise fervent French patriots of the older, republican variety, but this self-identification with France did not keep anti-Semites from thinking them aliens whose loyalties had to be elsewhere. Moreover, because Jews were seen supporting the Republic, anti-Semites could hate both jointly.

The stereotype of the Jew as a greedy, hard businessman was as important in France as it was in other countries. It was reinforced by the notoriety of a few, notably the Rothschild and Pereire banking families. Probably proportionately more Jews

went into business (and the liberal professions) than did Gen
tiles, but many were just ordinary workers. About 40 per cent of
Parisian Jews were poor. Of course, there was no genuine reason
to think Jewish and Gentile business practices differed significantly, and there were a great many more Gentiles around to
cheat and exploit the good people of France.

In France it was still more unrealistic than elsewhere to believe that Jews were harmful to the rest of society. Even if so
inclined, they lacked the strength of numbers. It required much
invention and still more credulity for anti-Semites to promote
belief that so few people constituted a menace, but the dearth of
Jews appears not to have deterred such promotion. France's first
anti-Semitic newspaper was established in 1881 by a priest—in
a town where no Jews lived. Western France became one of the
most bitterly anti-Semitic areas, but there were very few Jews
there, and none outside the cities. The region was also the main
stronghold of political conservatism and reactionary Catholicism.

The development of French anti-Semitism paralleled that in
Central and Eastern Europe, although the French version was
less virulent, rose a little later, and receded comparatively early.
Long-time social and religious animus was overshadowed as attacks upon Jews took on a fundamentally political character. They
were, for example, damned as exploitative capitalists, with governments damned simultaneously for being subject to their will.
The coupling of politics and prejudice eventually included election campaigns based primarily upon anti-Semitic appeals.

While political anti-Semitism elsewhere was a manifestation
of racist nationalism, in France it originated primarily in Catholic
counter-Revolutionary agitation, with nationalism a later addition. The few early instances of racism received very little attention until after Drumont's La France juive had helped to arouse
new interest in the theme.

This Catholic counter-Revolutionary foundation helps to explain the outstanding feature of French political anti-Semitism:
It was usually anti-Masonic and anti-Protestant as well. These
three sources of all misfortune and evil were seen as completely
intermingled. Most anti-Semitic tracts (including La France juive)
concerned themselves also with the menace of Freemasons
and Protestants. From the 1880s onward the extensive agitation
attacking Freemasonry became anti-Semitic as well. Political
anti-Protestantism received less emphasis, and there was com-

paratively little *separate* anti-Protestant agitation. However, it did occur regularly in combination with the other two.

As the more deadly and pervasive hatred, anti-Semitism has aroused concern and reaction, while anti-Masonic and anti-Protestant sentiments are disregarded or treated as minor, accessory matters. In the French situation, however, the linkage is so close that all three must be seen and explained together. This in turn should shift our gaze from Jews themselves to the condition of a society and political system in which such varied hate proliferates.

It has been common to examine anti-Semitism in terms of the actual relations between Jews and Gentiles. For example, much weight has often been given to supposed political consequences of the resentment of small businessmen and farmers against Jewish merchants and moneylenders. Similarly, it has been thought important that in many places Jews kept themselves a people apart, having little ordinary social intercourse with Gentiles. Actual economic and social relations were largely irrelevant to French anti-Semitism. Like Dreyfus himself, Jews were only symbolic objects for discontent whose real sources had little to do with them.

Conservatives had some genuine cause for hostility to the secret fraternity of Freemasons, although most of their fears were fantasies. Brought into France from England during the eighteenth century, Freemasonry embodied the rationalist spirit so important for the 1789 Revolution, liberalism, and republicanism. It was a secular cult of Reason complete with sacred rites, the freethinkers' alternative to a church. Protestants and Jews might reconcile their faiths with Freemasonry, but never a loyal Catholic. This was precluded by Freemasonry's aggressive anticlericalism, which in turn was a response to "superstition," dogmatism, and political conservatism in the Church.

All over Europe, Masonic lodges often engaged in political action, their members sometimes working to overturn monarchies and habitually militant about their anticlericalism. In the Third Republic Masonic lodges were clubs for committed republicans, who discussed and sometimes organized political action there. Even when not ranting about the order, French conservatives often spoke of the Third Republic as the *république maçonnique*. Since secrecy was the rule in the order and sometimes cloaked concerted political action, there was a germ of reality in the conspiratorial fantasies of the Masons' more extreme enemies.

For many devout Catholics, especially the clergy, the Revolution of 1789 and its sequels had been totally disastrous. The Church had been driven out of France and readmitted only with restrictions thought to diminish it severely. Apostasy, freethinking, and anticlericalism had grown ever more threatening. God's will had been denied by removal of the legitimate Bourbon dynasty, and the successor regimes had reigned over and been responsible for recurring disaster suffered by the faith and the nation. These true believers were counter-Revolutionary in their fervent desire to return France to rule by the dynasty, Church, ideas, and social relationships they thought had prevailed before 1789.

It was very difficult for them to understand how God could have allowed such calamity, so many sought to explain it in terms of occult and Satanic forces. Freemasonry fitted their need perfectly, and they made it into the monster of deviltry which had produced the entire catastrophe. The Masonic order was seen as quite literally the agency of Satan, its secret rites as devil worship.

Tracts to this effect first appeared soon after 1789 but began to come out with some frequency only in the 1870s. They were produced in ever larger numbers thereafter. Until the mid-1880s at least, the authors were all fervent Catholics in the counter-Revolutionary mold, most of them priests, and some bishops. The Catholic press gave a prominent place to anti-Masonic polemics, and in 1884 Pope Leo XIII formally denounced Freemasonry as anti-Christian and Satanic. By late in the nineteenth century anti-Masonic agitation was quite widespread, and a number of writers and periodicals were devoted to it. With the evolution of antagonism against the Third Republic, anti-Masonism became a standard feature of rightist politics; it was no longer exclusively a fantasy of counter-Revolutionary Catholics.

Anti-Masonic literature elaborated endlessly the tales of great evils due to the order, inventing a past for it that went all the way back to ancient times. More recent political events in which some Masons might have been involved were mixed in with every other sort of sin imaginable. Always there was the opposition of the forces of evil and Satan against those of good and of Catholic Christianity—and the corresponding opposition in politics of liberals and radicals against conservatives.

In the early 1880s anti-Semitic literature began to flow from the same sources. Anti-Masonic Catholic periodicals commented favorably on foreign anti-Semitic books and developments, and began to publish attacks on Jews by French writers. Authors of anti-Masonic tracts produced anti-Semitic ones and directed joint onslaughts against both.

The premise here was that Jews as well as Masons were anti-Christian, secretive, and inherently evil. Anti-Masonic obsession with the occult was extended to Jewish cabalism and ordinary ritual, about both of which inventions were especially fertile. Although not at first regularly a part of the myth, it soon became commonplace to claim that Jews played a leading part in Freemasonry, and even that the order was entirely the instrument of Jewry. In reality, there were some Jewish Masons, but they played only a minor role in the order.

In 1882 came the crash of the Union Générale bank, an event much celebrated afterward in the spurious view of the past promulgated by anti-Semites. Four years earlier the Union Générale had been formed to offer Catholics an alternative to a banking system thought to be dominated by Jews and Protestants. Its head and promoter was a high-flying wheeler-dealer named Paul Eugène Bontoux, who had learned banking as a Rothschild employee. He made the bank a citadel of conservative Catholics, especially royalists of the Legitimist party; they flocked to invest in the bank. For a time Bontoux's ventures were spectacularly successful, the bank became a real power, and its backers were delighted by what they believed to be political as well as financial victory.

However, Bontoux was reckless and made grave errors when caught by the effects of a general economic crisis. The consequent collapse of his bank came with extreme swiftness. While the bank struggled to survive, the government arrested Bontoux, who later was convicted for having squandered bank funds in a wild last effort to avert disaster. The Union Générale's failure was completed by Bontoux's arrest.

Neither Bontoux nor his backers could admit that he and his associates had been at fault. Initially they blamed the crash of the Union Générale entirely upon the Republic, which was supposed to have intervened in order to wreak havoc upon the Legitimist cause and the Church. Republicans had indeed been gleeful about the bank's ruin but had not acted to accomplish it, although the government had probably been influenced in its limited intervention by partisan politics. In particular, it had to deflect charges by militant anticlericals that it had favored a Catholic enterprise in trouble.

Likewise, there was no evidence that Jews or Jewish banks had schemed to destroy the Union Générale, through either financial manipulations or influencing government action. Yet a myth to this effect soon grew. The Catholic press was full of confused, self-contradictory analyses of the crash, in which the writers ignored the ample evidence that Bontoux was responsible. Instead, they spun out fictions about the deadly machinations of Jewish bankers and their instruments in the anticlerical regime. Evidence rarely mattered to such critics, whose often considerable talents were expended on the rhetorical development of ideas conceived without considering it.

Anti-Semitic literature grew steadily in volume, much of it emphasizing the Union Générale crash for having demonstrated the nature of the Jewish menace. With this came a significant shift in the burden of charges against Jews. As never before, anti-Semites became preoccupied with the supposed Jewish role in capitalism, and especially in finance.[3]

The writers initially producing this anti-Semitic literature exemplified both authors and audiences in the upsurge of political anti-Semitism that followed. Modern capitalism seemed increasingly to dominate their lives, and they neither understood nor accepted this. They witnessed the process as outsiders and sometimes victims, feeling themselves excluded from capitalist development's benefits by rapacious, ruthless operators. Instead of seeing a civilization transforming itself, it was easier to think in terms of small cliques machinating against a largely passive and helpless people.

Thus, images were readily formed of modernizing capitalism as a conspiracy, with small numbers plotting to victimize everyone else. Financiers had to be the primary culprits, and the big banks the chief power centers. Fears of occult and Satanic conspiracy fitted the picture well, as did the stereotype of the Jew as avaricious businessman and usurer. A pseudo-religious appearance was impressed upon the picture by recalling Church censure of usury and through Catholic theories of Jews as anti-Christian and corrupted by having denied the Savior and God's word.

Much was built upon a myth of the Rothschilds' controlling everything—not only finance and the Jewish conspiracy but also governments indebted to them. Although it was a caricature, the picture of Rothschild and Jewish hegemony in finance had elements of versimilitude. The substantial international scope of Rothschild banking operations was especially important for the myth. The delusion lay in thinking that the Rothschilds had grandiose designs for subjecting the world to Jewish dominion, and that they secured great political power by acting as financial agents for governments.

The crash of the Union Générale provided the critical link in the chain of fallacious reasoning. According to this, the bank's failure was a victory for its rivals: Jewish and Protestant banks. The disaster for Catholics meant victory for their enemies: Jews, Protestants, Freemasons, and other anticlericals. The collapse of this new source of royalist power gave victory to republicans. It seemed obvious that the victors must have conspired to accomplish this. At the same time, this league of intertwined, hostile interests appeared to the perfervid imagination as a band of puppets, with the Rothschilds the puppetmasters who schemed to subject the world to Jewry. The crash had exposed the monsters at work and given warning of the danger.

Anti-Semitism was now thoroughly political, the hostility to Jews thoroughly mixed with opposition to the Third Republic. The latter's promotion and protection of business and modernization made it a target for the anticapitalist, antiplutocratic passion that animated anti-Semitism with increasing vigor. The old antirepublican animosities reinforced this reaction. Henceforth, anti-Semitic polemic would shift freely back and forth between targets: Jews, Freemasons, Protestants, and the Third Republic. There was also frequent repetition of older fantasies about Jews, like tales of ritual murder, but that was mainly a matter of exploiting the sensational to arouse interest and anger, and few polemicists gave the tales the emphasis they received in some other countries.

Still more than in other lands at the time, French anti-Semitism was predominantly anticapitalist and antiplutocratic. The principal object was the very rich Jewish banker, stock market speculator, and industrialist. Typical cartoon stereotypes were fat and extremely well dressed. Stereotypes of grasping small Jewish businessmen—shopkeepers, moneylenders, peddlers— and costumed ghetto Jews were much less often employed. The close coupling of antiplutocratic and anti-Semitic sentiment gave anti-Semitic politics its real force. This helps to make more understandable the growing virulence of anti-Semitism in a country with few Jews. Not only were there some genuine Jewish financiers but, more important, the occult appearance to outsiders of high finance and its practitioners made the fantasy of Jewish control more credible, whatever the actual role of Jews.

Thus the process was one where first anti-Semitism was grafted onto a reactionary, primarily clerical politics, which had been directed at supposed enemies of Catholicism. Then came a more radical, populist anti-Semitism, which was tied to the older forms but more intensely concerned with modern plutocracy than with threats to the Church. In this, important parts were played by the crash of the Union Générale and the myth of "Rothschild"—the latter seen as a single Satanic figure even though there were actually several members of the Rothschild family playing distinct, significant roles.

At first anti-Semites did not succeed in exciting wide interest. Although some primarily anti-Masonic tracts went through many printings, those directed against Jews fared less well. Political anti-Semitism in France was an abstract doctrine offered to an audience who saw few Jews around them. Frenchmen could believe the theory without there being a substantial Jewish presence, as its eventual success in Western France demonstrated. However, first they had to feel that dread of modernity which anti-Semitism tried to express; then they had to have able propagandists connect their feelings to the doctrine. It did not take long for these developments to occur. With the appearance in 1886 of Drumont's *La France juive*, the doctrine came of age, finding a ready audience and an adroit propagandist to exploit the opportunity thus offered.

Drumont was then forty-two, a professional journalist with a modest middle-class background. Most journalism emphasized clever writing rather than accurate or full reporting of events; at this kind of work Drumont was experienced and able, but until then his career had not been especially successful. He was a big bear of a man with a bushy beard and an engaging personality, and his associates thought him a wonderfully good fellow. Drumont was sentimental and romantic, wielding his pen against Jews more in the spirit of a knight-errant than as a monster of hate. He also wielded a sword skillfully, in frequent duels against some of the many he defamed when *La France juive* had elevated him to paladin of the anti-Semitic crusade. His astonishingly vicious and destructive invective lashed out at both Jew and Gentile with apparent ferocity. Yet most of it seems less a matter of genuine feeling than of perverted rhetorical virtuosity.

After first gaining public notice because of growing controversy about it in the press, *La France juive* became a phenomenon of popularity. Not only did it sell like no other political work in the century, but it was very widely read as well, especially when serialized in a popular newspaper, *Le Petit journal.* Drumont followed it quickly with other books, several of which also sold well, in which he elaborated and repeated his charges. Other authors followed upon his heels, and some of them also became popular.

The imaginations of Drumont's readers were captured by his vivid writing, sentimentalism, and skillful use of juicy anecdotes. With delicious sensationalism he exposed the corrupt luxury of Paris society as well as the evil of Jews and their confederates. Drumont gave the appearance of substance to goblins people already feared might be around them. Celebrated men of letters, cultivated writers who should have been more discriminating, would later record how excited they had been by *La France juive.* Drumont did not have to deceive people, but only to help them deceive themselves.

He reiterated just about every allegation against Jews that others had advanced, but, though he wrote as a Catholic, he did not have the preoccupation with threats to the Church that typified clerical anti-Semitism. His main thrust was antiplutocratic, with strong sentimental populism and romantic nostalgia for a mythical past, when the French nation was supposed to have been an organic whole. With Drumont and the growing number of similar publicists, anti-Semitism had come from the province of traditional counter-Revolutionary conservatism to a comparatively radical variation of the new nationalist right.

While there was sympathy for anti-Semitism throughout most of the new right, the movement of professional anti-Semites around Drumont cultivated a semblance of populist radicalism. They usually rejected royalism, for they associated it with the supposedly corrupt upper classes, besides which they thought restoration no longer possible. Moreover, some of these anti-Semites valued the tradition of Jacobin democracy, despite their repudiation of other republican ideals.

Drumont and company liked to think of themselves as revolutionary and socialist, although they were neither. They declaimed about oppressed workers rising against their tormentors, about dispossession of the propertied and collectivization, but it was all just play-acting without serious intent to bring about any such change. While endlessly verbose in painting pictures of evil and good, they were exceedingly vague about specific political and social programs. For the most part they proposed nothing besides overthrowing enemies and punishing evil.

Some genuine socialists were attracted to Drumont and the anti-Semitic movement, because they seemed to share anticapitalism and championing of the exploited. These socialists thought that the populist anti-Semites could at least be useful allies. Yet, although socialists had rejected bourgeois liberalism in the name of genuine equality, they still remained true to most of its ideals and to its faith in progress through reason. The mentality of socialists was really quite opposed to that which generated anti-Semitism, despite the latter's affectations.

This was increasingly apparent to most socialists as they became more conscious of how closely associated was anti-Semitism with their old enemies on the right. Some anti-Semites tried to maintain fraudulent leftist credentials, but Drumont himself was too closely tied to clericalism. For most socialists the Church and its lay supporters were even more bitter enemies than the bourgeoisie, and Drumont could not escape the clerical stigma. There were a few onetime socialists who shifted their primary allegiance to the anti-Semitic cause, for it better expressed the dissatisfaction that had first led them to socialism. From about 1890 on, the ties between anti-Semites and socialists were progressively reduced, until the Dreyfus struggle brought socialists to full realization of how sharply opposed were their perspectives, purposes, and allies.

The populism of Drumont and company did alarm many conservatives, and caused some to keep the anti-Semitic movement at arm's length. Some also were bothered by the extremely defamatory and violent rhetoric—but they seem to have been disturbed much more by offensive political and literary style than by outrage to morals. Few rejected anti-Semitic extremism outright, and any misgivings about it appear minor beside simultaneous enthusiasm.

Despite their successes as propagandists, until the Affair anti-Semites were not able to accomplish much in organized political action. Anti-Semitic leagues formed in Paris and provincial towns got nowhere. There was some association with the Boulangist movement, especially through their shared hostility to the Republic, and the populist element important to much of Boulangism. With the collapse of the movement, some former Boulangists remained politically active as radical anti-Semitic nationalists. A number of onetime Boulangist and Bonapartist politicians achieved election successes as declared anti-Semites and even became formidable in the Chamber of Deputies. However, most accomplished this only when the Affair gave political anti-Semitism a more highly focused basis for organizing support.

Anti-Semitism's lack of any real political program was a disabling handicap. This was greatly magnified by having no effective organizers or leaders. The movement always lacked direction and was divided by personality clashes and other differences. Skillful organization and charismatic leadership might have capitalized on propaganda success, but the talents of Drumont and the others did not extend to this.

In one venture, however, they were able to use their abilities most effectively. Drumont in 1892 established a Parisian daily newspaper, *La Libre parole*. There were many dailies in Paris, most of them with small circulations and shaky finances. Drumont, however, obtained very substantial financial backing, and he attracted quite a few writers of real talent both for the regular staff and as occasional contributors.

From the first this band gave itself zealously to the sensational exposure of rot in French public life, corruption among the rich, and the menace of Jewry. *La Libre parole* was above all the organ of anti-Semitism, but it directed its venomous attacks more widely, raking muck wherever found and of course scourging Masons and Protestants at every opportunity.

A few months after its establishment, a *Libre parole* exposé produced the Panama scandal. Although many public figures were implicated, the paper made three Jews appear the chief villains. It could thus effectively combine anti-Semitism with condemnation of corruption in high places. *La Libre parole* enjoyed enormous success through its Panama campaign. Daily circulation went beyond 200,000—extraordinarily high for such a journal—and its onslaughts were much discussed by everyone concerned with current politics.

During the Panama scandal and at times thereafter, *La Libre parole* was a potent force because of its capacity for exciting great interest among readers, even those unsympathetic to it, and genuine fear among those subject to attack. Drumont in particular could daunt the boldest potential victim. He and his comrades knew no restraint. Neither truth nor ethics mattered at all. Libel brought frequent duels, lawsuits, and criminal prosecutions, but they were part of the game and often good for circulation. Rival publications did nothing by their examples to alter *La Libre parole*'s style.

Still, satisfactory subjects of scandal were often unavailable. Moreover, the newspaper's real attraction as the clarion voice of anti-Semitism was diminished by its taking some positions disliked by many of its sympathizers. By the fall of 1894 *La Libre parole*'s circulation had sunk to a very low level, and fresh scandal was desperately needed. The arrest of Alfred Dreyfus then provided the opportunity.

While populist anti-Semitism like Drumont's stood out most prominently, politically oriented hostility to Jews figured ever more largely on the right in general. Antagonism toward Jews, Masons, and Protestants fitted the new rightist nationalism too well for it not to be adopted, though perhaps in attenuated form. Those who might rarely have expressed such antagonism before did so with increasing frequency in the 1890s.

Anti-Semitic literature continued to flow also from specifically Catholic sources, most often from priests. A departure from the familiar counter-Revolutionary themes occurred with the formation, in early 1890s, of a Catholic movement led largely by priests and calling itself Christian Democracy. It was antiplutocratic, populist, and republican, spoke vaguely but earnestly of reforming both society and the Church—and was permeated with anti-Semitism. A short-lived political party was constituted in 1897. The movement was always crippled by disunity, and its radicalism inevitably aroused serious opposition from the Church hierarchy and important Catholic laymen.

Christian Democracy was diverted from its original purposes by the Affair, when many of its leaders were drawn to anti-Semitic and anti-Dreyfusard agitation. In the battle their radicalism and altruism, which never had been well matured, were compromised by alliance with conservative reaction. The conflict with Christian Democracy's egalitarian social mission seems to have been too great, and the movement soon died. It might be said that, while motivated by the gospel of love, their dread and the strangeness to them of modernity caused Christian Democrats to succumb to a doctrine of hate.

More important was yet another variant of Catholic anti-Semitism, one especially associated with the Augustin Fathers of the Assumption. French Catholicism knew much diversity in both political and religious beliefs. It did include liberals and others who thought their faith incompatible with anti-Semitism. Another wing, which represented a departure from well-established currents of Catholic thought and practice, was a popular movement of mystical piety, which took shape and grew to enormous proportions after 1870. Anti-Semitism came to it as an incidental matter, to which the Assumptionists gave prominence.

The pietistic movement spread renewed religious devotion centering upon cults, especially those of the Sacred Heart of Jesus and Our Lady, and pilgrimages to shrines. Hundreds of thousands from all over France crowded into Paray-le-Mondial, Lourdes, La Salette, and other shrines. Having been founded in 1847 to promote revival of popular religious fervor and destroy heresy, the Assumptionist order made the most of this mass phenomenon. It organized huge pilgrim groups, which traveled by rail with specially arranged cheap fares and with song sheets and other propaganda to enliven travel and arouse enthusiasm. Assumptionist priests addressed enormous audiences in a French equivalent to American fundamentalist revival meetings. The people were eager, and this order displayed real genius in mobilizing them.

Vital to this were the Assumptionists' extensive publishing operations, most notably a weekly newspaper directed at pilgrims, *Le Pèlerin*, and a daily, *La Croix*. Père Vincent de Paul Bailly founded the daily in 1880 and headed it for two decades. One of the great innovators of modern journalism, he made *La Croix* among the most widely read newspapers in France. Besides gaining a large circulation, it was disseminated throughout the country by specially organized local committees, which were intent upon seeing that its message reached as many people as possible. They also promoted satellite versions of *La Croix* produced in many provincial towns.[4]

The paper was pitched at the lowest possible level of sophistication in ways that greatly enhanced its popular appeal and impact. It was the standard source of news for the parish clergy, although its news coverage was rudimentary. *La Croix*'s politics was extremely simplistic, with the dominant consideration being defense of the Catholic faith against all perceived threats.

The pietistic revival aimed at atonement for man's transgressions. Living in a time of social upheaval and just after the national disaster of 1870, those drawn to the movement saw public misfortune as divine punishment for public sins, and the revival thus had a political character. "Anti-Christian" government and moral decadence in high places accounted for God's having visited his wrath upon the French. Satanism was seen to be at work, too, and apopcalyptic visions of the future were drawn from omens read into recent events. Current politics and modern history were regarded in mystical terms, which often meant that wildly unrealistic beliefs resulted, and evil was readily discovered without the inconvenience of referring to evidence.

La Croix was both active and highly effective in directing popular beliefs from simple religious piety into this mystical politics. The newspaper was basically conservative, populist, and nationalist, but its positions on issues often varied and did not match those taken by secular papers with comparable politics. In particular, while *La Croix* made familiar populist attacks on wealth, luxury, and plutocracy, in the 1890s it confined its anti-capitalism mainly to the "international" variety, while moderating its criticism of the French bourgeoisie.

At first *La Croix*'s expressions of anti-Semitism were erratic and usually not pushed hard. From 1889 on its anti-Semitism grew rapidly, rising to high intensity in the months just before Dreyfus's arrest in the autumn of 1894. From then on *La Croix* devoted its very considerable propaganda powers to continuous, ardent, and scurrilous attacks on Jews and the whole "trio of hate,"

> . . . which seeks with as much tenacity as hate the demolition
> of France and which includes; 1. Protestantism which wants
> to destroy Catholicism, the *soul of France*; 2. Judaism which

wants to rob her national wealth, *the body of France*, 3. Freemasonry, the natural compound of the other two, which wants *at the same time to demolish the body and the soul of France.*[5]

During the Dreyfus Affair, *La Croix* and *La Libre parole* were the most noisy and most noisome organs of anti-Semitism. Between them they articulated with real eloquence most of the sentiments and attitudes that gave force and popularity to anti-Semitism and kindred hate. They were dissimilar enough in content and diffusion that they probably reached different if overlapping audiences. Nothing else played a comparable part in stimulating popular anti-Semitism in the 1890s, and without these two newspapers the struggle of the Affair would surely have been very different.

A final insight may be gained from the remarkable story of Diana Vaughan, who revealed to an eager public the depths of Satanism in the Masonic order. Diana was promoted by a man known as Léo Taxil.[6] After a strict Catholic upbringing, Taxil had contrived to make a career and a good business out of anticlericalism. He was just as defamatory and even more ingeniously inventive at this than Drumont would later be at anti-Semitism. In 1885 Taxil created a sensation by sudden reconversion to Catholicism, after which he turned his considerable talent to anti-Masonry. The switch was undertaken solely because there was more money to be made on the other side. He multiplied his inventions of fraudulent stories—and his income—with a stream of anti-Masonic tracts. In 1893 his most successful one yet testified to many new discoveries about Masonic Satanism, including devils working in caves under Gibraltar, where they prepared epidemic diseases to overwhelm Catholicism.

Taxil's masterpiece was his invention in 1895 of Diana Vaughan, the descendant of an English Rosicrucian's union with the goddess Astarte. Diana was the fiancée of Asmodeus, the king of the demons, and the familiar of a variety of devils. She had been intended as high priestess of the Palladium, the inner, most Satanic circle of Freemasonry, but she was converted to Catholicism by Joan of Arc. The preposterous details of her story were piled up without restraint, in a grand prank burlesquing the whole anti-Masonic tradition in France. Taxil even had her born on February 29, 1874, without anyone's noticing that there had been no such date.

For almost two years he played out the game, creating anti-Masonic journals and books published in Diana Vaughan's name and promoting the enterprise with consummate skill. This included securing the explicit support of much of the Catholic press and Church hierarchy. He even obtained the Pope's blessings for one of her books. Though no one ever saw her, Diana founded anti-Masonic leagues across France and was widely acclaimed as a great crusader for the people and the Church.

Skepticism about Diana did arise eventually, for Taxil had not troubled to keep his stories consistent, and he had jealous rivals eager to unhorse him. With her actual existence at last in question, in April 1897 he called a meeting to introduce Diana publicly. The large auditorium was crowded with journalists and priests. Taxil told them that it had all been a hoax, and Diana Vaughan had never existed. He ridiculed and taunted his audience for its stupidity, then disappeared out a back door before the crowd, surging forward, could catch him.

Even so, there were those who continued to believe in Diana. Others turned from her to phenomena and crusades that were scarcely less preposterous. And their faith in Diana Vaughan had not differed very much from belief in the occult and evil deeds of Jews, Masons, and Protestants.

Critical reason could easily have demolished the Vaughan hoax, and critical reason did expose as fantasy the fears about the diabolical trinity. But such rational criticism could not shake the beliefs of the credulous. They desperately needed to believe the myths, and few of them knew how to appreciate or employ such reasoning.

Thus, it was natural that the same people and others like them clung tenaciously to the myths of Alfred Dreyfus's guilt and of the Jewish Syndicate conspiring to free him. Reason could not shake their convictions in this either.

6

Credulity and Conviction in the Affair

To form and maintain a conviction that Alfred Dreyfus was guilty, people had to believe an unending series of unlikely and incredible assertions and fables.

From the beginning there were wholly unsupported allegations about Dreyfus's supposedly sordid personal life and his history of treasonable deeds. While most of these stories were easily discredited, a continuing belief in them was needed. Otherwise there was no evident motive for him to have committed treason. He was too rich to have been spying for money, too upright to have been blackmailed, too successful to have acted because his career ambitions were frustrated. His supposed crime could be explained only by lies and by claims that *every* Jew prepared the betrayal of France.

Indeed, people could believe anything ill about Dreyfus but disbelieved or discounted all that incriminated Esterhazy. Yet there were many facts making the latter highly suspect: He was

86

obviously a dishonorable blackguard, whose speculation, gambling, and generally dissolute conduct left him perpetually desperate for money; he kept and lived with a registered prostitute, had swindled a host of victims, which included his own cousin, and years earlier had written letters in which he had fantasized about fighting on the side of the Germans, slaughtering the French, and pillaging Paris; he had been suspiciously inquisitive about military secrets, had copied secret documents, and was twice seen visiting the German embassy in Paris. While there was debate about the authenticity of the *petit bleu* (the document that first brought him under suspicion) his normal handwriting was identical to that of the *bordereau;* in contrast, the "experts" said Dreyfus must have disguised his hand when writing the *bordereau,* so remote was the resemblance claimed. When Esterhazy fled to England and confessed to having written the *bordereau,* anti-Dreyfusards believed either that he had sold out to the Jews or that he was truthful in claiming to have done it under orders, as part of a French counterintelligence deception.

Trial witnesses against Dreyfus gave testimony that plainly had no basis in actual experience. Some merely repeated gossip, and others were disreputable individuals whose word would not have been accepted elsewhere. Much testimony was simply irrelevant. None of the documentary evidence clearly had a bearing on the case against Dreyfus, and little of it would have demonstrated anything even if it were relevant. Authenticity of the documents was suspect anyway, since the forger Henry could well have altered or fabricated any of them. Yet there was widespread belief that testimony and documents proved Dreyfus guilty.

No one ever substantiated in any way the fables about the Kaiser's having written notes incriminating Dreyfus (and consequent threats by Germany of war if the documents were not suppressed), but belief in the existence of these notes remained wide and unshakable. Much was made out of Dreyfus's supposed confession on the day of his degradation. Yet, when first reported, the story had been scotched as worthless by none other than the War Minister, General Mercier, and the Deputy Chief of Staff, General Gonse; the tale's lack of a credible basis and its initial rejection by these anti-Dreyfusard heroes did not impede its later resurrection.

Exposure of Henry's principal forgery led anti-Dreyfusards

to be remarkably fertile with incredible explanations and justifications of his actions. Henry the confessed fraud and suicide was represented as an honorable patriot whose rectitude and veracity were otherwise unquestionable; one could not doubt his crucially important testimony at the first Dreyfus court-martial. This nonsense was believed, along with assertions that Picquart, until recently the most brilliant and promising of young officers, was a scoundrel who must have fabricated evidence on behalf of the Syndicate. (He was also said, falsely, to be a Protestant.)

There was scarcely more reason to believe in the existence of the Syndicate than in those devils under the Rock of Gibraltar, intent upon infecting Catholics with a plague. Indeed, there was hardly a Jew to be seen among well-known Dreyfusards, and many of the latter had long and honorable careers that testified to their patriotism. The extreme intensity of acrimony against Joseph Reinach reflected the lack of any better Jewish target; the Rothschilds carefully avoided involvement in the Affair. At least anti-Dreyfusard dreams of conspiracy had their counterpart in the conviction among Dreyfusards that General Staff officers conspired with Jesuits against them. This belief was not much better founded than the myth of the Syndicate.

Anti-Dreyfusards looked hopefully for revelations of additional, still secret evidence, which they supposed would finally yield decisive proof of Dreyfus's guilt. Yet reasonable men should not base judgment on speculative suppositions, which ought to have been discouraged anyway by the many worthless disclosures already made.

Some historians, perhaps compensating for Dreyfusard excesses, have claimed that there was uncertainty enough for doubt to be reasonable, or that the case was too complex for most people to understand. Doubt and confusion were possible until after the Esterhazy trial (January 10–11, 1898) or perhaps that of Zola (February 7–23, 1898). From then on continuing belief that Dreyfus's guilt was adequately established could only be a matter of refusal or inability to make a reasoned judgment, using the facts generally available to the public. One might have thought Dreyfus's guilt plausible though not yet proved, but even that position became unreasonable after the exposure of Henry and the flight of Esterhazy.

Moreover, French law required the reversal of Dreyfus's initial conviction, simply because the use of secret evidence kept

"Striking arguments," by Steinlen, in *La Feuille*, No. 6, January 21, 1898. (Houghton Library)

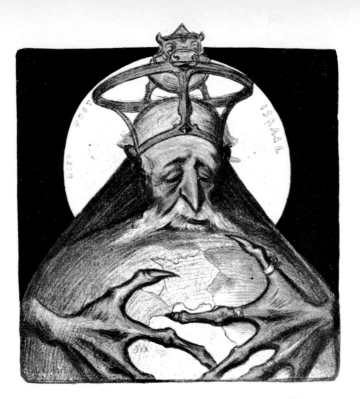

"Rothschild," by Charles Léandre, in *Le Rire*, April 16, 1898.

Deuxième Année. — N° 13.   15 centimes le Numéro.   30 Janvier 1898.

LES QUAT'Z'ARTS

Journal Hebdomadaire   Littéraire, illustré

Rédaction le Mardi, 62, boulevard de Clichy.

Rédacteur en Chef : ÉMILE GOUDEAU.   ❖❖❖   ABONNEMENTS
Administrateur-Directeur : F. TROMBERT.   Paris . . . . six mois : 5 fr. un an : 8 fr.
                                                          Départements . . —   5 »   9 »
                                                          Étranger. . . . —   6 »   11 »

Dessin de LÉANDRE

"Excuse, bourgeois, it seems that this is where they distribute ... bread?" By Charles Léandre, in *Les Quat' z' Arts*, January 30, 1898—a week after the battle of the Deputies in their Chamber. (Houghton Library)

LA LIBRE PAROLE

ILLUSTRÉE

La France aux Français!

RÉDACTION

Directeur : ÉDOUARD DRUMONT

ADMINISTRAT.

Quel temps de ch'en !...

Il pleut rudement sur le temple, depuis quelque temps.

"What beastly weather! It has been coming down hard on the temple for some time." In French, *temple* denotes both a Masonic lodge and, much less often, a synagogue. The Jew here wears a Masonic emblem, and the objects raining down mention Dreyfus and other affairs involving Jews. By Chanteclair in *La Libre parole illustrée*, January 5, 1895—the day of Dreyfus's ritual degradation. (Houghton Library)

"Popular amnesty!" Alfred Dreyfus, by Lenepveu, in his *Musée des Horreurs* (poster series), 1900. (Houghton Library)

MUSÉE DES HORREURS

paraît tous les Vendredis

Amnistie populaire!

n.º35

TRAÎTRE

1900

La collection des Numéros parus du MUSÉE des HORREURS est en vente à l'Administration : 58, rue Dulong et au Bureau de Vente : 10, rue du Croissant.

Le Prix des Abonnements à la Série complète de 200 Dessins est de 40 Fr.

"Let the wrecking begin!" Joseph Reinach, by Lenepveu, in his *Musée des Horreurs*, 1900(?). (Houghton Library)

After anti-Semitic rioting in Algiers, January, 1898. Sacked Jewish shop next to intact one with "[?French?] and Catholic" painted on it. Other unharmed shops had placards (which had been printed on a press) saying, "This firm is not Jewish." From Edouard Drumont's personal scrapbooks. (Houghton Library)

Pictures titled "Socialist agitation," in *La Vie illustrée*, October 27, 1898, two days after major riots in which most participants were from the right and most socialists kept away. Portraits represent socialist leaders (clockwise from top right) Paul Brousse, Jean Allemane, Edouard Vaillant, and Jules Guesde. (Houghton Library)

A 1904 post card with inscription, "Suicide of the brave Colonel Henry, author of the forgery presented as authentic by Cavaignac in the Chamber [of Deputies], July 7, 1898, and which tends to prove that Dreyfus was a traitor." (Houghton Library)

"Voice of the people."
"As one man ...
against one man." By
Hermann-Paul, in *Le
Sifflet*, No. 1, February
17, 1898. (Houghton
Library)

Comme un seul homme... contre un seul homme.

"A *radical* measure." "Sir X...,
member of the Institut, for
having pronounced the words
Justice and *Truth*, is pro-
visionally suspended. General
Didon and Father Jamont are
charged with the execution of
the present decree. Signed:
Bourgeois." Refers to actions
of Education Minister Léon
Bourgeois (of the Radical
party), suspending Dreyfusard
academics from their teaching
positions, and to *Father* (not
General) Didon's notorious
address in the presence of
General Jamont. The figure on
the gallows wears the costume
of a member of the Institut de
France. By H.-G. Ibels in *Le
Sifflet*, No. 27, August 4, 1898.
(Houghton Library)

Une mesure *radicale*.

"Election campaign."
"Finance—I am
Liberty! Clergy [liter-
ally: holy water
sprinkler]—I am
Equality! The Saber—I
am Fraternity! John Q.
Citizen—Fine . . . I
would never have
doubted it at all. . . ."
By Couturier, in *Le
Sifflet*, No. 9, April 14,
1898. (Houghton
Library)

TOURNÉE ÉLECTORALE

La Finance. — Je suis la Liberté !
Le Goupillon. — Je suis l'Egalité !!
Le Sabre. — Je suis la Fraternité !!!
Jacques Bonhomme. — Ben .. je ne m'en serais jamais point douté..

LA VÉRITÉ QUAND MÊME !

Méline — Malgré tout, j'ai bien peur qu'elle ne sorte, la rosse !...

"The truth in spite of
it all!" Premier Méline
says to Esterhazy,
"Despite everything, I
am afraid that she is
coming out, the hag!
. . ." Truth was con-
ventionally represented
as a nude maiden
rising from a well. By
Raoul Barré, in *Le
Sifflet*, No. 5, March
17, 1898. (Houghton
Library)

"For Truth." "The farewell cup." It is the well of Truth into which the Jew pours gold. By Forain, in *Psst. . .!*, No. 24, July 16, 1899. (Houghton Library)

Le coup de l'étrier

Au R. P. Du Lac

"I am the Truth!" The Jesuit Father du Lac sits on the well of Truth, above Truth's body, holding her mirror. By Louis Chevalier, in *Le Sifflet*, Vol. II, No. 11, April 14, 1899. (Houghton Library)

— La Vérité, c'est moi!

PSST...!

Images par FORAIN CARAN D'ACHE

N° 36
8 Octobre 1898

Le NUMÉRO : 10 centimes.

BUREAUX

"The détente"—
between bourgeoisie
and workers marching
together. Signs say:
"Long live Picquart.
Down with the Army."
"Down with France."
"Long live anarchy."
By Forain, in *Psst...!*,
No. 36, October 9,
1898. (Houghton
Library)

LA DÉTENTE

"The aristocracy of
tomorrow? But, we
are it!" The intellec-
tual's statue says,
"Truth on the march."
By Caran d'Ache, in
Psst...!, No. 61, April
1, 1899. (Houghton
Library)

L'Aristocratie de demain

L'Aristocratie de demain? Mais, c'est nous!

— Silence, Messieurs, j'aperçois un Français...

AUDIENCE DU 12 AOUT AU CONSEIL DE GUERRE DE RENNES. — LE CAPITAINE DREYFUS S'ADRESSANT AU GENERAL MERCIER
(Dessin d'après nature de notre envoyé spécial, Georges REDON)

At the second Dreyfus court-martial, August 12, 1899. Dreyfus upset by General Mercier's testimony, rushing toward him. Sketch drawn from life by Georges Redon, in *La Vie illustrée*, August 17, 1899. (Houghton Library)

Opposite Page (Top) "Silence, Gentlemen, I see a Frenchman." The costumes here are those of French magistrates. By Caran d'Ache, in *Psst . . . !*, No. 52, January 28, 1899. (Houghton Library)

Opposite Page (Bottom) Second Dreyfus court-martial, Dreyfus in background, and officer witnesses against him in front, left to right: Generals Billot, Zurlinden, and Mercier, Captain Junck, Major Lauth, General Roget, Major Cuignet, and, on right, General Gonse and Archivist Gribelin. By L. Sabattier, in *L'Illustration*, September 16, 1899. (Houghton Library)

One of Dreyfus's attorneys in the courtroom just after Dreyfus was convicted a second time, September 9, 1899. By Paul Renouard in his *L'Affaire Dreyfus* [Paris, 1899(?)], an album of lithographic reproductions of his pencil sketches. (Houghton Library)

from the defense had made the trial illegal. Nevertheless, most people managed to persuade themselves that the flagrant illegality did not matter, since the defendent had been guilty anyhow.

> ". . . they'se not a polisman in this counthry that can't tell ye jus' where Dhry-fuss was whin th' remains iv th' poor girl was found. That's because th' thrile was secret. If 'twas an open thrile, an' ye heerd th' tisti-mony, an' knew th' language, an' saw th' safe afther 'twas blown open, ye'd be puzzled, an' not care a rush whether Dhry-fuss was naked in a cage or takin' tay with his uncle at th' Benny Brith Club.
>
> "I haven't made up me mind whether th' Cap done th' shootin' or not. He was certainly in th' neighborhood whin th' fire started, an' th' polis dug up quite a lot iv lead pipe in his back yard. But it's wan thing to sus-pect a man iv doin' a job an' another thing to prove that he didn't. . . . . 'Let us pro-ceed,' says th' impartial an' fair-minded judge, 'to th' thrile iv th' haynious monsther Cap Dhry-fuss,' he says. . . . 'Cap, ye're guilty, an' ye know it,' he says. 'Th' decision iv th' coort is that ye be put in a cage, an' sint to th' Divvle's own island f'r th' r-rest iv ye'er life,' he says. 'Let us pro-ceed to hearin' th' tisti-mony,' he says. . . .
>
> 'Ah!' he says. 'Here's me ol' frind Pat th' Clam [Major Mercier Du Paty de Clam—see Chapter Ten],' he says. 'Pat, what d'ye know about this case?' he says. 'None iv ye'er business,' says Pat. 'Answered like a man an' a sojer,' says the coort. 'Jackuse,' says Zola fr'm th' dureway. An' they thrun him out. 'Call Col. Hinnery,' say th' coort. 'He ray-fuses to answer.' 'Good. Th' case is clear. Cap forged th' will. Th' coort will now adjourn f'r dools, an' all ladin' officers iv th' ar-rmy not in disgrace already will assimble in jail, an' commit suicide,' he says. [Martin Dooley, in the *Chicago Journal*, 1898].[1]

The judges of the Cour de Cassation were less anti-Dreyfusard than the one imagined by Mr. Dooley, but they were scarcely inclined to accept Dreyfusard contentions readily, and some were most reluctant. Yet all forty-six of them found in 1899 and again in 1906 that the case made against Dreyfus was entirely without merit. The second time they felt compelled to add that there was no basis whatever for even suspecting him. It should also be pointed out that there is too little ground for claims by some that the Affair demonstrated the bankruptcy of the French system of justice. Although slow, the *civilian* courts always found for Dreyfus and Picquart, and justice miscarried only in military tribunals.

At least the high court judges accepted only assertions that could be demonstrated by careful, reasoned assessment of evidence, and they cast aside the false and fabulous. Their preconceived opinions did not alter their final judgment. All this was their calling and responsibility, and they had the training and experience to accomplish it.

But what about the rest of the French? Why were they so credulous?

One might say that the critical faculties of most of them were not sufficiently cultivated. Few could be as logical and discriminating in forming their beliefs as were the justices of the Cour de Cassation. Thus, anti-Dreyfusard propagandists could persuade the public with sophistic argument and demogogic appeals. Perhaps so, but then one must ask why were the credulous receptive to *this* propaganda and not that of its opponents.

Knowledge of actual mass opinion in the Affair is limited and indirect. Most attention has been directed at those who were actively engaged in the struggle and who were articulate about their opinions and experiences. Most of them were cultured men and women, accustomed to discerning the credible in the midst of polemic. Why did they accept the incredible so readily and persist in their convictions so steadfastly?

In France educated persons have long cultivated virtuosity in expressive speech and writing, to such an extent that verbal eloquence and felicitous style often cover extremely superficial or fallacious thought. Perhaps anti-Dreyfusard discourse was only an outstanding example of that, with audiences so beguiled by words that they cared too little for discovering truth. We can call to mind images of clever conversation in the fashionable salons and clubs where the best Parisian society met to discuss the latest sensations. In public, extraordinary eloquence was achieved by many anti-Dreyfusard journalists, most notably Drumont of *La Libre parole*, Rochefort of *L'Intransigeant*, and Cassagnac of *L'Autorité*. There were also anti-Dreyfusard masters of oratory, especially the Comte Albert du Mun in the Chamber of Deputies. With verbal artistry so much appreciated, the morning's striking article or speech was savored at that evening's social gatherings and reprinted in tomorrow's newspapers all over France. One can not disregard the power of words themselves, however deceptive, foolish, or groundless critical examination may find them.

Yet one must ask here too why audiences were receptive to the discourse of anti-Dreyfusards and not to that of their opponents. The Dreyfusards had many masters of eloquent and clever discourse; for examples, Clemenceau could match anyone with his biting invective, and Jaurès was an unrivaled orator and a brilliant writer. (De Mun was praised by calling him "the Jaurès of the right.") To be sure, they won converts also and their words were suitably appreciated in some circles, but the acceptance was much narrower and more slowly accomplished.

Nobody indiscriminately believes whatever is well said. Pitchmen and swindlers dupe only those already accessible to the particular line employed. It is much the same in public affairs: Everyone has beliefs predisposing responses to political issues and making them similarly accessible. There is little that even the most intelligent and experienced people will refuse to believe if it appeals sufficiently to their prejudices and personal interests.

This should be evident from the numerous anti-Dreyfusards who were distinguished by their proven political acumen, intellectual brilliance, or both. The anti-Dreyfusard camp contained a larger number of people with real intellectual and artistic achievement than did the opposing camp, despite the great and much-discussed intellectual strength of the latter. These anti-Dreyfusards were not simple, gullible dupes or mere facile manipulators of words. They included many or even most of those alive who had created the glories that made French high culture pre-eminent in Western civilization. Most men of proven accomplishment and judgment in national politics also opposed the Dreyfusards until very late in the drama, although many moderated or reversed their stands eventually.

Intelligent and astute anti-Dreyfusards did believe Dreyfus guilty, and they did accept their side's impossible claims while refusing to entertain seriously those of the opposition. Yet they were less concerned with guilt or innocence than with what they saw as the consequences of the Dreyfusard campaign. They often had little to say about Dreyfus and proofs, although most discourse on both sides concentrated upon this. In their declamations the ex-captain's guilt was simply assumed, perhaps with some minimal argumentation, and they moved impatiently on to confront the *real* issue: The Dreyfusards were destroying France.

In fact, for all the committed anti-Dreyfusards the Affair finally reduced to this. Dreyfus was only the occasion for the struggle, and argument about why he had to be guilty was only a way of fighting. Belief in his guilt came easily and persisted, for anything else was intolerable, given their perspectives on contemporary politics. Dreyfus had betrayed France because he was a Jew, but what mattered most was national betrayal by his champions. The epithets regularly employed in reference to the Dreyfusards are revealing: They were *vendus* and *sans-patries*— "sellouts" (to the Germans and the Syndicate) and "men without a country."

Just as the anti-Dreyfusards' nationalism involved much more than a simple love of country, so did their animus against the Dreyfusards involve more than distress about supposed betrayal. For all the talk of proofs, the main purpose of their polemics was insistence upon the damage done by the crusade for Dreyfus; when we examine what they thought destructive we may discover what on their part made the Affair so intense and vicious a struggle.

In regarding the extent of the combat over Alfred Dreyfus, we should be struck not only by the persistence of belief in his guilt but also by the importance both sides attributed to a mere espionage case. Other instances of spying did not arouse intense and prolonged controversy; they caused short-lived, limited sensation, and then the press of other events caused them to be largely forgotten. To be sure, alleged treason by a General Staff officer and a Jew mattered more, but in the usual tumult of events there were many more important developments to occupy attention.

After Dreyfus had been sent to Devil's Island, his story was indeed slipping into obscurity. Then, beginning in September 1896, there was an extended sequence of developments involving Mathieu Dreyfus and his few sympathizers on the one side, and outraged patriots on the other. Through mutual interaction a conflict grew in intensity and public visibility, and led to the major engagement of forces a year and more later.

The involvement of anti-Dreyfusards may be explained in terms of reaction to the campaign for Dreyfus, but there remains the question of how and why others became so deeply engaged on behalf of the prisoner of Devil's Island. Most of those eventually thus engaged had first supposed Dreyfus guilty—and had no interest in the case after the initial furor of 1894 subsided. Mathieu Dreyfus had been turned away in 1895 when seeking help from some who later would become Dreyfusards, including two of the most important, Senate Vice-President Auguste Scheurer-Kestner and Yves Guyot, a prominent politician and chief of an old republican newspaper, *Le Siècle*.[2]

Evidence and its critical assessment did matter very greatly to those drawn to the Dreyfus crusade. So also did the injustice done to the innocent captain. When they learned facts persuading them that justice had miscarried, they were drawn into the Affair, but it was not simply a matter of righting the wrongs done to Dreyfus and, later, Picquart. There must be an explanation of why so many became so deeply, so very passionately involved that the Affair obsessed them and engaged most of their energies over an extended period. Many years later, after World War I and much else had intervened, onetime Dreyfusards would say the Affair had been the most important experience in their lives. Dreyfus alone could not have mattered that much.

Moreover, one must discover why the critical assessment of evidence was so important to the Dreyfusards when it seems not to have mattered to their antagonists. And why did the Dreyfusards value justice so highly, when their antagonists seem to have preferred for the sake of *la Patrie* that Dreyfus remain condemned even if innocent? Clearly the Affair was a struggle of general political importance and not just a matter of criminal justice. It is not so clear how attitudes about evidence and the priority of justice should be connected to the larger political questions that simultaneously stirred the combatants. Yet the ways both sides mixed expression of these attitudes with their political words and deeds shows that the connection was intimate and vital, and has to be clarified.

Dreyfusards also assumed their positions in reaction to the anti-Dreyfusards, whose concerted clamor alarmed them. Socialists and anarchists, who at first turned away from Dreyfus, the rich bourgeois officer, were especially affected by the character of the anti-Dreyfusard effort. Although ordinarily opposed to those whom the Affair made their allies, these men and women of the left overcame their aversion to siding with the bourgeoisie in order to fight the more immediately dangerous enemy. Most went from abstention to active partisanship for Dreyfus, and they formed a large segment of the most militant support for the Dreyfusard cause.

Thus in the Dreyfus Affair on the one side we find credulity and tenacious retention of patently false beliefs about guilt and proofs, and on the other a faith in the logic of facts and a passionate drive to make the logic prevail. Each side formed these approaches and reacted against the other on the basis of deeply held prior convictions. Their convictions were so sharply opposed and so mutually incomprehensible that the combatants often appeared to come from different worlds. Both sides wanted desperately to sustain their own positions and confound their enemies. This urgency leads us to a presumption that the convictions in question must have determined or reflected what was most vitally important to them in life as a whole.

When learning about the Affair one ordinarily is first bewildered by the astonishing complexity of arguments over proofs and guilt. When it becomes clear how poor was the case against Dreyfus, one becomes bewildered instead about how so many could have kept fighting on so bitterly and persistently anyway. The result is a tendency to suppose that they were overwhelmed and confused by a factual complexity much compounded by forgeries, lies, and wild charges.

Yet the complexity was not *that* confusing; indeed, at the time quite a few published efforts to disentangle the case achieved a remarkable degree of clarity. Complexity was like a smoke screen, and clearing it away did not change what it had covered. Behind lay the convictions that actually motivated those engaged in the struggle and made it so intense and prolonged.

Then making sense of the Affair requires knowing what those convictions were and how they operated. If they were as fundamental as the magnitude of the struggle suggests, then this knowledge should reveal much to us about what France and the French were at the end of the nineteenth century. Since the anti-Dreyfusards thought they acted as a result of the Dreyfusard crusade, then further examination must begin with the Dreyfusards.

> A man unjustly condemned, how often has that been seen? How often will it yet be seen? The laws even violated by their guardians, a daily spectacle! All society's cruelty raging

against the victim, the usual effect of the anonymous cowardice of the interests in power! But when, with the condemned, with the *condemners*, a whole established order stands indicted, when behind them the great social forces are engaged in close combat, when for him law has only to be the law [in order for him to go free], when the whole administration of justice is in danger of having its various organs fall to pieces, when individual conscience sees rising up against it the formidable apparatus of the State, supported by the conscienceless crowds, then everything becomes magnified, everything assumes inordinate proportions, and the combat mounts to epic scale where all humanity appears before the bar.

The victim in this case, whatever pity he inspires, is established as a living symbol of all failings of spirit and of heart. This transient representative of an unjust human justice suddenly appears as the synthetic witness of all the iniquities of the past, against all the forces of social dominance, which an injustice redressed threatens with other, more formidable redress. The representative injustice has to remain in order that the league of the principal powers not be broken. The religion of charity brandishes the iron and says, "Misfortune to the Jew." The mind of the military castes will not allow force to be subject to reason. Against liberty searching for its path there rises up the authority of dogma and of iron, implacable because infallible. The inquity *is:* an immense force in comparison with the justice sought. The arbitrary establishes itself over the law, the lie over the truth, and force crushes thought.

And, in this frightful combat of all the tyrannies on earth against the creature in distress, what recourse for the weakness of one man alone come to grips with the vastness of the sovereign powers? Nothing but ideas, abstractions. . . . Ideas, words, but magical words all the same. . . .

Justice, a little word indeed! The greatest of all. . . . A fine word . . . which man cannot hear without finding himself larger, without feeling himself better. . . . Word stronger than force, by means of hope.

With this word for our entire armament, we have joined battle.[3]

7

The Crusaders for Dreyfus

"Ideas, abstractions . . . magical words. . . . Justice . . . with this word for our entire armament, we have joined battle." In saying this, Georges Clemenceau marked the links of the chain binding together the diverse individuals in the Dreyfusard campaign. Words and ideas were precious also to their opponents, but in crucially different ways.

It has long been virtually a cliché to say that the Dreyfusards were crusading "intellectuals." That term, scarcely ever used in the French language before 1898, was first taken by Dreyfusards for themselves, then used against them by enemies. *Intellectuel* joined *vendu* and *sans-patrie* as a favorite pejorative noun. (Because of this usage, in this book the *noun* "intellectual" never refers to anti-Dreyfusards, who are included in less politically charged expressions like "men of letters.") Much has been made, with reason, of the role played in the cause by writers and academics. Yet such great intellects as the historian Gabriel Monod, the novelist Anatole France, the poet Charles Péguy, and the scientists Emile Duclaux and Henri Poincaré had only secondary though significant parts. Most of the knights leading the crusade were not quite the sort of people many of *us* usually think of when speaking about "intellectuals."

We might just as well call the Affair a crusade of journalists, whose number included nearly all the most vocal and active Dreyfusards. In the campaign the endless discussion, the planning, the decisions, and the action took place for the most part in the offices of Paris daily newspapers, especially *L'Aurore* and *Le Siècle*. Paris dailies also battling for the Dreyfusards were *Les Droits de l'homme*, *Le Radical*, *Le Rappel*, *La Fronde*, *La Petite République*, *La Lanterne* and *Le Journal du peuple*. Much of the campaign was waged through the forum these newspapers provided, as well as in other, less frequently published periodicals and through a stream of pamphlets and books written by the same authors and issued by the publisher P. V. Stock.

Nevertheless, the role of journalists is also subject to misunderstanding. They were not quite the sort of people we usually think of when speaking of journalists, either. And, as will be seen, the Affair was not simply a creation of the press.

Yet another view might be derived from the dominant part played in Dreyfusard inner circles by professional politicians, above all Joseph Reinach, Auguste Scheurer-Kestner, Georges Clemenceau, Jean Jaurès, Ludovic Trarieux, and Arthur Ranc. The professional politicians either served in the national legislative chambers during the Affair or, if excluded by election loss, hoped to return there (most did). While some were mavericks in one way or another, most were political insiders who helped build and sustain the regime of the Third Republic. Their use of the Affair for partisan and personal political advantage may be thought to strain the image of a crusade waged by intellectual idealists; some Dreyfusards would in time come to believe that it had done so.

In reality, the categories "intellectual," "journalist," and "politician" overlapped so much that they were at times indistinguishable. Moreover, it should be recognized that, while intellectuals were individually most prominent, the Dreyfusard crusade gained many supporters who were not intellectuals but were drawn in either to defend the Republic or to fight its enemies. Anarchists and, to some extent, socialists acted for the

latter purpose but not the former. Both groups were composed
for the most part of nonintellectuals, and both were important in
the Affair. Their engagement will be examined in the next chapter, in the context of the combat they felt compelled to join after
initially abstaining.

In order to clarify the involvement of intellectuals, we shall
look here at some exemplary figures, beginning with three who
were simultaneously intellectuals, journalists, and professional
politicians, each with a different partisan perspective. Clemenceau was a left republican, Reinach a moderate one, and Jaurès a
socialist. Their ties resulted from a shared culture, which will be
examined with emphasis upon the distinctive place of journalism.

The process by which Dreyfusard intellectuals were engaged
is analyzed chiefly by seeing what happened with these three,
plus three others. Each of the second trio was young and came to
politics from deep involvement in literary criticism. Bernard-
Lazare was engaged especially because he was Jewish and increasingly preoccupied with what place in the world Jews might
have. Léon Blum, although also Jewish, was engaged by the rational force of Dreyfusard arguments and by political ideology.
Daniel Halévy, while he also was swiftly engaged for much the
same reasons as Blum, exemplifies the ambivalence that many
intellectuals felt at the time.

Clemenceau was a one-time physician with training in psy-
chiatry, who had early been fascinated by political ideas and as
a young man had translated John Stuart Mill (*Auguste Comte et le
positivisme*, 1868). A professional politician from age thirty onward, he continued to write voluminously and in many different
forms, including a novel and a play. The play was performed
with music by Gabriel Fauré and was made into the libretto for
an opera with music by Charles Pons, which was performed at
the Théatre de l'Opéra-Comique. Clemenceau was a prolific journalist, writing about anything and supporting himself thereby
when out of office, but writing daily newspaper articles when in
office as well. Moreover, he became in many ways *the* outstanding politician of the Third Republic, who served five years in two
terms as Premier—including the crucial final year of World War
I and the making of the Versailles Treaty.

Most of Clemenceau's writing was undistinguished, except
for pieces on political issues that really engaged him, releasing

his remarkable, passionate energy. So one might say he was no intellectual, but just a very clever man dabbling in the writer's game. Or one could say that he was too extraordinary a personality to illustrate a type. But such objections would overlook the character of thought that informed his literary efforts and the character of the culture for which he produced them.

Joseph Reinach provides another illustration. Reference works identify him as a journalist, but in that role his pen was given to a clearly conceived political purpose. As a young man he was the secretary of the principal founding father of the Third Republic, Léon Gambetta, and succeeded him as editor of the newspaper *La République française*. From this forum Reinach fought Boulangism, and went on to serve Gambetta's party of moderate but devoted republicanism in the Chamber of Deputies from 1889 until defeated by anti-Dreyfusard fury in 1898, then serving again from 1906 to 1914.

Yet Reinach was also a highly accomplished scholar and brother of two distinguished scholars, Salomon and Théodore, who were active and prolific in the Dreyfusard cause as well. Théodore also was a Deputy from 1906 to 1914. A Dreyfusard sketching Joseph Reinach mentioned his skill with horses and hunting, then added: "The bicycle tempted him: through curiosity, *in order to know*, he practiced the modish sport, but he returned to the horse with passion. Intensely cerebral, with uncommon aptitudes, he writes constantly. Deprivation of pens, of paper, of ink, would be for him most cruel!"[1]

Reinach was a man with multiple occupations and a single vocation. Another such figure provides the next example: Jean Jaurès. He was educated at the Ecole Normale Supérieure, France's most selective and prestigious institution of higher humanistic learning. He had the best entrance examination score in his class, and while there his only rival in brilliance was Henri Bergson, who was destined to become France's most celebrated philosopher. Jaurès himself went on to become a university professor of philosophy before he turned to elective politics and political journalism. With two breaks when voted out of office, he served in the Chamber of Deputies from 1885 until assassinated in 1914. For all the animosity of partisanship, he has been the most admired political figure of his era, and for some years before his death he may have been the most influential. He also wrote and spoke so much that the mass of it discouraged later publication of his collected works; an estimated eighty or ninety large volumes would have been needed. Most of this was newspaper articles and speeches, but his work also included two doctoral theses in philosophy and a history of the French Revolution published in four- and eight-volume editions. Jaurès's oratory was spellbinding and largely extemporaneous; he used minimal notes and elaborated his themes brilliantly through matchless force and fertility of intellect. Many of his speeches survived nevertheless because stenographically recorded, even outside the Chamber of Deputies, for his words were considered too fine to be lost.

The "great socialist tribune" was an idealist who devoted himself to making ideas practicable. Unlike most French socialists of his time, he had closely studied and understood Karl Marx's system in good scholarly fashion, as well as the ideas of other major theorists of socialism. From them he formed syncretic, nondogmatic convictions of his own. Jaurès believed in socialism because he thought that only through it could true democracy and traditional republican ideals be realized. This idealistic approach did not find wide favor among socialist militants, but there were other intellectuals with similar views of socialism, and they were among the first who rallied to the Dreyfusard cause.

Jaurès, Reinach, and Clemenceau could thus exercise their versatile talents because of the distinctive opportunities open to men of ideas in their country. This was the "Belle Epoque," when French culture scintillated most brightly and Paris knew itself to be the center of the civilized world. While most of the French devoted themselves to tending their fields, their cash boxes, or their bosses' machines, a surprisingly large number had access to and took pride in the wonders of that bright culture. Many endeavored to make their own amateur contributions. Publishing was comparatively cheap, and from the flood of things printed it seems as if *everybody* fancied themselves writers. Innumerable dilettantes helped learned societies to flourish all over France. More than seven hundred had been formed by the end of the nineteenth century, 452 of them founded in the century's second half.[2] There were ready audiences for the bountiful creations of the Belle Epoque. Exhibitions of the visual arts drew large crowds. The performing arts and lesser recreations attracted many more. Literature, criticism, history, philosophy, and science all found abundant consumers.

Artistic and intellectual accomplishment was so highly prized in this society that the ambitious sought fame and fortune through writing and art. Fortune usually did not come swiftly if at all, but many opportunities were offered to writers by the periodical press. There the aspirant could gain recognition, useful connections, and a little income. The already successful writer could greatly enlarge his reputation there, and perhaps acquire the power of real cultural or political influence; a few earned large incomes as well. Weekly and less frequent journals of ideas and the arts were very numerous and sometimes influential; these reviews were the principal vehicles for many writers.

However, in many respects the most important vehicles were the daily newspapers. One did not find a simple division of "serious" writers to one side and journalists to the other. The two vocations were so nearly interchangeable as to make such a division impossible.

In that era French newspapers were very different from the press today, anywhere. "News" as such played only a limited part in them. They were short, only four pages, with six pages just beginning to be adopted, slowly. Much of that space often was taken up by advertising and data, mainly financial market quotations. Plain, factual news reports were usually very brief and not numerous. Few newspapers or journalists took care to verify any facts mentioned, or even to estimate the reliability of information acquired through secondary sources.

Most newspaper space was given over to what may best be called literary efforts. There were, most obviously, the feuilletons, sometimes serialized novels and often essays where the main criterion was cleverness and elegant style; depth of thought and even significance of subject mattered much less, if at all. Then there was criticism of contemporary arts and letters, with regular critics potent figures indeed. Both occasional and regular writers of criticism and feuilletons were extensively employed by the daily press, and it was a real mark of success to have one's pieces appear in the more prestigious papers.

Cultural matters were given great prominence, but politics was also presented as literature. Most political journalism did not simply report what had happened but recreated it imaginatively, and according to the preconceptions of the writer or his editors. A good example is provided by the flights of facile eloquence describing Dreyfus's degradation and reproduced in Chapter Three. Rhetorical virtuosity was all-important; elegant style and seemingly brilliant intellect were essential; overt prejudice was normal and inescapable. Instead of synthesizing information, they editorialized, often with a verve and even splendor rarely seen in the press today.

There were scores of daily newspapers in Paris and countless others in the provinces. Three of the Parisian multitude had circulations from half a million to over a million (*Le Petit journal*, *Le Petit parisien*, and *Le Journal*), competed energetically for readers, and found increasingly large proportions of them outside Paris. Three others printed between one and two hundred thousand (*La Libre parole*, *La Croix*, and *La Petite république*), as did some of those in the larger provincial cities. Three more (*Le Temps*, *Le Figaro*, and *Le Journal des débats*) were very high in quality, very respectable, and very influential despite small circulations (fifteen thousand to forty thousand). The rest all had small, select clienteles, whose prejudices they addressed with similarly slanted journalism.[3]

Nearly all the newspapers actively promoted a particular political point of view, although some variation was often allowed to contributors. Most papers had been created or taken over by new owners with this promotion as a central or sole purpose. They were often losing business ventures in consequence, and some survived only by means of the prepaid subscriptions of ever loyal supporters. Political identity was established in several ways: control by interests, like a business or political group, with particular propaganda purposes (for example, the Assumptionists' organ, *La Croix*); establishment and control by a dominating political figure who made a paper his personal organ (Henri Rochefort's *L'Intransigeant*); the will and vision of a powerful editor (Ernest Judet and France's largest newspaper, *Le Petit journal*); or through the collaborative efforts of a band of like-minded journalists (*L'Aurore*).

The multitude of newspapers provided abundant opportunities for writers to market their ideas and display their verbal facility. Even small circulation papers made attractive forums, both because a select readership could be an important target and because newspapers extensively repeated and commented upon each other's material. Rochefort's startling invective in *L'Intransigeant* was widely familiar, although the paper printed only thirty thousand to fifty thousand copies daily. With only six thousand to ten thousand, *Le Siècle* built upon loyal readers and outstanding writers to make itself an effective force in the Affair.

Many newspapers gave much of their space to occasional contributors and employed as regular writers people whose primary employment was elsewhere. There were many professional politicians like Clemenceau, Reinach, and Jaurès writing regularly for and editing newspapers. With the press so frankly partisan, words they printed there were as much a part of executing political purposes as words spoken in the Chamber of Deputies or Senate.

Journalism was also important as a vehicle to figures much engaged by politics and wanting a potent role in it, but unable or unwilling to do so through serving in public office, although some made occasional forays there. Some of these individuals devoted their primary energies to other writing, to academe,[4] or to the practice of law, but they found time for political journalism also, especially when aroused by specific issues. The Dreyfus Affair excited many such people to exercise their skills.

Before the Affair, the daily press's opportunities for writers attracted many men of letters and ideas whose immediate concerns were not primarily political. They may have concentrated their journalism on art and literary criticism and on feuilletons, or they wrote about politics because doing that was the job available. Yet in their world the arts and letters were not distinct from politics, and a novelist or poet might readily turn his pen to comment on public affairs, or make fiction or verse into political statements. Academics saw teaching and scholarship as a civic function and could likewise slip readily into political advocacy, either in the press or through their academic and scholarly functions.

Then the Affair burst upon them and occupied the center of the stage. For many, the ideas and values that oriented their approaches to their usual endeavors seemed very much at stake in the drama's contest, their beliefs challenged by a situation where the wrong man had been condemned and seemingly vast forces were united in angry refusal to change anything. And thus they rallied to the Dreyfusard cause: men, and some women, of politics, of journalism, of letters, of ideas, of the academy—categories that were not really distinct. They were linked by a common faith in the power and virtue of words and by a belief that the key words had the same meaning and degree of importance for all of them. Accustomed to employing words with facility and style, they moved naturally to journalism as their main instrument of combat, especially in the daily press and also in the reviews and separately issued tracts (many of them compilations of newspaper pieces). Parliamentary debate was long an unequal contest, for they were too few there, and they fanned out across the country in a well-organized and well-executed campaign using the spoken word to excite additional support.

One can refer briefly to the reasons for their coherence and determination by saying they were "inspired by a common ideology." However, that phrase represents a situation that cannot be fully understood so simply, for neither the inspiration nor the ideology of the Dreyfusards was uniform. Besides obvious differences, like those between centrist republicans and anarchists, when the combatants thought they shared beliefs their understanding of ideas was often very different. The meaning an individual ordinarily gives to central abstract ideas like "justice," "liberty," and "equality" depends on just how one associates it with a wealth of other ideas, attitudes, and experiences. People using the same words may think they speak of the same conceptions when they do not at all. Modern French political discourse relied upon the emphatic use of such words denoting great abstractions but did not lend them anything like exact definition. "Liberty! Equality! Fraternity!" remained an effective slogan, but with too little recognition that it did not really mean very much, besides the rich connotations of historical experience. Surely the Dreyfusards were moved by such connotations, but not in the same ways.

Words and their ambiguous meanings must be emphasized here, for specifically defined doctrines did not much matter to most Dreyfusards. Many had definite negative convictions—about whom and what they did not like—but in the Affair they were also fighting *for* something, and that something was entangled in these ambiguities. Some Dreyfusards were directed by religious or Marxist doctrine, but their part was not large, and the connection of the Affair to their doctrines was for the most part indirect and uncertain. While even the most dogmatic ideology is not uniformly understood, French political beliefs in that era were particularly indefinite and varied.

No doubt vagueness of belief was important to the Dreyfusard combination of diverse support, for in that way actual differences could be submerged to make the common cause. They had enough similar elements of thought to join together, and a sense of grave crisis to prevent division.

Instead of a definite doctrine, Dreyfusards shared general values and attitudes, the products of modern, urban, bourgeois French education and culture. These established their preconceptions and expectations, and thus the ways they responded from late 1897 on to a dispute over a criminal case supposed to have been long since settled. The values of their shared culture determined the degree of importance they attributed to words and abstract ideas, as well as how they conceived them. That may have been a vague sort of ideology, but it was a real one.

Joseph Reinach belonged to the party of republicans who so frequently followed the course of expediency that they have often been referred to as the Opportunists. Yet these Opportunists had fought hard for many years to establish republicanism in France against a determined and potent opposition. Their vision of republicanism was conservative compared to that of a Clemenceau or a Jaurès, but it was ideals they fought for against the royalists, and not merely political power. Such an idealistic vision always directed Reinach's actions and discourse. In 1889 he had fought the authoritarian thrust of Boulangism in the same spirit as he fought the anti-Dreyfusards and what he saw as the entrenched authoritarianism of the Army and the Church.

Of these three exemplars, Jaurès's self-directing idealism is the most evident—but mainly through our knowing of his brilliant early academic career and his conscious formation of political ideas through careful study of theoretical systems. His profession was turning philosophy into practice; while his knowledge of philosphy was exceptional for a professional politician, his use of ideology did not really differ in kind from that of either Clemenceau or Reinach.

There may have been differences among these men and with others when any of them was confronted by apparent conflict between abstract principle and immediate practical considerations. Yet such differences must appear as personal or ideological, and not between those actually engaged in public affairs and the ones isolated in ivory towers. Until late in the struggle it was not expedient to fight alongside the Dreyfusards; practical considerations alone would have kept people in any quarter from rallying to the cause and did hold back many until it no longer seemed so hazardous.

The ones who entered the fray despite the dangers were moved by intellect: "with this word [Justice] for our entire armament we have joined battle." Thus we can freely name them "intellectuals," whatever their nominal professions. Yet there were many other, anti-Dreyfusard men and women of intellectual talent and accomplishment who scorned both the name and the ones who bore it. The very notion of "intellectual" itself appears to be at the heart of the opposition between Dreyfusards and anti-Dreyfusards. Thus we must see what made the Dreyfusards' intellect different by seeing how they were enrolled and how they fought, and by examining the words they found precious.

Efforts to free Alfred Dreyfus naturally began with family and friends, who could not believe him capable of the crime. These included Zadoc Kahn, the Grand Rabbi of France, whose steady support was cherished by the family but not of much help otherwise. The commandant of the military prison where Alfred Dreyfus had been kept while in Paris, Major Ferdinand Forzinetti, had been convinced by his conduct there that he was innocent. Forzinetti became close to the Dreyfus family, illicitly gave them crucial documents, spoke to others openly of his belief, and eventually was dismissed from the Army for his actions.

From the beginning a few others believed Alfred innocent or at least doubted his guilt. For some the most effective consideration was belief that only an innocent man could act as he had at his ritual degradation. His lack of apparent motive and the closed trial were troubling, as were the nastiness and anti-Semitism of the press campaign occasioned by the case. This last was an important factor in enlisting support for the cause when it became a major struggle.

Within a short time after the court-martial, Mathieu Dreyfus had learned of the illegal use of evidence there and knew enough of the secret evidence itself to think it could be discredited. With this knowledge Mathieu slowly secured additional support, beginning with Bernard-Lazare. Forzinetti had said there were just

two men capable of conducting the propaganda campaign necessary to shake the government into allowing a new trial: Lazare
and Edouard Drumont. The latter was not quite a likely ally, but
Lazare agreed readily, in the spring of 1895, although Mathieu's
caution did not allow action then.

Thirty years old at the time, Bernard-Lazare was an avant-
garde literary critic, well known and in some circles considered
most important. He was a committed anarchist, but his literary
activity and bourgeois personal style made most people take him
for the sort of intellectual called *anarchisant* ("anarchizing"): having rebellious inclinations rather like those of anarchists, but
perhaps vague and often mainly aesthetic, and without commitment to an anarchist movement or recognition by anarchists
themselves as one of their number.

As a seemingly *anarchisant* man of letters, Lazare was representative of a significant number of later Dreyfusards. He was
also like some others in being a nonbelieving, assimilated Jew
who found that the Affair transformed his own sense of Jewish
identity. In 1894 he had published a book about anti-Semitism,
in which he criticized the voluntary distinctiveness of Jews refusing assimilation and identified anti-Semitism as conservative
nationalist reaction against Jewish nationalism. Anti-Semitism
would be overcome and Jews protected only by social revolution.

However, by the time the first published version of his pamphlet, "A Judicial Error—The Truth About the Dreyfus Affair,"
appeared in November 1896, Lazare's view had shifted. He wrote
that Dreyfus's arrest, condemnation, and continued imprisonment were due to anti-Semitism, a persecution unprovoked by
the victim or his co-religionists. Lazare was arriving at the conviction that in the face of such hatred Jews could not assimilate
and should instead make the most of their distinctiveness. Their
common background and culture made of Jews a nation, and
their salvation lay in their own nationalism. Lazare's changing
views came close to those being developed at the same time and
for much the same reasons, including the stimulus of the Dreyfus
Affair, by the Viennese intellectual Theodor Herzl, who became
the principal founder of twentieth-century Zionism. While always remaining nonreligious, Lazare devoted himself thereafter
to Jewish causes—to him the Affair was a battle for all Jews—
and especially to Zionism, until his early death in 1903.

Bernard-Lazare's emphasis upon anti-Semitism to explain

action by the Army and the State against Dreyfus was miscon-
ceived, but it was given wide credence by Dreyfusards and did
much to arouse their outrage against their opponents. However,
after early 1898, Bernard-Lazare himself withdrew from public
view, although he continued to work behind the scenes on organization of the crusade. Apparently Mathieu Dreyfus thought
him too provocative a figure, and by that time the cause had
many other eloquent champions.

Some Dreyfusards were drawn into the crusade because they
had been troubled by the case from the beginning, and then
were convinced early by the exculpatory evidence they learned
of privately. Reinach was one of these, as were Senators Trarieux
and Ranc, who also became important leaders of the campaign
for Dreyfus. Lazare's pamphlets and other publicity converted
still more.

Probably the most effective mechanism for enlisting support, however, was persuasion by individuals who drew in
friends and associates through conversation and argumentation.
Many a Dreyfusard would later write about just who enlisted
him and under what circumstances, usually in the fall and early
winter of 1897. Typical but more detailed than most were the
reminiscences of Léon Blum, written in 1935, just before he became French Premier.

Blum was vacationing in the country near Paris in September 1897. At the time he was twenty-five years old and fast rising
in the world of literary criticism. He was visited there most after-
noons by Lucien Herr, the librarian at the Ecole Normale Supérieure. While a student there Blum had become one of those for
whom Herr was a valued mentor and friend, in both scholarship
and politics. One day Herr rode out on his bicycle as usual to see
Blum. Herr asked him point blank, "Do you know that Dreyfus
is innocent?"

In 1894 the librarian had been alerted to the possibility of
Dreyfus's innocence by the assurances of Lucien Lévy-Bruhl, a
Sorbonne philosopher who was a cousin by marriage of Dreyfus.
Herr was finally convinced by examining evidence, both that
presented by Lazare in his tracts and that communicated privately by the route Picquart to Leblois to Scheurer-Kestner to
Mathieu Dreyfus to Lévy-Bruhl to Herr. Arguing with the extraordinary logical skill of which he was master, Herr set out to
convince his large circle of intellectual friends, including a num-

ber of distinguished academics, former and present students at the Ecole Normale, and Jean Jaurès himself.

When confronted by Herr's question, Léon Blum was at first nonplused, for he had simply given no thought to Dreyfus since his conviction. Then Blum remembered incidents to which he had attributed little significance at the time they occurred; recalling them now heightened his concern with Herr's arguments.

At the time of the Dreyfus court-martial he had been told by a close friend, Michel Bréal, who was a linguist and professor at the Collège de France: "I do not believe or disbelieve in the innocence of Dreyfus. And I do not understand because, up to now, they have provided me no intelligible motive. I reject the hypothesis of a human action to which it is impossible to assign reasons."

To this intellectualistic statement Blum added the memory of encountering Bernard-Lazare one morning at the offices of *La Revue blanche*, the leading avant-garde literary review. Lazare, who was accompanied by Major Forzinetti, had affirmed his convictions about Dreyfus; Blum had been incredulous and paid the arguments little heed. Now, when hearing Herr, Blum remembered the incident and his usual great respect for Lazare's intellect and critical acumen, and regretted that he had been so obtuse and indifferent.

Finally, Blum remembered being told by an acquaintance just come from a dinner party of a conversation heard there. Among the dinner guests had been a Colonel Roget, probably the same officer who shortly would play a substantial part in the Affair (as assistant to War Minister Cavaignac, General Staff spokesman, and troop commander upsetting Déroulède's coup attempt). Roget said that, as chief of a General Staff bureau, he was on the track of an international Jewish syndicate with unlimited funds that sought to free the traitor Dreyfus. Another dinner guest, unnamed, had asked who was this person Dreyfus, whose name he could only recall vaguely. Roget gave the whole story in detail, "with elegance and precision." The other man had next caused a furor at the party by saying he knew nothing of the case other than what the colonel had just told him, but if this information were all accurate, then "there can be no doubt for anybody with good sense: Dreyfus is innocent."

As Blum walked in his garden with Herr, the latter employed cogent reasoning from evidence to persuade his friend, who had been prepared by these previous intimations of the truth.[5] It appears that the engagement of many or most Dreyfusards followed a comparable pattern.

The growing uproar of the Affair, still relatively subdued when Herr enlisted Blum, added force to logic and made active participation in the struggle more urgent. Yet for these intellectuals what mattered most in their recruitment was the evidence, the consequent argument, and the personal influence of respected friends.

Blum and Herr were already politically engaged and committed to republican values through a socialism closely akin to that of Jaurès. Although not always socialists as well, the substantial circle of Herr's friends and protégés had similar values, and most were soon drawn into the Dreyfus cause. There were other groups with comparable positions, some of them linked by friendship and political or professional association to Herr, his friends, and the Ecole Normale Supérieure. Among these were a remarkable coterie growing up around Charles Péguy, who was a recent student of the Ecole Normale and a Herr protégé, and the band of academic social scientists centered upon the pioneer sociologist Emile Durkheim, who was then teaching at the university in Bordeaux.

These were all men whose education and intellectual activity had emphasized reasoning from evidence, as well as the political ethos of a militant, anticlerical republicanism. All this was typical of the Ecole Normale Supérieure, where many of them had studied and a few taught. Since politics was already central in their lives, they did not have to drag their attention away from remote concerns. In consequence they were more readily drawn to the Dreyfusard cause than others with less definite or fully developed political attitudes, or with less concern for this critical reasoning.

Fear of being hurt by those hostile to Dreyfusards as well as other practical considerations would deter many from open commitment to the Dreyfusards, especially in the first critical months. Nevertheless, the early Dreyfusards just mentioned and others felt impelled by logic and politics to rush forward, though some were vulnerable to retaliation. There were some Dreyfusard Army officers and priests, and many Dreyfusards were civil servants, including all academics. Some retaliation did occur, and there was much anxiety. Clemenceau reported early in the Affair:

"Yesterday, one of our most distinguished teachers in secondary education said to me, 'You will have no one from *lycées* [state secondary schools]. If you give my name, that imbecile [Education Minister] Rambaud' (I euphemize) 'will send me to rot in the depths of Brittany.' "[6] Acting despite such hazards added immeasurably to a sense among Dreyfusards that they were heroes, beleaguered but invincible.

Parliamentary politicians whom ideology inclined to the Dreyfusards ran other risks. Their responses ranged from the handful who openly committed themselves as soon as it became an issue to those who avoided a stand or opposed the Dreyfusards until it was profitable to do otherwise—after Dreyfus had been released through Presidential clemency. Each of those who made early commitments seems to fit the patterns of intellectual background and political perspective of the exemplars examined here.

Clemenceau's own involvement has been regarded by many as the cynical expediency of a man who tried to recoup the political capital he had lost through his implication in the Panama scandal five years earlier. This judgment results from recognition of the man's cynicism and chauvinism on other occasions, but it underestimates the extremity of the anti-Dreyfusard reaction from the first. No one stood to gain enough from supporting Dreyfus to outweigh the harm likely to be suffered, until the drawing of the battle lines began to make it clear, by the summer of 1898, that the future of republicanism itself might well be at stake. Clemenceau's whole-hearted involvement can be seen in his newspaper articles from the way his initial reservations fell away, beginning with the first article on November 1, 1897. Just before then he had been persuaded by Scheurer-Kestner that justice had miscarried, though the latter's inability at the time to reveal Picquart's confidences kept Clemenceau unsure about Dreyfus's actual innocence. It is not clear just when he did become sure, but he was soon moved to fight unreservedly, the issue of the unjust 1894 court-martial being sufficient to engage him.

Jaurès very carefully went over the known evidence and consequent arguments with Herr, Lévy-Bruhl, Scheurer-Kestner, and Leblois. He saw the necessary conclusions, but he held himself back in order the better to bring into the fray with him other socialists, who were reluctant to enter what they saw as a dispute of the bourgeoisie. By late November 1897 a Jaurès newspaper article criticized the illegal court-martial and anti-Semitism. A few days later he wrote of the necessary connection between the Esterhazy and Dreyfus cases, and damned Premier Méline and the War Minister, General Billot, for denying it. On January 19, 1898, the parliamentary socialists made a tentative first step toward commitment, and three days later Jaurès cast aside restraint in an inflammatory address to the Chamber of Deputies. His thundering charge provoked a brawl, discussed in the next chapter, in which Deputies pounded each other and prevented the session from continuing. It was the end of any semblance of restraint or civility in the Affair.[7]

In retrospect it does not seem difficult to perceive, when one is familiar with the figures in questions, why some chose to be Dreyfusards and others to be active in opposing them. Yet the ambiguities of the situation were substantial enough for the combatants themselves often to be surprised by the choices made. Dreyfusards hoped to secure the support of two of the most eloquent warriors of the political press, Henri Rochefort and Paul Cassagnac. Rochefort seemed likely because of his leftist affectations and his fondness for pillorying the government for supposed misdeeds. Cassagnac, though a conservative nationalist, was highly independent in his views and since 1894 had often been severe in criticizing the government for unfair conduct of the Dreyfus case. Also hoped for was Maurice Barrès, a writer who was enormously influential among men of letters on both the left and the right; it was thought that his ideas made him a likely recruit. Then there were Ferdinand Brunetière and Jules Lemaître, the greatest living critics and historians of French literature. Surely their cool, superior rationality would compel their support of the Dreyfusards; not incidentally, Lemaître was a graduate of the Ecole Normale Supérieure and Brunetière a professor there.

All five of these men became leading anti-Dreyfusard spokesmen, and all remained unshaken by the ever mounting evidence that the case against Dreyfus was worthless. On the other hand, Dreyfusards thought the novelist Anatole France would be unreachable because of his skepticism and detachment from politics, as well as his attachment to a social and cultural milieu whose comforts might be denied him were he to be engaged. Yet France joined the Dreyfusards immediately when approached and was outspoken in their cause.

There were many Dreyfusards who found the choice difficult for reasons other than fear of harm by anti-Dreyfusard reaction. Ambivalence among them is illustrated by Daniel Halévy, who powerfully evoked the time in recollections written a decade later.[8] Twenty-five years old in 1897, he became an early Dreyfusard, but a major part of his experience and thought had acted to keep him from this course.

For generations his family had been one of the most distinguished in French letters and art, and included a number of major writers and composers. The Halévys were Jews who had intermarried with Protestants and had become fully assimilated into the highest level of Parisian bourgeois society. Daniel grew up familiar with the greatest figures of the French cultural scene, who often were guests in his father's house (where he continued to live during the Affair) and at that of his cousin, Geneviève Straus, who maintained one of Paris's most splendid literary salons. There is unlikely ever to have been a society more sophisticated, urbane, cultivated, and supremely self-assured than that which frequented the Halévy and Straus mansions.

Daniel Halévy undertook his own serious literary pursuits very early, in close company with a number of young men destined for celebrity, among them Léon Blum, André Gide, Paul Valéry, and Marcel Proust.[9] Like the rest of the society he knew, these were people with highly developed literary sensibilities, but most of them had scant concern and much disdain for politics. Halévy himself was little involved by politics before the Affair. As it would also be later, his political perspective was anomalous. On the one hand he shared the elitist liberalism that seemed so natural to his family and much of their upper-class circle. On the other, he had substantial *anarchisant* inclinations, which in most respects were quite opposed to the attitudes his upbringing had instilled.

The milieu in which Halévy had grown up was open to the values of republican ideology that moved many Dreyfusards, but it had not until then embraced them. He could not readily feel the reflexive impulse that excited action by a Reinach or a Herr. With his limited concern and disdain for ordinary political affairs and his complex and ill-developed ideas about politics, it required the urgency of crisis to press Halévy into adopting a position.

Moreover, this milieu itself was divided by the Affair, so that taking a stand meant alienating precious friends and acquaintances. Halévy later said they were all having a fine, soft time enjoying their intellectual and aesthetic pursuits and their urbane company, when everything was disrupted by the intrusion of the Affair. A large portion of the society frequenting the Halévy and Straus residences did move sooner or later into the Dreyfusard camp, and the Straus salon became one of the most important gathering places for Dreyfusards. However, many of their valued friends and guests departed forever, becoming anti-Dreyfusard. Daniel suffered an especially painful loss through the alienation of the painter Edgar Dégas, whom he had loved as a second father. Dégas cut himself off from the Halévys in November 1897 out of an anti-Semitism become acute because of the Affair.

Many of Daniel's friends had ambivalent attitudes analogous to his, and they too were pulled in opposite directions by elements of life important to them. Ultimately most of his circle of younger friends did choose to involve themselves in the Dreyfusard crusade, with the earliest converts like Léon Blum helping to bring the others to decision.

In his memoir Halévy recalled that before Scheurer-Kestner's intervention one did not know or want to know what had happened. "a prudent instinct counselled" them to remain ignorant, complacently accepting the sentence rendered. But Scheurer-Kestner's intervention brought forth facts and furor which together awakened them. After careful study, the meaning of the facts seemed quite clear, and the anti-Dreyfusard clamor made it impossible to ignore them. Like many other refined intellectuals, Halévy's Dreyfusard motivations included an elitist element that is apparent in this memoir, even though it was written after he had spent years trying to cross the gulf between his world and those of the masses.

> From that moment our liberties were suspended, through the madness of public opinion. We had to excommunicate ourselves, or humiliate ourselves before the fanatics and profess the religion of a savage patriotism for which Dreyfus guilty symbolized faith. . . .
>
> The chiefs of the General Staff, not knowing how to keep

their secret, sought to get the country naively to do it for them, and through its press, its orators, kept up this illusion. Frivolous and ill-fated enterprise! Revelation of error and injustice, producing their effects, dragged the entire country toward stupidity and wickedness. . . .

[All injustice has two victims, the second being] the one who inflicts it; his misfortune is not so visible, but it is more formidable. [Here more than Dreyfus] another victim laid claim to our concern: it was France, which a small number of men have poisoned with fear, with hate, and disgraced. . . .

It was a question . . . of the spiritual health of France. The cause of its alteration was, we knew it, this Dreyfus affair, quite obscure, from which unwholesome odors rose. Anti-Semitic fury, anti-militarist fury; fanaticism of affirmation, fanaticism of critique; humanitarian delirium, patriotic delirium; nothing emanated from there that was not intoxication, fury, fanaticism, hatred, or delirium. What remedy for this evil? We say only one: to go to the source, to purify the very foundations. People did not know: from that, all the violence. It was necessary to know; not to take revenge or to punish, but to restore clarity and, through it, in the masses some peace, in the elites some serenity. . . .

[This was a] singular revolution, the most strictly religious, perhaps, of all the wars of religion, where so many men, without shedding their blood, gave their lives.[10]

8

Combat Joined

Those who have not known the joy of standing up for a great cause of justice have not known what makes living worth while [Attributed to Paul Painlevé].[1]

Standing up for the cause was no easy matter. The conflict was too bitter and too often violent. On both sides antagonism was so sharp and so deep-seated that a would-be contestant might well flinch and retreat in the face of it. "Civil war" is hardly a metaphorical term for describing what happened.

French politics and journalism were not distinguished by their moderation in any event, while the divisions in the French people exhibited themselves through extremes of violence. Street riots were all too frequent, and since 1789 France had known four bloody revolutions and a number of episodes of murderous mass terror. In the usual course of affairs political discourse was often marked by eagerness to humiliate and destroy opponents, and the vendetta could seem more natural than the compromise.

Still, despite all the persistent divisions and hostilities, a society ordinarily has to find ways most of the time for tolerating differences and restraining people in conflict from open warfare. Compromise and customary forms of civility do moderate conflict and cloak it under covers that most individuals find more comfortable than frequent bloodletting. Even while conscious of their differences, opponents can learn to recognize their simultaneous affinities and to see the mutual value of restraint.

Severe tension between the opposed modes of aggravated hostility and conventional restraint was the usual condition of public life in this divided France. During the Dreyfus Affair all were conscious that restraints had failed and antagonisms had been fully released. The Affair's most characteristic and famous cartoon (by Caran d'Ache, in *Le Figaro*, February 14, 1898) brought this home to people. Ten well-dressed persons are shown at dinner with the gentleman at the head saying, "Above all! Let us not talk about the Dreyfus affair!" A second picture shows them attacking one another, strangling, stabbing with forks, raising fists. This picture's caption is, "They talked about it."

Zola's scarcely restrained attack in "J'Accuse!" was followed immediately by violent meetings and riots almost daily across France. In Algiers the riots went on for days, with the authorities unable or unwilling to stop them. Jews suffered badly through both personal injury and property damage. While the Algiers riots were going on, the Chamber of Deputies met for a key debate about the Affair on Saturday, January 22, 1898.

The spectator seats were filled by an eager crowd, including the Italian poet of conflict and violence, Gabriele d'Annunzio. Under attack by nationalists for inaction, Premier Méline successfully defended himself by insisting once more that the Dreyfus condemnation was beyond question, referring vaguely to Dreyfus's "confession," and by attacking the Dreyfusards. He said that the socialists, above all Jaurès, were preparing France for a new version of "the Debacle"—the 1870 humiliation of the French army by Prussia.

Nationalist Deputies were wild with enthusiasm, and Jaurès was wild with indignant rage. He rushed to the tribune and launched himself into a tirade. "The debacle was due then to the court's generals, protected by the Empire, as today it is in danger of being due to the Jesuits' generals, protected by the Republic!"

(*Commotion on the right and in the center; applause on the extreme
left.*) The presiding officer, Henri Brisson, remonstrated: "I beg
of you, Monsieur Jaurès, to watch your language; your talent has
no need of violent expressions." (*Applause.*) But Jaurès continued, red in the face with anger, and charged Méline with lies,
equivocation, and cowardice and with having supporters who
rioted while howling, "Death to the Jews!" Jaurès ignored Brisson's efforts to call him to order.

The commotion he provoked increased, and then a monarchist Deputy, the Comte de Bernis, shouted above the clamor, "You
are part of the Syndicate . . ." (*Animated interruptions.*) Jaurès:
"What did you say, Monsieur de Bernis?" Bernis: "I said that
you must be part of the Syndicate, that you are probably the
advocate of the Syndicate!" Jaurès: "Monsieur de Bernis, you are
a wretch and a coward!"

Bernis rushed toward Jaurès, apparently to hit him. A socialist Deputy, Gérault-Richard, leaped up and struck Bernis
with his fist. Dozens of Deputies from the right of the Chamber
and socialists jumped into a quickly expanding melee. Sergeants
at arms immediately joined the mob, trying without success to
restrain the men of France's governing assembly, some of whom
turned to wrestle with these officers. A militant socialist, Jules
Coutant, fell upon a group of visiting Senators, beating them as
hard as he could. "I'm a Senator!" cried one. "I don't give a
fuck!" replied Coutant, pounding him all the more. Another man
shouted, "Hit me, wretches! Hit me!" and friends obliged by
tapping him lightly. Bernis cried despairingly as socialists pum-
meled him. "And into the middle of this swarm of heads con-
gested with fury," *L'Intransigeant* later reported, "we saw, to our
amazement, a dervish whirling with frenzy!"—an Algerian in
white burnoose had jumped into the battle.

Unable to affect anything by ringing his bell, Brisson put on
his hat, the conventional signal declaring the session adjourned,
and crept on all fours to his seat. Jaurès was still at the tribune.
Bernis sidestepped the whirling dervish, climbed the stairs,
slapped Jaurès, and left before the surprised orator could respond. Jaurès made a grand gesture of helplessness in the face of
the uproar and departed. The battle's frenzy intensified still
more. Even after the military guard had pushed the combatants
out into the corridors, the fighting continued for some time
longer.[2]

On Monday the session resumed in somber silence, with Jaurès again at the tribune. The riot in the Chamber had been a comedy compared to the simultaneous pogrom in Algeria. In Paris, the center of world civilization and political liberty, the Chamber's riot mattered much more.

Violence in the streets did alarm the government, whose social conservatism induced an exaggerated anxiety about popular upheaval. Dreyfusards expressed outrage over the opposition's viciousness and provocation of barbarous violence, and the resulting victimization of Jews. Nevertheless, in the capital most people regarded street rioting as incidental, especially when it occurred elsewhere. It seemed significant mainly for its contribution to the general atmosphere of crisis and anguished antagonism. Rioting in the center of the organized political process, the Chamber of Deputies, appeared to be another matter altogether.

The furor that broke out in the Chamber on January 22 was the culmination of months of intensifying conflict. The Affair had many climactic moments, as truly sensational events crowded upon one another in rapid succession until the sustained excitement became quite exhausting. Together with completion of Jaurès's speech when the Chamber reassembled on January 24, this fracas was especially crucial because of both its timing and the involvement of Deputies, particularly the socialist ones.

From the time that Scheurer-Kestner's intervention for Dreyfus had first become publicly known, late in the preceding October, the nationalist press had been hard at work denouncing him and all who were thought to support him. Most of his political colleagues would no longer talk to him, even though until that moment Scheurer-Kestner had been one of the most respected men in national political life. *Le Journal* on November 12 called him an "idiot," a "senile old man," and "the most striking example of contemporary stupidity." In *La Libre parole* on October 30, Edouard Drumont gave the most immediate reason for the acrimony against the once-esteemed Senator: "What constitutes the security of the State is the confidence soldiers have in their officers. Now officers who condemn one of their comrades when he is innocent are either rogues or idiots. In asserting the innocence of Dreyfus, M. Scheurer-Kestner conspires against the security of the State." This was one of the milder criticisms.

Henri Rochefort ridiculed Scheurer-Kestner almost daily, in the most extreme terms, and many other journalists followed his lead.

In addition to Bernard-Lazare's pamphlet (November 6, 1897), other Dreyfusards published almost daily disclosures and comments about facts exculpating Dreyfus. This aroused the opposing journalists and politicians to counterattack with invective, argument over the allegations of both sides, and unfounded or distorted claims about damning evidence.

The most extraordinary and mischievous of these assertions was a story by Rochefort in *L'Intransigeant* on December 12. Rochefort claimed an unimpeachable source; Dreyfusards believed the story to have been given him by the General Staff. Rochefort said that years before Dreyfus had decided to move to Germany and adopt German nationality. He wrote directly to Kaiser Wilhelm asking to enter the German Army officer corps. The Kaiser instructed him to remain in the French Army as a spy, while secretly holding a German officer's commission, and Dreyfus did so. Before arresting him, French counterintelligence had stolen eight letters from the German embassy in Paris. Seven were from Dreyfus and the eighth was the Kaiser's instructions to the ambassador on information to be collected by Dreyfus, who was named. Germany had threatened war if these letters were not returned; they were, but not before they had been photographed. Naturally, this definitive evidence had to remain secret, lest war result.

To this incredible story the anti-Dreyfusards added another (supposedly also from the General Staff) about the *bordereau annoté*, a copy of the *bordereau* with marginal notes by the Kaiser incriminating Dreyfus. The fact that none of these imaginary documents could ever be produced did not keep them from being ever persuasive for the credulous and most important for the Affair.[3]

The Dreyfusards had their correspondingly sensational revelation—a genuine one—two weeks before, with the publication in *Le Figaro* on November 28 of extracts from the "Uhlan letters" of Esterhazy. He had written them between 1881 and 1884 to his mistress of that time, and her lawyer had just given them to Scheurer-Kestner. The letters were so named through Esterhazy's having said in one that "if this evening I were told that I would be killed tomorrow as a captain of Uhlans [German cavalry] sabring the French, I would be perfectly happy." He had also written that he "would kill a hundred thousand Frenchmen with pleasure" and that he dreamed of "a red sun of battle, in Paris taken by assault and turned over to pillage by a hundred thousand drunken soldiers." There was much more in a similar vein.[4]

Le Figaro printed a facsimile of the most striking letter next to one of the *bordereau*. The handwriting in the two pieces looked identical. Esterhazy was still being represented as a fine officer victimized by the Syndicate. The Uhlan letters hardly fitted that image, and there was much effort to prove them forgeries, although in fact they were adequately authenticated. One might say that no one would dare to *invent* anything so outrageous, were it not for the inventions so freely proclaimed by the anti-Dreyfusards. Rochefort would even assert in his December 12 story that Dreyfus, having been denied success as a French officer because he was Jewish, thought he could achieve it in that well-known refuge of tolerance for Jews, the German Army officer corps!

While dismayed by the sharpness of the conflict and their status as a small, beleaguered minority, the Dreyfusards were most upset by the refusal of so many to listen to reason. Perhaps people might remain skeptical about some of the Dreyfusard contentions, but certainly they should admit that Esterhazy's implication in espionage had a direct bearing on the Dreyfus case, especially given the close resemblance of his normal writing to that of the *bordereau!* Yet this obvious rationale was denied or simply disregarded. Such denial was what Premier Méline meant by his famous words to the Chamber of Deputies on December 4, 1897: "There is no Dreyfus affair." After much applause from the right and center, he insisted once more: "There is not, at this moment, and there can never be a Dreyfus affair." There was more applause from right and center, and protests from the left. Méline went on: "An accusation of treason has been brought against an officer of the Army [Esterhazy]; this particular question has nothing to do with the other."

Declarations like this infuriated and frustrated Dreyfusards more than invective and lies possibly could. They cared so much about reason that it was intolerable to see it thus violated. While they could discount with scorn the outrages of polemicists and the vulgar mob, here they confronted what usually passed for reasonable men. If politics was no longer a rational process, then what was left to them?

Later in the same December 4 debate, Comte Albert de Mun spoke on behalf of the Army. He was neither a crass demogogue nor a Minister defending himself, but an upright gentleman and statesman. Yet he spoke of "an occult and mysterious power" undermining the Army leaders upon whom the country had to rely. This moment was recalled by Joseph Reinach, who was present as a member of the Chamber:

> Emotion choked the throat of the admirable actor [*comédien*]. He stops. An intense epidemic suggestion, fulminating, took over the entire Chamber. What! the legend of the Syndicate, this invention of the Jesuits, it is the republicans who ratify it! No longer are there republicans in the Chamber, but only a mob, incapable like all mobs of reflecting, to whom reasoning is something as alien as it is to those decapitated animals whose ganglionic and spinal life no longer feels anything but the exaggerated, disordered action of the reflexes. I feel upon my head the hate of three hundred hypnotized men who turn toward me, in a single imitative demonstration, when they are tired of applauding. I cross my arms; one word, one gesture would have changed this madness into furor. How can one struggle against a whirlwind? Jaurès, perhaps, could have attempted it; he was absent.[5]

Still later in this debate Reinach was verbally attacked by Alexandre Millerand, who exchanged gunshots with him in a duel the next day. Millerand and his seconds in the duel, Gérault-Richard and René Viviani, were leading socialist Deputies who, like most socialists, were then still hostile to the Dreyfusards.

With the struggle waged at first mainly through the press, the Dreyfusards found few newspapers at all open to them. The most important was *Le Figaro*, but protests by subscribers against its publication of Dreyfusard material caused the editor, Fernand de Rodays, to be forced out on December 13, 1897. Like many journalists, his successor also believed Dreyfus innocent but felt constrained not to let his paper say so openly. *L'Aurore* had been established shortly before, on October 1. Its founder and head was Ernest Vaughan, Rochefort's brother-in-law and former manager of *L'Intransigeant*. Despite this connection, Vaughan made *L'Aurore* a left republican journal, with Clemenceau as political editor and an excellent group of left-wing intellectuals for the staff. Though not instantly Dreyfusard, the paper moved quickly in that direction.

On December 9 Marguerite Durand established a left republican daily, *La Fronde*, with a highly talented all-woman staff. These women were Dreyfusards from the first, especially the most able of them, Séverine, who came from *La Libre parole*, of all places! Another odd switch was that of Joseph Cornély, an editor of the anti-Dreyfusard and royalist *Gaulois*, who moved to *Le Figaro* and before long to very active involvement as a Dreyfusard. And on January 9, 1898, Henri Deloncle established *Les Droits de l'homme* as a Dreyfusard daily, also with a staff of dedicated left-wing intellectuals. At the same time Yves Guyot brought his old republican daily, *Le Siècle*, into the fold.[6] A very few other newspapers and some journalists were Revisionist—believing that the illegality of the first Dreyfus trial made a new one necessary, but without affirming Dreyfus's innocence. Revisionists could be critical of the Dreyfusards for waging a harmful campaign, but their criticism was comparatively restrained, as was that of journalists who secretly sympathized with the cause.

On January 7, 1898, *Le Siècle* published the *acte d'accusation*, or formal indictment, upon which the 1894 Dreyfus court-martial had been based. Although the document had been secret, Mathieu Dreyfus had obtained it from Major Forzinetti, the former prison commandant who thought Alfred innocent. It consisted merely of speculation about the character of the accused and about the nature and authorship of the *bordereau*, the only documentary evidence cited. This indictment demonstrated publicly for the first time that the other documents supposedly proving Dreyfus's guilt had been introduced illegally, because they had been omitted from the indictment. Moreover, the indictment made so poor a case that anyone critically examining it had to be forcibly impressed with how ill-founded the prosecution had been. Publication of the *acte d'accusation* was the final stroke winning for the Dreyfusards the support of many who had wavered until then.

On January 9, 1898, *Le Temps* published a letter to Scheurer-Kestner about this indictment from Emile Duclaux, who was France's most eminent biologist and director of the Institut Pasteur:

. . . if, in the scientific questions we have to resolve, we conducted our investigation as it seems to have been done in this
affair, it would indeed be only by chance that we would arrive
at the truth. . . .

[Our research follows definite rules and then,] when we
have searched and believe we have found the decisive proof,
when we have even succeeded in getting it accepted, we are
resigned in advance to seeing it invalidated in a trial of revision over which we often preside ourselves.

. . . one has to ask himself if the State is not wasting its
money in its educational establishments, for the public mind
is scarcely scientific at all.[7]

Duclaux's words were characteristic of the typical Dreyfusard
perspective and wholly alien to the mentality of most anti-Dreyfusards. For the latter, proofs were instruments for contention,
not guides to thought, and judgments were final, not provisional
and subject to re-examination. Few statements in the Affair reveal so well the difference in thinking between the two sides.

Writing a few years later about this first week in January,
Reinach said that the turn toward the Dreyfusard cause was
above all a revolt of reason against the reactionaries for being too
quick, too arrogant, too insolent in their seizure of victory, in
their treating the public as if it were quite stupid.[8] These anti-
Dreyfusard characteristics made all the more forcible an impact
in connection with the farcical Esterhazy court-martial on January 10 and 11, 1898, and in the crowing by the right over this
"victory." Some, notably Drumont, had the audacity to sing even
louder than before in praise of that most excellent officer, the
Comte Marie-Charles-Ferdinand Walsin-Esterhazy.

Thus the acquittal of Esterhazy did not discourage the Dreyfusards but drove them to renewed effort, especially since the
last necessary fragments of evidence had been disclosed at the
trial. Emile Zola's words a few days before expressed their collective mood: "Truth is on the march, and nothing will stop it."[9]
After Esterhazy's acquittal Zola worked as if possessed to produce a stirring credo for the faithful. Once finished, he took it to
the offices of L'Aurore, where he read it aloud to the editors and
others gathered there. They burst into applause and printed it on
January 13 under the headline "J'Accuse!"

Zola's role has been so much exaggerated by so many that

one is tempted to write about the Affair without mentioning him at all. But "J'Accuse!" was a splendid polemic and a most effective catalyst. Others carried the burden of the fight afterward, even at Zola's own trials, but with this one declaration he provided the main provocation for excitement of emotion all over France, and even around the world. For one side, Zola was the "conscience of humanity," and for the other . . .

Cartoons represented him as a pig. Some of the crowd gathered outside during his first trial burned Dreyfusard newspapers and sang,

> *Zola is a fat swine,*
> *The older he gets, the more beastly he gets.*
> *Zola is a fat swine,*
> *When they catch him, we will toast him.* [10]

In one caricature, vividly rendered in a large color poster format, Zola appears as "King of the Pigs." He is painting a map of France with a brush dipped in a chamber pot marked "International shit [*caca*]." The elements of pig, brush, map, and chamber pot were repeated in other cartoons, and in some circles chamber pots were spoken of as *zolas!* Emile Zola was in good company, as many other Dreyfusard champions of Justice and Truth were savagely caricatured in pictures, verse, and story. [11]

"J'Accuse!" received much international attention, and expressions of sympathy and support for the Dreyfusards arrived from many countries. The Affair was regularly and widely reported in the press abroad. Except for anti-Semites, the more evident foreigners commenting almost always supported the Dreyfusards, since they lacked the nationalist concerns of the French anti-Dreyfusards and often had liberal perspectives. They simply could not understand the resistance in France to justice for Dreyfus. [12]

For many weeks before "J'Accuse!" appeared, manifestos and petitions seeking a new trial for Dreyfus had been circulating among French men of letters and science. During the fast-paced developments of January, the number of signatures rose by hundreds, as many of the best in the quite remarkable assembly of intellect then to be found in France committed themselves. The first of these declarations of commitment appeared in *L'Aurore* the day after "J'Accuse!" under the headline "Manifesto

of the Intellectuals." This was the occasion that made a shibbo-
leth of the word "intellectual." More manifestos and many more
signatures were to follow.

It can be difficult for anyone without a comparable experience to recognize fully what is involved in such a public commitment. In the face of a popular hostility frightening in its intensity
and near universality, a published signature made an unequiv-
ocal and open declaration of defiance. Even attendance at a meeting (or sometimes refusal to attend one) could be a gesture of
defiance and commitment. Such a move was all-important to the
one making it, whatever others thought. Once the initial leap
into commitment had been made, then one's ambivalence was
put aside and full, continuous involvement was comparatively
easy. Léon Blum wrote of the intellectuals' experience:

> The generations which have followed us can no longer realize
> that for two interminable years, between the beginning of the
> revision campaign and the pardon, life felt as if it were sus-
> pended, that everything converged toward a single issue, that
> in intimate feelings and interpersonal relations, everything
> was interrupted, upset, rearranged. One was Dreyfusard or
> one was not. . . . An explorer of Antarctic regions, after win-
> tering on the ice pack, asked this question first of the relief
> expedition: "Is Dreyfus free?" [13]

One large segment of the Dreyfusard forces was not composed primarily of intellectuals: the socialists and anarchists.
Their numbers gave the movement a mass of active supporters it
would not otherwise have gained. This was important for allowing the Dreyfusards a sense of collective strength as well as for
giving them added force in parliamentary politics. Anarchists
and socialists—especially the former—were the ones who did
most of the fighting with anti-Dreyfusards in the streets and
meeting halls, as they proved no less militant in their fashion
than were the cultivated men of words who fought with pen and
tongue.

Socialists and anarchists did not adhere to the cause readily,
however. Few were intellectuals like Herr and Blum, or Jaurès,
whose socialism resulted from study and reflection and who
were easily moved by the same process to Dreyfusard activism.
Most were veterans of what they regarded as a class war in which
the bourgeoisie was seen as the enemy of the masses. They had
no working accommodation with the bourgeois republicans who

were sounding the clarion to rally support for Dreyfus. Socialists and anarchists had preconceptions about society and politics that initially barred their participation. Yet their perspectives proved close enough to the views of the bourgeois intellectuals for an urgent need for collaboration to be discovered. In this way intellectuals found themselves closer to plebeian socialists and anarchists than they were to anti-Dreyfusards who had once cultivated the fields of arts and letters with them.

In 1898 French socialists constituted a small but substantial political force; though a minority, they were numerous enough to be weighty in the much fragmented political system, and they were a growing movement. Among the indications of this were election successes: In municipal elections they doubled their vote from 1893 to 1896, when socialists received about 1,400,000 votes, and from 1893 to 1898 their representation in the Chamber of Deputies rose from thirty-seven to forty-two (out of 581), even though several socialist leaders were not re-elected in the latter year.[14]

The socialists were divided into many factions by ideological and other differences but were on the way to achieving some unity, which would be marked by formation of a single party in 1905. Most of the leaders were also in the course of a retreat from revolutionary militancy, as prolonged experience and the apparent opportunity of electoral politics induced moderation. Winning elections and thereby causing the government to direct gradual social change seemed more promising than cataclysmic revolution. In 1896 all the important socialist leaders had joined in support of a programmatic statement of this legal reformism, the "Saint-Mandé Program."[15]

While the Republic's democracy could thus moderate socialist militancy, anarchists believed that this supposed democracy was a fraud that perpetuated repression without allowing real self-government. They were the pure rebels, whose unwavering militancy attracted those who had too much anger and too little hope to think the prevailing state and social systems could ever become what humanity most needed. To conservatives and moderates, anarchists were the most frightening element in the land, because they would never compromise or surrender, because of the threat of their violence, because their purity in rebellion might be too attractive to the discontented masses.

At first anarchists refused to give attention to the Dreyfus

case, regarding it as solely the affair of despised enemies of the
people, the bourgeoisie and the Army. Socialists shared the anarchists' antibourgeois and antimilitarist attitudes. Dreyfus was
not a victim but a rich bourgeois officer. In addition, the nationalism of some socialists made them angry about the "traitor"
Dreyfus and slow to be aroused by the injustice supposedly done
to him. Anti-Semitism among some socialists had the same effect. Thus, while anarchists ignored the Affair, initially many
socialists were stirred to fight the Dreyfusards, not the anti-
Dreyfusards. Some Dreyfusard leaders, notably Scheurer-
Kestner, Reinach, Trarieux, and Guyot, had been especially
antagonistic to anarchists and socialists, and both groups remembered that bitterly. In addition, a few moderate socialists in
the Chamber of Deputies were, like many of their nonsocialist
colleagues on the left, hesitant about risking defeat in the elections coming in May 1898.

Both socialists and anarchists began their shift toward the
Dreyfusard cause in the first weeks of January 1898, although in
both groups disagreement over participation continued for a year
and more. Anarchists moved first; on January 8 one of the most
influential, Sebastien Faure, announced in his organ, *Le Libertaire*, that there would be a big protest rally on behalf of the
Dreyfusard cause. It was held a week later with Faure and other
anarchists addressing the crowd. Although initially criticized by
some prominent anarchists, Faure devoted himself thereafter to
the cause, organizing and addressing a great many public meetings (about two a week) all over France and rallying support
through *Le Libertaire*. He made himself the heart of an anarchist
Dreyfusard campaign that reached a substantial popular audience, much of which probably would not otherwise have been
touched.

At first Faure and his anarchist allies did not know or much
care whether Dreyfus was innocent, and they scorned the legal-
ism important to other Dreyfusards. For these anarchists the Affair was an occasion for revolutionary agitation, both by
advocacy of general revolutionary theses and by arousing the
people against the forces that always repressed them and now
were arrayed against the Dreyfusards. Later these reasons for
engagement would be complemented by sympathy for Dreyfus
as the victim of these forces, on the principle of compassion for

all humanity victimized by oppression, and fury for the oppressors.[16]

Socialists developed similar reasons for action, but with a less revolutionary emphasis and with an additional consideration, defense of the Republic. They were drawn toward the Dreyfusards when they saw that the other side was clearly a combination of enemies still worse than bourgeois republicans —the Army, the Church, the monarchists, the antiparliamentary nationalists, the vicious anti-Semites. While liberals had taken repressive measures against the left and had served exploitative capitalism, at least they had some tolerance for the left and accepted some progressive change. The reactionaries arrayed against Dreyfus were completely hostile to the left and its goals.

Jaurès tried to lead the way to acceptance of this position and Dreyfusard commitment. He also believed, as would many other socialists, that the Dreyfusard drive for justice and reason was as much the socialists' cause as anybody's. Socialists deferred to Jaurès's leadership in the Chamber of Deputies and when he exercised his oratorical talent upon them elsewhere, but he was an independent, without a party following.

On January 19, 1898, the socialist Deputies issued a manifesto signed by all of them and urging workers not to involve themselves with either side. However, it also called for an unending struggle against the reactionaries who subverted justice. The next day the leader of the Marxist faction, Jules Guesde, said in *La Petite république* that proletarians should not join "any of the clans in this bourgeois civil war" but at the same time should utter "a triple war cry: war on capital whether Jewish or Christian, war on clericalism, war on military oligarchy."

Thus socialists as a group took the position of remaining neutral while fighting hard against one side—a paradoxical position perhaps, but a tenable one. Jaurès wanted fuller commitment, and as time passed more and more socialists joined him. At least two of the smaller factions fully committed themselves at once. Guesde and the leader of the other major socialist faction, Edouard Vaillant, privately agreed with Jaurès on many points, including Dreyfus's innocence, but long kept their factions "neutral" through refusal of collaboration with bourgeois Dreyfusards.

In 1898 and 1899 it seemed increasingly as if reactionaries

might well advance to exclusive power by means of their agitation in the Affair. Aroused by this, nearly all socialists and anarchists become fully committed Dreyfusards, the anarchists by
January 1899, the socialists by June. The mass demonstration of
100,000 for the Republic, at Longchamps on June 11, 1899, was
the moment symbolizing the unity of all forces from the left of
center, including anarchists, socialists, and bourgeois republicans, against the menace of the reactionary right.

The rush of events in January 1898 had set the pattern, however. Attacks and counterattacks followed each other in such profusion that brief citations of them for this one month occupy
fifteen closely printed large pages in the principal chronology of
the Affair.[17] Once moved by what was happening, anarchists
and socialists were in the thick of the conflict. On January 17,
1898, there was an anti-Dreyfusard rally in the Tivoli Vaux-Hall,
called by Drumont, Rochefort, and the Ligue Antisémitique
chief, Jules Guérin. Anarchists and socialists urged their comrades to pack the house. The crowd that evening overflowed
much beyond the 6,000-person capacity of the hall. No meeting
could be held, as the opposite sides fought each other in a chaotic
riot inside and out, lasting much of the night. It established a
pattern for many of the rallies organized by both sides in the
days and months that followed.

Rioting in the Chamber of Deputies on January 22 focused
nationwide and even worldwide attention upon the resumption
of Jaurès's speech on the twenty-fourth. He was at the peak of
his form, his oratory attacking the Méline government on the one
hand and the Army on the other. Méline was not only Premier
but also the chief symbol of the many who, while not raging
against the Dreyfusards, resisted them in stony indifference to
their claims of justice and reason. For the Mélines, keeping the
political process under orderly control and avoiding public reaction at the polls mattered most. In the view of Jaurés, the government had long swindled the people through turning away from
the proper work and spirit of the Republic, which was the assurance of justice to all, whatever their race, religion, status, or
wealth.

The indictment drawn by Jaurès concentrated upon the fact
that the Army chiefs had been placed beyond the law, their judgments immune to review by civil courts and ministries. The
Army constituted an authority that remained untouched by rea-

son in the form of law and judicial process or popular will in the form of elected government. To Jaurès and all the Dreyfusards this was representative of the entire threat of rightist politics: the imposition of rule by exclusive authority that scorned both reason and the will of citizens.

Conversely the initial reaction of the anti-Dreyfusards concentrated upon precisely this Dreyfusard challenge to the independent authority of the Army. The anti-Dreyfusards might not really scorn reason and law, but for most of them reason and law were only convenient tools, transcended and superseded by that which was essential to the vital spirit of man and the nation. The Army was thus essential. Likewise, many anti-Dreyfusards might not scorn popular will, but they still thought *some* authority had to remain beyond it, and that authority was above all the Army.

Anatole France perfectly captured the temper of the anti-Dreyfusard reaction in one of the novels in which he satirized aspects of the Affair:

> "I say again," said the Duc de Brécé, "the agitation about this affair is, and can only be some abominable scheme by the enemies of France."
>
> "And of religion," gently added the Abbé Guitrel, "and religion. One can not be a good Frenchman without being a good Christian [i.e., Catholic]. And we see that the scandal has been fomented mainly by the freethinkers and the Freemasons, by the Protestants."
>
> "And by the Jews," continued M. de Brécé, "by the Jews and the Germans. What unheard-of audacity to question the decision of a court-martial! For in fact, it is inconceivable that seven French officers could be deceived."
>
> "No, assuredly, that is inconceivable," said the Abbé Guitrel.
>
> "Generally speaking," put in M. Lerond, "a judicial error is most unlikely. I will even say it is impossible, so much protection does the law offer the accused. I am speaking of civil law, and of military law as well. Before courts-martial the accused, if he finds less protection in the somewhat summary procedural forms, does obtain it through the character of his judges. To my mind it is a flagrant insult to the Army that doubt is expressed about the legality of a verdict rendered by a court-martial."
>
> "You are quite correct," replied M. de Brécé. "Besides,

can it be admitted that seven French officers could be deceived? . . . The syndicate of treason! It's outrageous!"

Later, the Duc de Brécé says to Lerond:

"For in fact, the Army is all that is left us. Of all that formerly made up the strength and grandeur of France, absolutely nothing survives except the Army. The parliamentary Republic has shaken the government, compromised the magistracy, and corrupted public morals. The Army alone remains upright upon the ruins. That is why I say that it is sacrilege to meddle with it." [18]

9

The Rage Against Things
Modern

We want an army, and have to have one, because we want to
continue to be a nation, a nation and not an insurance association, a juxtaposition, a syndicate, an aggregate of interests.
We want an army, because we are and we want to continue to
be a living organism . . . a true organism, whose parts are all
hurt by the mutilation or withering of just one of their number. . . . we want an army because, in a democracy, we believe that a national army alone is capable of forming,
maintaining, and drawing closer the bond of unity. In a democracy, it is the national army which binds, so to speak, the
extremities of the common territory to their center, communicating and propagating the pulsation of life [Ferdinand Bru-
netière].

In fact the revolutionaries, who want permanent armies destroyed, have made use of the Dreyfus Affair as a potent
means to achieve their goals. They immediately perceived,
indeed, that by discrediting the army's principal chiefs, by

violently attacking their honor or their intelligence, by thus
throwing suspicion and scorn on the High Command, a fatal
blow is struck upon the military institution itself. For an army
is an organized body whose head and members cannot be
separated, and its principle is destroyed by setting the chiefs
and the troops against each other [Albert de Mun].

*Intellectual: individual who persuades himself that society must
depend upon logic and who fails to recognize that it rests instead
on necessities which are prior and perhaps alien to individual
reason. . . .*

    As for us, it would suit us better to be intelligent rather
than intellectual, and we would want in all circumstances to
keep a clear notion of the role that each one must fill in the
social order, according to his predestination and his function
[Maurice Barrès].

A Dreyfusard is a parricide who contemplates the assassination of the mother country [*la mère patrie*] [Henri Rochefort].[1]

The preceding quotations are presented as a display of anti-
Dreyfusard variety: Brunetière, the cool rationalist and an "intellectual" in all but name and party; de Mun, the "Jaurès of the
Right"; Barrès, the antirationalist and mystical Don Quixote; and
Rochefort, the comedian with a gift for destructive play-acting.
    Ferdinand Brunetière was probably the most respected man
of letters in France—literary critic and historian, editor of the
very influential *Revue des Deux mondes,* teacher of the elite at the
Ecole Normale Supérieure (appointed there despite his lack of
the academic credentials necessary for anyone else.), and one of
the Immortals of the Académie Française. Comte Albert de Mun
was the most celebrated paladin of French Catholicism: the chief
spokesman of traditionalist conservatism, formerly devoted to
the Legitimist royal dynasty, but obeying the Pope's command
to rally to the Republic, and dedicated to relieving the misery of
the masses through Christian charity and paternalism. De Mun's
discourse upon reception into the Académie Française on March
10, 1898, struck a blow for the anti-Dreyfusard forces. Maurice
Barrès was the French man of letters most influential upon his
generation and the next one, author in several genres, sometime
elected politician, journalist, soul-stirring advocate of cults of
both the self and the nation, sorcerer who could enchant men of
ideas from positions across the political spectrum. He entered
the Académie Française in 1906. Henri Rochefort was . . . well,

himself. Any brief description would misrepresent the man, as he so often gleefully misrepresented both himself and others.

In a strict sense these quoted statements are themselves more broadly representative of anti-Dreyfusards than are those who wrote them, for each of these men was too outstanding and idiosyncratic to be a model. Nevertheless, each man can also be taken as a prominent though distinctive example of a type important among the anti-Dreyfusard legions. Brunetière was the cultivated man of letters, well established in elevated social and cultural circles, and customarily balanced, judicious, and learned in his discourse. De Mun was the conservative politician, bound to respond to the Affair in terms of its bearing on issues regularly contested in partisan politics, especially in the parliament. Barrès was the imaginative writer, capturing readers with the magic of his vision and the ardor of his rebellion against the many stultifying aspects of modern life. Rochefort was the journalist who depended on his wit and evocative power, and enjoyed employing them. He was also the political activist who was "radical" because wild attack was virtually the only action conceivable to him; he fought at different times on both the left and the right but could not have helped to build a new order if he had ever succeeded in tearing down the old one.

When one counts Rochefort as example of two types, journalist and "radical" political activist, then these four very dissimilar men can examplify the bulk of those who played prominent parts in the anti-Dreyfusard fight. There were variations on these types, such as politicians less conservative than de Mun, or journalists less wild than Rochefort, but driven like them by nationalist ardor. There were also Army officers like General Mercier, whom the Affair had implicated in alleged crime or stupidity and who fought in self-defense as well as through conviction. Many more who were not of these types also fought, such as retired officers, parish priests, and anti-Semitic workmen from the Paris slaughterhouses; they were the rank and file, who did not set the style of combat or determine the positions taken.

Barrès defined a position upon which they all could stand, in unbending opposition to those intellectuals, those *sans-patrie* Dreyfusards:

> The release of the traitor Dreyfus would after all be a minor matter, but if Dreyfus is more than a traitor, if he is a symbol, it is another affair: it is the Dreyfus affair! Halt! The triumph

of the camp which holds up Dreyfus as symbol would firmly
install in power the men who are after the *transformation of
France according to their own logic* [*esprit*]. And me, I want to
save France.[2]

Now, after so much time has passed, one may approve
Barrès's intention to save France, but not believe with him that
it was threatened by the Dreyfusards. Likewise, one is not likely
to accept Brunetière's assertion that only the Army could unite
the nation, or de Mun's repetition of the common claim that
criticism of some officers would mortally wound the entire Army.
Nevertheless, a great many contemporaries of these men found
such statements quite plausible. It is important to see how.

If we look again at contemporary journalism we see an obvious pattern that fits other writing also, but not so obviously.
Facts were collected haphazardly and were not critically examined for reliability and accuracy. Articles used them in whatever
ways they could conveniently fit a picture, which itself was
formed from unexamined premises without careful reflection.
Often, published pieces were essentially elaborations, without
substantial addition or refinement, of opinions first advanced in
the thoughtless ways people often talk in casual conversation.
With many journalists there was little deliberate effort to con-
struct articles primarily on the basis of facts and the conclusions
following logically from them—although they might have
achieved something like this despite themselves.

Drumont's *La France juive* provides a good if extreme example, for it is essentially an extension of the approach regularly
used by contemporary writers in both journalism and more "serious," reflective compositions. Basically historical in form, this
book is a compilation of stories that Drumont very studiously
gathered to support his anti-Semitic, antiplutocratic position.
Working in an unconscious parody of scholarship, he adapted
whatever suited his preconceptions and ignored whatever did
not. He generalized without reason to do so, imputing to the
many the sins supposedly committed by a few. For the most
part, Drumont's discourse was reasonable in apparent form, and
not mere ranting. His "logic" was usually fallacious, but recog-
nizing this required critical faculties his readers usually had not
cared to develop fully.

Moreover, readers were receptive to Drumont's unexamined premises. Since they could start from much the same point as he, they were more comfortable in following him uncritically than an unsympathetic audience could ever be. For a more extreme example of the same process, one need only recall the widespread uncritical acceptance of the preposterous history of Diana Vaughan.

Drumont's "history" should be compared to that of the greatly admired Hippolyte Taine (d. 1893), whose work anti-Dreyfusards often referred to for wisdom and inspiration. His *Origines de la France contemporaine* (1875–93) was in large part a reactionary polemic against the French Revolution of 1789 and the republican political tradition stemming from it. Powerfully written and supposed to be firmly grounded on fact, the work was enormously influential through providing an intelligent foundation for political convictions opposed to the Republic and popular democracy. Yet Taine's method was little more than a sophisticated refinement of Drumont's. To be sure, the former used genuine historical documents, but he selected only those which suited his prejudices and polemical intent, and he elaborated his theses with little regard for achieving fundamental validity beneath the rhetorical form of his arguments.

Taine's history was repeatedly assaulted by Alphonse Aulard, a committed republican and from 1891 professor of the history of the French Revolution at the Sorbonne. Aulard emphasized the distortions introduced by Taine's prejudice and his carelessness about facts. In one attack Aulard wrote of his finding documents in the archives that had been thrown into complete disorder; the archivist told Aulard that Taine had done that because he was furious whenever he could not find in a box of documents anything against the Revolution. Aulard's polemic went on to say of Taine:

> He was impassioned and prejudiced to the point that it became *materially impossible* for him to see anything which offended his passion or opposed his prejudice. He had so much ardor and in reasoning his brain raged so powerfully that he confused everything, mixed up his notes, jumbled his numbers, no longer knew from where he had taken a text. It even happened that, believing he transcribed a real text, he wrote out what his romantic and unbridled imagination dictated to

him. It is Taine who has deformed, with an air of erudition,
the history of the origins of this democracy. . . .

Taine is not an historian: he is a pamphleteer, a pamphleteer of the right.[3]

In the most common retrospective view Hippolyte Taine was
a very great conservative historian and man of letters, while
Edouard Drumont was a loathsome and destructive bigot, or
worse. Taine may have been the more talented of the two, but it
is difficult to see how their intellectual perspectives differed very
much. Drumont attacked Jews more and the unwashed masses
less than did Taine, but they formed their views of the world in
much the same manner. So too did other anti-Dreyfusards, and
in that lies their principal difference from the Dreyfusards, as
may be evident from the considerations implicit in the quoted
criticism by Aulard.

Like every historian, Aulard's own history was shaped by
preconceptions, especially political ones. He was more preju-
diced and less objective than he would have liked to admit. Both
he and many other like-minded historians had very definite,
conscious political purposes in their teaching and writing of history. Yet their methods were really different from Taine's, which
anti-Dreyfusards immediately recognized, so that many were
bitter in attack upon the Aulards of the world.

Despite their prejudices and purposes, Aulard and company
tried to be scientific, to form their conclusions only after careful,
discriminating assessment of all available evidence, with the
most fastidious efforts to determine the reliability of each item of
evidence and to weigh conflicting items against each other. Ac-
counts of their findings might be embellished for literary effect,
but not if this corrupted the primary purpose of telling the truth
about man's past. Indeed, their histories were often too matter-
of-fact to have much literary appeal.

Their idea was that their political purpose would best be
served by telling that truth, and they were prepared to accept
correction of errors they might have committed, should evidence
prove them wrong. This openness to revision was essential to
the modern scientific spirit. It had been the principal point made
by the natural scientist Emile Duclaux in his letter of January 9,
1898, quoted in the preceding chapter, in which he damned the

official investigation of the espionage for which Alfred Dreyfus had been condemned.

The consequence of these disparate points of view for the Dreyfus Affair should be immediately obvious. Dreyfus's prosecutors had leaped to premature conclusions on the basis of insufficient evidence. Anti-Semitic prejudice need not have been involved. They did not know how to weigh the meager evidence adequately, and their initial snap judgments became decisive prejudice in evaluation of additional evidence. No effort was made to assess all the evidence available; in fact, this was not done before the final revision, beginning in 1903. The exculpatory was ignored, while anything that might conceivably incriminate was accepted without critical evaluation of reliability or relevance.

Once the original court-martial had made its judgment, it was final, never to be revised whatever contradictory evidence or arguments were developed. Both the soldiers concerned and the civilian anti-Dreyfusards *needed absolutes*. They could not tolerate tentative opinions and did not understand that judgments could be probable, not certain.

Similarly, anti-Dreyfusards could not regard criticisms of specific actions by particular Army officers as anything but absolute repudiation of the entire Army, despite the sincere protests to the contrary by many Dreyfusards. In this the anti-Dreyfusard delusion was aggravated by the antimilitarism of some of their opponents, while the longtime steady support of the Army by other Dreyfusards was ignored or thought to be deceitful.

Of course the elaborate marshaling of evidence and argument by Dreyfusards could not alter the stubborn views of the anti-Dreyfusards. They rejected whatever did not fit their previous convictions, or distorted it to fit, just as Taine did with his documents on the French Revolution. And they uncritically accepted whatever would fit, like the legend of the Kaiser's incriminating notes or the sophistic justifications of Henry's chief forgery.

Moreover, anti-Dreyfusards made the contest one of personalities and supposed underlying motives. Many of the Dreyfusards were people they detested in any event. For this reason, and because the anti-Dreyfusards believed their opponents sought to use the Affair for nefarious purposes besides the traitor's release, they could not think Dreyfusard contentions might possibly have merit. Thus anti-Dreyfusards made little attempt to meet the opposition on its own ground by showing its claimed proofs to be logically and empirically defective. Anti-Dreyfusards had no use for the sensible advice of one Dreyfusard, Julien Benda, when he pointed out that it did not matter if Zola, Jaurès, and the rest *were* paid huge sums by the Syndicate, for their arguments had the same validity and consequences regardless of their morals and motives.[4]

The words most often used by the anti-Dreyfusards may well have been "fatherland," "treason," and "Syndicate"; the word most used by their opponents probably was "proof." Dreyfusards also made personal attacks upon their enemies, complained about how the other side was a menace to France, and railed against a conspiracy—that of the Army and the Jesuits. Nevertheless, the bulk of Dreyfusard polemic was their effort to prove by evidence and reason that they were right and their opponents wrong. Thus it was that, when he made his most important effort to win wide support for the Dreyfusard crusade, Jean Jaurès addressed proletarian readers with an assembly of powerful arguments titled *The Proofs*. This appeared as a series beginning August 10, 1898, in the mass circulation socialist newspaper *La Petite république* and soon was also published in book form.

Writing in response to an article by Brunetière, the Dreyfusard scientist Emile Duclaux said in May 1898:

> A prime minister, who controls the applause [in the Chamber of Deputies], can be content to say from his lofty height, "The intellectuals are the ones who have done all the evil"; he is not obliged to prove it. When one writes in the *Revue des Deux mondes,* and one is named Brunetière, one cannot dispense with a theory and a demonstration. . . . there are so many people who say: "We have the proofs!" without really wanting to say what these are. An apple is an apple, by definition; but a proof becomes a proof only after discussion, and only for those whom it has convinced.[5]

One might suppose, cynically, that Dreyfusards harped upon proofs only because they recognized them as their best weapons in the political battle. Yet the key factor here is that intellectual Dreyfusards *did* believe that their proofs were potent weapons, no matter how much the opposition disregarded them. Socialist and anarchist Dreyfusards who were not intellectuals made little use of proofs. The intellectuals were baffled and enraged that their opponents remained quite unshaken by proofs.

On the struggle's two sides intelligence simply functioned in quite different ways. There was a dichotomy in how reality was conceived. To achieve the fruits of intelligence, anti-Dreyfusard men of letters depended on heightened aesthetic sensibility, intuition, and the inspired insight that was not discovered through deliberate, conscious logical process. Reason could be useful for refining insight, for filling in gaps in a picture, for presenting a view to others and persuading them. These men of letters might feel aesthetic delight in the logic of an argument or in rationalized literary style, but only as long as the view expressed was not contrary to their own pre-existing ideas and tastes. For most of them, the forms of a vision were constituted and approved within oneself, and reason could not be a neutral means of discovering and verifying it, nor could external factors supersede intuition and inspiration.

Each of the quotations that began this chapter revealed openly or implicitly an organismic vision of society. Anyone may find society-as-organism to be effective as a loose descriptive metaphor, which captures meaningfully some of what we sense or know about social relations. But most anti-Dreyfusard men of letters thought society *really* to be an integral living organism. This view was an essential element in their new nationalism and in their profound resentment against the Third Republic.

However appealing intuitively, this organismic conception is devastated by analytical examination, for analogues between a society and an individual organism prove to be much less significant than differences. But for anti-Dreyfusards critical analysis mattered here no more than it did in judging Dreyfus. They wanted to believe that their society, nation, and culture formed a natural, integral entity with a vital spirit that transcended the individual. They felt that modern urban civilization was dissolving bonds that made their people a whole, leaving isolated individuals adrift in an artificial setting. One can speak analytically of social atomization and alienation without resort to organic metaphor, but these men felt most comfortable with their organismic vision and elevated it to absolute doctrine.

This conception of society as organism had gained currency

long before the Dreyfus Affair. Conservatives reacting against the French Revolution had regarded that whole process as the disastrous result of *mechanistic* thinking: that human society and institutions are the artificial constructs of human intelligence, to be reconstructed whenever and however reason determines. To conservatives this was a vast delusion and an abuse of reason, for mechanistic thinking departed too far from reality, with intellect mistaking its own fictions for rational knowledge. Thus the liberal and republican political ideas associated with the tradition of the French Revolution were false because they were mere abstractions, which had little to do with what man really is, individually and collectively.

In these conservative terms the condemned ideas were *abstract*, as opposed to the approved ones, which were *natural*. Natural ideas were the genuinely rational and realistic ones, not the constructs of mechanistic rationalism. This "natural" view of the world effectively excluded comprehension of the rationalist approach it repudiated; it could not see that the organismic metaphor, the associated idea of the Nation, and all the rest were still further abstracted from nature than the often empirically based ideas of the rejected rationalism.

Conservatives did respect pure natural science, although few understood what was most essential to its method. However, they distinguished emphatically between the application of scientific reasoning to nonhuman subjects and the use of anything like it in human affairs, as in philosophy, social science, or scholarship in areas like literature and Biblical criticism. They did not object to erudition itself. Like Brunetière, many of those criticizing modern rationalism were themselves quite erudite. Instead, they opposed the substition of rational system for insight and the use of system to erect artificial constructs that were false and harmful. Their common caricature of the type of savant they despised was a man who reduced everything read or observed to countless record cards, then mechanically built from his cards an abstraction he claimed to be truth.

When a Dreyfusard demanded a hearing for his proofs, it looked to anti-Dreyfusards like a Sorbonne professor lecturing from his record cards, an empty pretense not worthy of an audience. They had made "intellectual" a much-used term of opprobrium precisely because intellectuals were supposed to be the ones proliferating all that was worst about modern thought and, indeed, about the modern world in general. Intellectuals were not just symptoms of the disease corrupting the social organism, they were its principal agency.

Instead of emphasizing the artifacts of modern intellect as the objects of complaint, these conservatives concentrated on the forms of thought supposed responsible for what civilization was becoming. Ineffectual parliamentary government, French humiliation in international power struggles, rapacious capitalism, dark and dingy mines and factories, teeming urban masses wallowing in misery, the disruption of idyllic rural communities, persecution of Christians and their Church—all this and so much more had to be the consequences of abstract rationalism.

Anti-Dreyfusards did not act with desperate force only because Dreyfusards threatened the Army's integrity, or because the campaign for Dreyfus could be used to secure greater power for the left, however important these elements of the conflict seemed. The intellectuals had initiated and led the campaign and had made the most they could of their deadly rationalism. That turned the struggle over Alfred Dreyfus into a full confrontation between two hostile forces that could neither comprehend nor tolerate each other.

In the course of an attack upon the intellectuals, Maurice Barrès lamented that the French nation lacked "moral unity," since it had surrendered the dynasty and traditional institutions that held it together before 1789. He continued by pointing out that

> . . . it is indeed natural that pernicious metaphysicians assume influence over our imaginations, provided that they are eloquent, persuasive, "liberal" [généreux]. In proposing us an ideal, they undertake to restore moral unity to us. But far from delivering us from our uncertainties, they only cause them to multiply by their contradictory affirmations.
>
> That is what must be remedied. Only a faint heart and a spirit positively corrupted by anarchy can be happy in this dissociated and decerebrated France.
>
> But what means is there to redeem this consciousness which the country lacks?
>
> Let us repudiate the philosophical systems and the parties that generate them. Let us attach our efforts again, not to one of our mind's visions, but to a reality. . . .
>
> In order to accept this reasonable, realistic vision of the Fatherland, it is necessary to develop ways to feel what exists natu-

rally in the country. We cannot form the union from ideas, in so far as they rely upon reasoning; they must be doubled in their sentimental power. At the root of everything, there is a state of sensibility. One strives vainly to establish the truth through reason alone, since intelligence can always find a new motive to call things into question once more.[6]

Words like these resonated powerfully among the contemporaries of Barrès, even when they did not fully share his mystical vision. This was how he and others like him could be so influential in an age when Science, enlightened Reason, and the dream of Progress supposedly prevailed. Not only cultivated men of letters accustomed to playing with words and ideas but also others who were ill at ease in this modern age often found such pronouncements appealing, by articulating what they felt better than did critical reason.

There were legions of schoolmasters preaching the secular rational faith of science, republicanism, and progress, and they had their converts. Other advocates preached the variant rationality of Marxism, and they too had their converts. Together these and like apostles did prevail increasingly as the nineteenth century gave way to the twentieth, but the great mass movement of late-nineteenth-century France comprised the throngs going in pilgrimage to shrines of religious mysticism and simple piety; they were moved by what they *felt* about their faith and their world.

In looking back at that age, we have too readily accepted the assumption that resistance to modern rationalism was mainly a matter of popular ignorance, and perhaps some few diehards among the educated. Thus a Barrès appears to us an aberrant figure, one who indulged himself in mad nonsense and sustained it by literary virtuosity. Such a man is repellant and dangerous if his maunderings can be connected to political evil, and a picturesque oddity if they seem confined to art.

This view is an illusion produced by shifts in literary tastes, political perceptions, and theoretical concerns. Of all the men of letters and ideas who flourished in France at the end of the nineteenth century, readers today take only a selected few who suit their current interests and preferences. When one looks at authors then who achieved critical or public favor—for example, literary prize-winners—very few of the names are familiar now to anyone except, perhaps, an occasional scholar. Thus we magnify the authors we can still admire into the typical figures of their age and, when we do notice someone like Barrès, we think him aberrant.

Earlier in this book it was said that, among persons with real intellectual and artistic achievement, anti-Dreyfusards outnumbered Dreyfusards. Strictly speaking, that statement was not factual, for there is no way of identifying and counting all the heads in the two camps. And if we counted only those figures who remain known today, Dreyfusards would probably comprise the larger number. Nevertheless, there is much reason to think that anti-Dreyfusards were more typical of the era. This becomes apparent when we examine the extensive information that can be assembled about who adhered to each side at all cultural and social levels. Before examining further the ideological bases of division, we can do well to explore some of this information and what it suggests.

The division followed social class lines very little. One expects the aristocracy and much of the upper bourgeoisie to have been conservative and consequently anti-Dreyfusard. This seems usually to have been the case, but there were many exceptions —for example, in Geneviève Straus's salon—so that we should look for an explanation besides the connection of the upper classes to conservatism. To the extent that we do know where people stood, the rest of the population was split.

Despite the usual obscurity of the "voiceless masses," we can tell something of how they reacted. There are the ambiguous but still significant indications suggested by the dissemination around the country of publications that reached a mass readership. These were generally anti-Dreyfusard. Chief among them were *La Croix*, its provincial satellite newspapers, and the three giant Paris dailies; these papers were distributed all over France. *La Croix* (about 170,000 circulation), its satellites (circulation figures not exactly known but large), and *Le Petit journal* (about 1,100,000) were always violently anti-Dreyfusard. *Le Petit parisien* (about 750,000) and *Le Journal* (about 500,000) were less violent but also anti-Dreyfusard; the former became comparatively impartial after Henry's exposure. Dreyfusard newspapers counted only a tiny part of all circulation, most of it accounted for by socialist papers.[7] One might also point here to Drumont's *La France juive*, which was still widely read by all classes. While the connection obviously is not a necessary one, it can be tentatively supposed that there was a correspondence between popular opinion and opinion in the popular press, especially since the latter was aggressively competing for readers.

Another way to unveil mass opinion might be to see where people gave support to political leaders active in the Dreyfus struggle. However, election results are largely deceptive without detailed knowledge, which usually is deficient, of how campaigns were waged in individual districts. This is especially a problem because in some districts local notables won without their political positions mattering much, or mattering only because they were identified with a general stance, like conservative Catholicism.

Something can be gathered, nevertheless, from the experiences of candidates (all anti-Dreyfusard) campaigning as nationalists, anti-Semites, and "revisionists" (that is, seeking constitutional revisions because the Republic was so rotten). In parliamentary elections of 1898 and 1902 and municipal council elections of 1900 and 1906, these candidates enjoyed a large upsurge of voter support, especially in Paris. From 1900 on nationalists assumed control of the Paris municipal council and its delegation to the Chamber of Deputies; Paris had long been a stronghold of the left. (Senate elections were indirect and not very responsive to the currents of popular opinion.) The bulk of these successes were gained in districts where conservatives usually were strong, but in Paris the "new right" made big gains in quarters that had been held by the left, including one area (the Eighteenth Arrondissement) with a poor, mainly proletarian population.

The apparent rough correlation of anti-Dreyfusards, old conservatism, and new nationalism is significant, although predictable. Especially interesting, however, is support won by nationalists in Paris quarters formerly held by the left. Neither the nonsocialist nor the socialist left had effective party organizations in these quarters; the best-organized party of the left, the Marxists led by Jules Guesde, functioned almost wholly outside the capital. The Eighteenth Arrondissement, the one proletarian area that elected nationalists, was a district of workers who were organized neither by parties of the left nor by trade unions.

A comparable phenomenon can be seen with supporters of the Ligue Antisémitique, which flourished only during the Affair. Unlike other organizations important in the anti-Dreyfusard campaign, this one drew a substantial portion of its members from among urban workmen. Among its main strongholds was this same Eighteenth Arrondissement. Once more, the bulk of the workers attracted to the Ligue appear not to have been organized by parties or unions; consequently they were vulnerable to the radically antiplutocratic and antigovernment demogoguery of the Ligue Antisémitique.[8]

Although there must remain much uncertainty, it does appear that, wherever in France socialists and anarchists had already won working-class support, they were successful in getting those workers to fight the anti-Dreyfusards. The Ligue des Droits de l'Homme et du Citoyen addressed a mainly bourgeois clientele, one which was especially receptive to Dreyfusard appeals. Many of the rest of those who had sometimes supported the left were open to appeals from anti-Dreyfusards, whose politics of antagonism could seem much more attractive than the leftist alternatives.

Because most of the election campaigns in which districts shifted to the right took place after Dreyfus's release, many probably made little or no reference to the Dreyfus Affair, although the rightist candidates would have all been anti-Dreyfusards. (In the 1900 Paris municipal council elections, however, the Affair was very important.) Still, the candidates' attitudes and often their basic issues remained the same. The left had promised people a better world; when for many that proffered hope had been frustrated, the left's vision must have seemed a delusion. Then relief had to be sought in very different ways. The right claimed precisely this, and they won votes and shock troops to fight in the Affair's street battles and rally confrontations. Neither this support nor the large circulation figures for anti-Dreyfusard publications are proofs of popularity, but they are suggestive.

Rallies, public meetings, demonstrations, and riots in the Affair seem to have been frequent, although knowledge of them is fragmentary. Available reports indicate that such events occurred in nearly all parts of France, that they often involved groups numbering more than a thousand, and that many were violent. In some violent incidents there were unprovoked assaults on Jews or Dreyfusards; in others, anti-Dreyfusard and Dreyfusard forces clashed. Reports of battles most often mention participation by workmen—socialists, anarchists, or those led by anti-Semites—and by students. Too little is known for a clear picture, but from this fragmentary information it does appear that engagement in the Affair extended well beyond Paris and beyond the men of words who have left most of the record of the struggle.[9]

More can be gleaned from lists to which people believing something in the Affair added their names. The most remarkable of these is the list of 25,000 contributors to the "Monument Henry," a collection organized by *La Libre parole* on behalf of Lieutenant Colonel Henry's widow and child. While collecting 131,000 francs in December 1898 and January 1899, the newspaper published all the contributors' names, along with the self-revealing remarks they often sent with their money, and notation when submitted of occupations and places of residence. All this constitutes a wealth of information, which scholars have subjected to extended analysis. The contributors were overwhelmingly urban (88 percent), from both medium and large towns and cities. Compared to their numbers in the whole French population, disproportionately large percentages were workers (39.25 percent) and professionals (8.25 percent), as well as the more predictable military personnel (28.6 percent), students (8.6 percent) and priests (3.1 percent).[10]

Also predictably, remarks of contributors most often echoed the right's published propaganda, especially that of *La Libre parole*, but did so with many individual twists which suggest that the propaganda not only shaped but also reflected popular opinion. The remarks become especially significant for regions and occupations that were not usually very conservative but from which the proportions of contributors were exceptionally high. Many of the districts in question shifted to the right in the 1898 election of Deputies, with some moving leftward in later elections.[11]

These were areas and occupations suffering from or feeling themselves threatened by economic decline and intrusion by "outsiders"—foreigners, agents of the State, and commercial interests—who disrupted or were thought to disrupt their customary ways of life. The remarks of these people repetitiously disclose profound disturbance, dread, and anger over the social upheaval they felt, their feelings cast in cries of hatred against the "Diabolical Trinity" and against that parallel trio: intellectuals, rapacious capitalists, and the Republic.

Another large and revealing list brings our attention back to

the cultivated middle and upper classes. This one, from January–
February 1899, gives the names, often with occupations and
places of residence, of the first adherants to the founding manifesto of the Ligue de la Patrie Française, the largest organization
formed to fight the Dreyfusards. In all, 17,033 individuals and
4,279 groups are listed; occupations are listed for 9,921 individuals. Nearly all were middle and upper class, about 70 percent of
them in occupations requiring a good education. Eighty-seven
belonged to the Institut de France (national academies of learning
and arts) and the Collège de France, including twenty-six of forty
members of the Académie Française. (But one of the Académie's
most celebrated members, Anatole France, was an active Dreyfusard.) The bulk (65.4 percent) of those listing their occupations
were academics from higher and secondary education (905), men
of letters (368), artists (588), journalists (699), law (1,330), medicine (1,012), and students (1,590).[12] Clearly the Dreyfusards had
no monopoly on learning.

There were Dreyfusard equivalents to the list of adherants of
the Ligue de la Patrie Française. One, the membership rolls of
the Ligue des Droits de l'Homme et du Citoyen, was destroyed
in World War II. Another, a tribute to Picquart with more than
fifteen thousand names, often accompanied by notations of oc-
cupation and places of residence, appears not yet to have been
subjected to thorough analysis. However, more limited examination of this and other, shorter lists provides a well-defined
picture of the signatories. With the previously mentioned lists
and other information, we can see clearly who fought on each
side.[13]

In belles-lettres and fine arts, the anti-Dreyfusards generally
were those who conformed to prevailing critical standards and
public tastes, including most of those established in positions of
eminence. Most men of letters and art were conventional in these
ways, and few of this sort became Dreyfusards. In scholarship
and science, the anti-Dreyfusards typically were those who did
not fully employ rigorous scientific methods, or did so without
consciousness of and commitment to the critical rationalism that
underlies that method. They included scholars who relied more
upon insight and literary skill than on empiricism, and scientists
who wandered up blind paths through not seeing how to proceed. There were still a great many such savants in France.

Most of these men were conservative both politically and in

their intellectual or artistic endeavors. Partial exceptions to this rule were reactive individuals, who often were conformist in many respects but despised much of what the modern world seemed to have become. A good example is Jean-Louis Forain, a very well-established artist who was also a prolific and wonderfully effective political cartoonist, attacking all those he supposed to be victimizing ordinary folk. Some of his cartoons would have fitted well in anarchist publications, but he was much more at home with the radicalism of populist anti-Semites.[14]

Unable to comprehend the rational approach of the intellectuals they condemned, these men of ideas and art thought they had no need themselves of such rationalism. Much the same can be said of many others who were educated to use reason in some form but had not really learned to do so in thoroughly critical and empirical ways. Here should be included many or most of those in journalism, teaching, law, medicine, and both state and business administration. If background and established positions inclined them to be conservative or reactive, then no amount of talk about proofs was likely to make them Dreyfusards.

On the other hand, the Dreyfusard pattern was the inverse of that described for their opponents. In belle-lettres and fine arts they were most often those who had advanced beyond prevailing critical standards and public tastes, and they usually were not well established in conventional ways, although "advanced" culture had its own system of recognition and establishment on a lesser scale. Most Dreyfusards whose work had achieved substantial public acceptance before the Affair were still unconventional enough to have been controversial. Zola was an example. Scholars who became Dreyfusards were ones who had deliberately committed themselves to scientific rigor in their work: That was their "advanced" departure from convention. Despite the many years in which men of ideas had been trying to adapt scientific method to social and humanistic studies, scholars committed to this were still struggling to define and establish use of such method in their disciplines. Dreyfusard involvement of other men of ideas can also be described as the inverse of the pattern for anti-Dreyfusards.

One expects education to have been important in shaping the differences distinguishing the opposed sides, especially since academics and students were very active in both camps. Of these, Dreyfusards were concentrated in university divisions of letters and sciences and in some secondary schools, especially the most prestigious Paris *lycées*, whose teachers differed little in their intellectual attainments from those at the Sorbonne. While the Ecole Normale Supérieure was predominantly Dreyfusard, the Ecole Polytechnique definitely was not: It was under control of the Army, and most of its students prepared for Army careers. Elsewhere in higher and secondary education anti-Dreyfusards prevailed. We know too little of the elementary school teachers to see how they divided; the usual image associating teachers in state schools with doctrinaire republicanism is neither sustained nor contradicted by the available evidence on partisanship in the Affair.

This differentiation of secondary and higher education institutions was not related to the social class of their clienteles, which was homogeneous. Very few youths from the lower and lower middle classes found a way into higher education or the secondary schools preparing students for it. While public higher education was free, in all secondary education there was expensive tuition, with very few scholarships. Pecuniary inability to complete secondary school was a bar to higher education. Even if this hurdle could be surmounted, lower-class and lower-middle-class youths usually lacked the enriched cultural background necessary to succeed in academic competition with their social superiors.

However, the institutions and the professions they prepared students for did have distinctive characters. Letters and science divisions in universities were becoming citadels of scientific rationalism. The Ecole Normale Supérieure and some of the best secondary schools heavily emphasized free critical discussion in classes and written exercises. Some institutions, including the Ecole Normale, had reputations as strongholds of ardent republicanism and anticlericalism.

Secondary and higher education was limited in its capacity to shape the political and intellectual outlooks of students, since parents avoided letting their children attend schools whose images did not suit their own political and intellectual prejudices. Very few practicing Catholics or sons of Army officers went to the Ecole Normale, despite its enormous prestige. Of course, parents often transmitted their prejudices to the students, thus establishing their receptivity to education's shaping of their perspectives.

Thus, family background became highly important in establishing and maintaining the intellectual differentiation important for splitting cultivated Frenchmen in the Affair. Education developed and sharpened the differences but was not well able to create them. Nor could educators devoted to scientific rationalism change the views of their countrymen quickly. With so great a reservoir of conservatism in the upper and upper middle classes, one should expect most well-educated Frenchmen to have retained the intellectual perspective reflected in the quotations with which this chapter begins.

This book's effort to understand the anti-Dreyfusards leads at last to a conclusion that might have been more obvious at the beginning, were not most of us who look at the Affair so caught up by quite modern points of view. At the end of the nineteenth century, France had not yet transformed itself into a country that was fully imbued with the qualities we understand to be "modern." To many of its citizens it *seemed* to have become modernized, for so much of the modern already appeared to be well established, from democratic government to rapid transport to domestic gas service to extensive mechanization of work. The excitement of the Affair gave way to the grandest of all celebrations of modernity, the Paris Exposition of 1900.

Yet the country remained much divided, with many of the divisions resulting from resistance to aspects of modernization. Despite great strides, industrialization remained retrograde in key respects, and its impact was only beginning to be felt by much of the population. That very modern government was so ill-established that its survival was threatened by reactionaries, who would have replaced it with something they imagined to be drawn from the past. A major part of the French population was devoted to a church which at that time still resisted with much of its considerable might suggestions that the Middle Ages were gone forever.

Most of all, "modern" entails a mentality, one which assumes innovation to be the norm, even if sometimes still reacting uneasily against it. This mentality assumes that knowledge is acquired through scientific reason, even if people are often governed by emotion instead. The mentality assumes that egalitar-

ian democracy and universal, rational law must be the basis of
politics, even if not always allowing these ideals to regulate practice. In short, the mentality is that of those persons who in 1898
were bitterly damned for being *intellectuals.*

Anti-Dreyfusard men of letters and ideas did not share this
mentality, and they fought with such determination because
they could scarcely begin to comprehend it. They spoke in this
instance for many more people than just the well-educated.
Dreyfusard intellectuals were "advanced" thinkers—too advanced for most of their countrymen. And that would not have
mattered so much had not the intellectuals seemed so dreadfully
dangerous, whether in academe, the press, or the halls of government. They were spoken of as "sellouts" to Germany but, much
worse still, they were selling out the nation to the twentieth
century.

> This century, advancing into the tempests born by rational-
> ism as on a fragile barque, must crash onto the inevitable reef
> [Albert de Mun, upon his reception into the Académie Fran-
> çaise on March 10, 1898].[15]

10

"Aux Armes, Citoyens!"

It is a strange and prolonged war where violence tries to crush
the truth. All of violence's efforts can not weaken the truth,
and serve only to give it more strength; all the light of the
truth can do nothing to stop the violence and can only aggra-
vate it still more. . . . Let no one claim from that, nevertheless, that things are equal; for there is that extreme difference
that violence has only a course limited by the command of
God, who directs its effects to the glory of the truth it attacks.
Truth instead endures eternally and triumphs finally over its
enemies, for it is eternal and mighty like God himself [Blaise
Pascal writing in 1656, quoted by Joseph Reinach in *Le Siècle*
on July 7, 1898].[1]

Looking at a survey of the Affair's decisive events, it can be
difficult to see what people found occasion to fight over for two
years. In particular, one may wonder what there was to contend
about once the government had given in and sent the Dreyfus

case to the Cour de Cassation for review. That might seem to have removed the matter from the political arena, creating an extended lull.

Actually, something *was* happening all the time. Most of the controversial events that stirred people had little consequence for the final outcome and have often been ignored in later years, but to many at the time they seemed important. For example, on May 23, 1898, *Le Petit journal* published a story signed by the editor, Ernest Judet, which falsely claimed that Emile Zola's father had embezzled funds from his company treasury when he was a Foreign Legion officer nearly six decades earlier.[2] On subsequent days Judet added charges of other dishonorable conduct by the elder Zola. There was an extended storm, with the two sides exchanging charges and Zola bringing action against Judet and the paper's owner, Hippolyte Marinoni, for criminal libel. After a three-day trial in August, Zola won a substantial judgment, on which occasion there were violent altercations in the courtroom, causing a Dreyfusard editor, Emile Michon, to challenge a leader of the radical right, Marcel Habert, to a duel.

There were newsworthy, often controversial, Affair-related trials going on most of the time. Formal charges were filed and verdicts rendered at the rate of about one a week for nearly two years, because there were so many secondary crimes and libel suits. Some of the preliminary examinations by magistrates aroused more interest and controversy than the trials themselves.

An originally minor event could become magnified into the occasion for major and extended conflict. Secondary and tertiary characters in the drama became principal villains or heroes, about whom there were widespread strong feelings.

Major Mercier Du Paty de Clam was a General Staff officer who had been important in the 1894 investigation of the *bordereau* and Dreyfus. Later he was entangled in Henry's intrigues, some of which were really quite comical. Venting fury at Du Paty helped Dreyfusards to sustain their ardor, but after 1894 his role in the case was minor. Although he was actually guilty of little besides very bad judgment, many Dreyfusards thought him the key figure in the General Staff conspiracy, a criminal equal to Esterhazy himself, and perhaps his partner in espionage. They wasted much emotion and effort against him, and the feelings endured for years, even forcing the resignation of War Minister

Alexandre Millerand in 1912 for having appointed the by then retired Du Paty to command of an Army reserve regiment.

Another remarkable instance of much ado about little was occasioned by Jules Quesnay de Beaurepaire, a courtroom mountebank who had a long personal history of disrupting judicial process with self-inflating demogogic claptrap. After a disgraceful career as the principal prosecutor in Paris, he was of course appointed chief judge of the Cour de Cassation's civil appeals chamber. While the criminal chamber of the court was considering the Dreyfus case in January 1899, Quesnay de Beaurepaire successfully sought to make himself a right-wing hero by trumpeting false charges of partiality and impropriety against the criminal court judges and by resigning in protest. His charges occasioned two months of extremely agitated nationwide controversy, with the Dreyfus case eventually transferred in consequence to hearing and decision by all three chambers of the Cour de Cassation.

Even without the sophisticated techniques for manipulating public opinion that would be developed in later years, contestants in the Dreyfus struggle had many instruments to excite public interest and influence opinion. In particular, this was a golden age of satirical cartoons: Many exceptionally fine artists in France were cartoonists, and they created a profusion of cartoons whose combination of artistic and satirical merit probably has not been equaled in any other time or country. Much of this talent was engaged in the Affair.

Forain and Caran d'Ache produced an anti-Dreyfusard satirical cartoon weekly called *Psst . . . !*, beginning on February 5, 1898. Hermann-Paul, Ibels, Couturier, and others responded quickly with a Dreyfusard cartoon weekly, *Le Sifflet* ("hiss" or "whistle"). Cartoons were often featured in the posters, broadsides, pamphlets, and postcards that proliferated in the Affair. Some of the material was issued in series, notably the remarkable anti-Dreyfusard poster caricatures of *Le Musée des horreurs* and superb cartoons in the nihilist, often Dreyfusard broadsides of *La Feuille*. A large number of other cartoons were vulgar and artistically crude, especially but not only when directed at a lower-class audience; however, many excellent artists were *anarchisant* and contributed to the popular Dreyfusard campaign of the anarchists.

Other pictures were also widely circulated, both graphic art work and photographs. Individual portraits and scenes figuring in the news were not only printed in the periodical press but also issued separately. Publishers produced many different photographs and picture postcards, the latter being so numerous that a collector's catalog of them was also published. Foreign interest in the Affair was great enough to result in the origination of many cartoons and postcards abroad as well.

To some extent the publicity crossed over from propaganda to commercial exploitation, which no doubt was involved in much of the sale of photographs and postcards. There were also Dreyfus Affair toys and games, and the packaging of commercial products, like soap bars and absinthe bottles, with Dreyfus Affair icons.[3]

In 1899 cinema pioneer Georges Méliès made eleven short motion picture films re-enacting scenes from the Affair, but fighting in the audience forced withdrawal of the films from public exhibition. It was fully three-quarters of a century before a motion picture about the Affair could be produced or shown in France. Live dramas also became occasions for partisan demonstrations, notably two plays performed in 1898 at the Théatre de l'Oeuvre—Romain Rolland's *The Wolves* and Henrik Ibsen's *Enemy of the People*. Neither drama concerned the Dreyfus conflict directly, but both were understood as allegories of the Affair, Rolland's play intentionally so. Even in 1931 a German play about the Affair, produced in French by old Dreyfusards, was forced by Action Française demonstrations to close after only three performances.[4]

However, this was most of all a war of words printed in newspapers and separate tracts, and spoken to crowds at rallies, to courts, to parliamentary assemblies. Someone was always *saying* something to keep the battle going. In addition to the polemical declamations and carefully reasoned arguments, literary talents were applied in fiction, verse, and personalized sketches of events experienced.

Anatole France, whose novels had long been much admired throughout cultivated society, created quite a stir with his *Histoire contemporaine*, a sequence of novels being serialized in a daily newspaper while he wrote it. He converted the serial into a satire about the Affair, beginning on November 23, 1897. (This installment is quoted at the end of Chapter Eight.) From February 18, 1898, the serial was definintely Dreyfusard. On February

21—three days later—*La Libre parole* had the following to say about Anatole France (whose real surname was not France, but Thibault):

> *By falling in step with the author of "Paris" [i.e., Zola],*
> *The one we loved has won our scorn.*
> *He now has only to cut off . . . his* capuce *["hood"—i.e., his prepuce]*
> *And his name today is: Anatole Prusse ["Prussian"]!*

The newspaper serializing the *Histoire contemporaine, L'Echo de Paris,* was strongly anti-Dreyfusard but endured France's partisan fiction until January 1899, when the paper dropped him; the serial resumed in *Le Figaro* six months later.

And each side in the Affair had its catechisms; the following are excerpts from a Dreyfusard "catechism" of 1898:

> *Who are you?*
> Child of France loving his fatherland.
> *What do you want?*
> To be of the Syndicate.
> *What do you understand by that?*
> To associate myself with men who sacrifice their well-being, their tranquillity, their relations, their reputations, their liberty for the triumph of the idea of justice. In short I want to be among the intellectuals such as Bernard-Lazare, Zola, Duclaux, Yves Guyot, Jaurès, and others.
> *What is an intellectual?*
> He is a man whose brain refuses to function *by order,* and whose smallest actions are inspired by the greatest principles.
> *Then a worker can be an intellectual?*
> From the moment that a member of the Institut like Brunetière can be an ass-ual, nothing is opposed to a worker being an intellectual. . . .
> *What opinion have you of Colonel Henry?*
> The same he had at the moment he cut his throat.[5]

On each side polemical declamation was the chief weapon, wielded daily in the multitude of newspapers and from many a speaker's platform. While Dreyfusards relied more than their opponents on rational argument, and anti-Dreyfusards relied more on invective, neither had exclusive title to either rationality or vituperation.

Invective was often simply vicious attack on individual enemies, as when *La Libre parole* referred to "the drunken Guyot, the sinister Brisson, the womanizing Bourgeois, the forger Picquart, the morphinomaniac epileptic Pressensé."[6] Rational argument was not essential to asserting significant, coherent positions, and vituperation added force to assertions where logic was lacking. As an example, there are the following assertions from *La Libre parole* of September 28, 1898, that the Dreyfusard-Jewish enemy really controls the courts and the State. The author here, Gyp (the Comtesse de Martel de Janville), was reacting to the Brisson government having just sent the Dreyfus case to the Cour de Cassation for review:

> They are a State within the State, Them, the people of the Affair!
> They triumph! and the force of their insolence seems to grow greater every day.
> . . . [In the court] the extraordinary power of the Jews is confirmed once more. [An anti-Semitic diatribe follows, then:]
> They are in Their own place, the *hog-snouts!* Picquart is Theirs.
> It is THEIR Palais [de Justice]! It is Their affair, which must lay its course between the State that They are, allied to the Foreigner, and the supposed State that they are annihilating little by little.

It appeared that this sort of declamation and pandering to prejudice did more to form opinion about the Affair than did carefully reasoned pronouncements. That much seemed clear to Dreyfusards from the way they heard people around them talk. This amazed and outraged the Dreyfusards, as can be seen from an article by Paul Brulat titled "Crétins!" in *Les Droits de l'homme* on February 19, 1898:

> One remains stupefied by what passes for reasoning, coming even from those who ordinarily reason. . . . One could suppose that all these people are joking. Not at all. They speak seriously, their faces swollen with rage.
> There are countless examples I could mention. Everywhere one hears the same stupidity, the same extravagances. It is the bankruptcy of common sense, a wind of absurdity and folly which passes over the nation, which carries beyond our frontiers that old French spirit which was made of reason, balance, and solidity . . .

Stupidity and mediocrity of mind are, alas! Bastilles more
difficult to take away than Bastilles of stone and iron.

There were anti-Dreyfusards who could remain beyond the
appeals to passion of a Gyp or a Rochefort, but they proved also
to be beyond Dreyfusard appeals to reason, a frustration no less
"stupefying." Paul Cassagnac, the anti-Dreyfusard editor of
L'Autorité, was himself unexcelled in polemics, but he was also
extraordinarily astute and independent. Throughout the Affair
he maintained that the government and Army leaders had handled the case wrongfully and that the known proofs of Dreyfus's
guilt were insufficient. He even went so far as to say (on November 1, 1898) that *if* Dreyfus were innocent, the five War Ministers
from Mercier on should be sent to Devil's Island in his place.
Nevertheless, Cassagnac continued to believe Dreyfus guilty: He
claimed that this belief and anti-Dreyfusard militancy were the
duty of all who loved *la Patrie*. The brilliant rationalist Ferdinand Brunetière insisted that he was not competent to evaluate
evidence and had to rely on the court-martial's judgment. De
Mun claimed that one should believe Dreyfus guilty because no
one had proved him innocent.

Cassagnac's "moral conviction" about Dreyfus's guilt, Brunetière's profession of incompetence, and de Mun's demand for
proofs of innocence were all positions regularly taken by "reasonable" anti-Dreyfusards, who maintained them long after
most of the case's facts had been fully unveiled and Henry's
forgery had been exposed.[7] Cassagnac alone made explicit the
reality that convictions depended upon prior political beliefs, not
upon the facts.

Perhaps these three and other anti-Dreyfusards suffered because the dictates of political conviction were contradicted by
those of reason. One can imagine that this conflict caused deep
anguish for some of them, yet it is difficult to detect signs of this.
The self-deceptive power of political commitment can be very
great, especially for those to whom critical reasoning was largely
alien. Whether the Cassagnacs and Brunetières hid their anguish
or simply did not experience it, we cannot tell.

Most oral declamation and much of the written propaganda
were parts of organized campaigns. In addition to the anarchist
and socialist efforts discussed earlier, there were several impor-

tant groups in the field. Of these, the first to go into action was the Ligue Antisémitique Française.

This league had been developing since early 1897, but it led a shadowy existence until the anti-Semitic and Zola trial riots of January and February 1898. Initially its role in the riots probably was not large, but the league swiftly seized the opportunity, capitalizing on popular sentiment to foment trouble and recruit members. Estimates of its size vary widely, but it probably had at least five thousand to ten thousand members during much of the Affair and may have had substantially more. While concentrating its operations in Paris, it had active branches and affiliates in many other cities and towns, with large numbers in some of these.

Jules Guérin, the league's chieftain, was an adventurer who had been in trouble for his business swindles. He exploited anti-Semitism for his personal profit and seems to have been motivated in large part—perhaps entirely—by this rather than political conviction. Guérin obtained very large secret subsidies on a regular basis from the main royalist pretender, the Duc d'Orléans, who hoped that anti-Semites would so disrupt the political situation that royalists could seize power. The principal Bonapartist pretender, Prince Victor, refused Guérin's request for simultaneous subsidies from him. Guérin spent much of the league's income on himself. He and his Algerian confederates also sought profit by buying the business properties of Jews ruined by riot attacks.

The Ligue Antisémitique's propaganda emphasized economic issues; it directed its radical populist appeal at urban workers, although it also obtained much of its support from middle- and upper-class anti-Semites. However, the league's ideological position was vague, and its planned remedies for national ills still more so.

Guérin was an authoritarian leader who insisted upon complete control but lacked the ability to exercise it effectively. He could not keep bitter squabbles from dividing his associates, and his judgment in deciding campaign actions proved to be poor. The league was always disorganized, and it had virtually collapsed by the end of 1899. Nevertheless, in the heated conditions of the Affair it did flourish in its haphazard way, making itself a significant factor, not only by causing street violence but also through abundant printed propaganda and a large number of public rallies and demonstrations.[8]

Somewhat similar, but larger and apparently less corrupt, was the Ligue des Patriotes. It had been established by the patriotic poet Paul Déroulède in 1882, was an important Boulangist organization in 1888–89, then was dissolved when that movement failed. Déroulède and Marcel Habert reconstituted it in September 1898. In this reincarnation the group was determined in its hostility to parliamentary government as practiced in the Third Republic, as well as to the Dreyfusards. It sought drastic change in the constitution—by violence if need be—but not royal restoration. It typified the populist radical right.

At the time Déroulède attempted a coup d'état in February 1899, the Ligue des Patriotes seems to have had about sixty thousand members, although that figure could be exaggerated; perhaps three-fourths were in Paris and many of the rest in Marseille. In Paris the Ligue included groups of onetime socialists, some of them following Henri de Rochefort; their anti-Republic, reactionary nationalism and Boulangism had led them to depart from conventional varities of socialism. Members who are known tended to be concentrated in the same Paris districts as were known members of the Ligue Antisémitique. However, the Ligue des Patriotes probably depended more on the support of the middle-aged and middle class, especially 1870–71 war veterans and the lower middle class, and less on young workers.

Action by the Ligue des Patriotes also followed the anti-Semites' pattern of extensive printed and oral propaganda, with frequent rallies and demonstrations that tended to be violent. It fought the Republic more and Jews less, and seems to have been less involved in fomenting riots and breaking up Dreyfusard meetings. Its agitation was extensive, highly visible, and probably more important than the involvement of some from the group in plots to seize the State by force. Like the Ligue Antisémitique, the Ligue des Patriotes flourished during the Affair, then declined when the situation cooled after Dreyfus's release.[9]

The Ligue de la Patrie Française was formed at the very end of 1898 by men of letters and elected politicians for whom the Ligue des Patriotes was too extreme. Its president was Jules Lemaître, a literary historian and critic comparable in stature and rational powers to Ferdinand Brunetière, who also was a member. As can be seen from the analysis in the preceding chapter of its early adherants, this league enjoyed very wide support among the educated elite of France. It has been estimated that the league had 100,000 members by March 1899, and four to five times that number a year later.[10]

Adherants of the Ligue de la Patrie Française represented a major bloc of opinion which tends to be underestimated in the face of more extreme views and events. League spokesmen probably expressed the most broadly typical anti-Dreyfusard outlook. They professed to be sincere republicans, and in their fashion, so they were. On anticlericalism and anti-Semitism they claimed neutrality, although they inclined away from the one and toward the other. At least their anti-Semitism usually was comparatively subdued and confined mainly to complaints about the Syndicate and suggestions that Jews were often greedy, foreign, or otherwise cause for concern and perhaps contempt.

However, the league's spokesmen damned corrupt parliamentary government; they sought constitutional revision to eliminate this corruption and to replace the creation of theoreticians reasoning abstractly. They would replace party politics with "national" politics—that is, with a more authoritarian regime that better embodied the national spirit. Nationalism was defined as the sentiment of good Frenchmen disgusted with the existing state of affairs and opposed to the Freemasons and Jews who were ruining the country. In a speech of November 13, 1899, Lemaître said:

> We want a republic which merits the name and is not contradictory to its principle. The republic is the government of all in the interest of all. . . . It is we, the opponents who are the republicans and democrats: those governing us and their accomplices are at present only a factious oligarchy.[11]

It may be noted that, while the tone differs, the idea expressed here is similar to that of the quoted passage by Gyp.

The anti-Dreyfusard Ligue de la Patrie Française emulated the tactics of the Dreyfusard Ligue des Droits de l'Homme, with an extensive, organized propaganda campaign conducted in its own publications and in meetings held around the country. While the anti-Dreyfusard organization did much of this, it was not as active or well organized as its Dreyfusard counterpart. The Patrie Française, as it was usually called, also tried to organize

election campaigns for nationalist candidates in 1900 and 1902.
Despite some success in 1900, the Patrie Française did not make
a good political party, and it was torn by internal discord; by late
1902 it was inactive, an empty shell.

The most impressive propaganda effort was that of the Dreyfusard Ligue des Droits de l'Homme—although the separate effort of the anarchist Sebastien Faure (discussed in Chapter Eight)
was also most extraordinary. The Ligue des Droits was established in February 1898 by a group of republican intellectuals,
nearly all of them academics. With the battles of the Zola trial
going on both in the court and in the streets outside, and the
police tolerating frequent assaults on Dreyfusards, it seemed that
there was great danger to republican principles, as expressed in
the 1789 Revolution's Déclaration des Droits de l'Homme et du
Citoyen. During a trial recess Senator Ludovic Trarieux proposed
the league to companions in the waiting room for witnesses, and
it was established at a meeting in his home the following Sunday, February 20.

The league's program was given in its full name, the Ligue
Française pour la Défense des Droits de l'Homme et du Citoyen
(French League for the Defense of the Rights of Man and the
Citizen). To the members the Déclaration des Droits was the
"soul of the New France," incarnating all the aspirations of a
more just and humane world, not only for France but for all
humanity. The league sought to rally all "true republicans and
democrats" against the threat of reactionary politics to civilization and progress. A June 17, 1898, league manifesto asserted
confidence in the future and in the power of reason and promised
to defend all those whose rights were threatened. From the beginning the league did seek to defend many besides Dreyfus,
especially through campaigning against anti-Semitism.[12]

While Dreyfusard support was drawn from a wide range of
diverse political opinion, league members united in defense of
the ideals—though these often were vague—that for more than
a century had defined the republican tradition. Republicans of
this sort responded to messages like that of Paul Brulat, of the
newspaper Les Droits de l'homme: "When they violate justice,
when they violate reason, then it is more than a right, it is a duty
to protest."[13] By the end of 1899 there were about twelve thousand dues-paying members and local committees in 298 towns
and cities.

Compared to most of their opponents, Dreyfusards were more fully involved and worked much harder in the struggle. The Ligue des Droits campaign was more extensive and better organized than anything on the other side. Dreyfusard memoirs often speak of doing little else but fight for two years, while most anti-Dreyfusards appear to have diverted much less of their energies to the struggle.

The Ligue des Droits carried on a massive campaign of public meetings with what amounted to a traveling road show of Dreyfusard celebrities, who seem to have spoken wherever a hall could be obtained for a night. The league also gave wide distribution to printed material. In October 1898, when few newspapers were reporting what actually was said in sessions of the Cour de Cassation—which was then demolishing the case against Dreyfus—the Ligue des Droits sent transcripts of these sessions to all the teachers, municipal councilors, and *juges de paix* (lower-level magistrates) in France. The league distributed 400,000 copies of a reply by its president, Ludovic Trarieux, to War Minister Cavaignac's speech of July 7, 1898. It sponsored publication of books like Jaurès's *Les Preuves* and commissioned Pierre Quillard to make his 715-page analysis of the Monument Henry.

There was a potentially receptive audience, which the league tried with some success to win for the Dreyfusard crusade. Many of the French were nominally republican only because that was conventional and because they associated republicanism with the social order dominated by the bourgeoisie in place of the aristocracy. But there remained a substantial number whose love of republican ideals was alive or could be revived: It was they who rallied in response to the call of the Ligue des Droits.

The idealistic republicans were also the type most likely to become Freemasons, those satanic figures who so disturbed many of the French. It seems that most Masonic lodges did eventually become Dreyfusard, but how soon and what they did about it remain obscure. There were some Dreyfusard meetings in Masonic lodges, and presumably much informal communication there, but it seems unlikely that Dreyfusards depended on the links and influence the order provided.

Some Dreyfusards can be identified as members of the Masonic order. Dreyfusards already mentioned here who were Masons include: Aulard, Deloncle, Gérault-Richard, Guyot,

Millerand, Ranc, Joseph and Théodore Reinach, Trarieux, Viviani, and Zola. Presidents Faure and Loubet were Masons, as were four Premiers in the period of the Affair—Dupuy, Bourgeois, Brisson, and Combes—and a number of their Ministers. A few anti-Dreyfusards were also in the order, notably Cavaignac and Rochefort.[14]

Anti-Dreyfusards railed against Protestants in the Affair as well as against Jews and Freemasons. An 1899 book entitled *The Protestant Peril* agonized over the "accursed trio" of Jews, Protestants, and Freemasons trying to rehabilitate Dreyfus. "Whether you like it or not, the Judeo-Masonic Protestant coalition is powerful. The number of Dreyfusards grows each day. The university is Dreyfusard, notably Protestant academics." Another 1899 book, *The Protestant Treason* (with a Forain cartoon on the cover), skillfully spun out a detailed and persuasive picture of Protestant involvement in the Dreyfusard conspiracy and described the aim of all Protestants in France to betray the nation to Germany and England.[15] In fact there were a few Protestant Dreyfusards, including Scheurer-Kestner, Leblois, Pressensé, and a number of academics. Of course their presence did not constitute a Protestant league, conspiratorial or open.

Mention should be made of the "league" formed around Charles Péguy. Having just dropped out of the Ecole Normale Supérieure, in the spring of 1898 he established a small book shop and publishing business, the Librairie Georges Bellais. This was the principal gathering spot of many intellectuals active in the Affair, and the publisher for some of their works of combat. Daniel Halévy became an intimate of Péguy there. The shop was also a military command post, from which Péguy led sallies to fight off incursions threatening physical attack on Dreyfusard professors at the Sorbonne, a few yards away. The shop had failed as a business by August 1899, but Péguy followed with a journal, the *Cahiers de la Quinzaine*, whose office and book shop continued to be a central gathering place for intellectuals until Péguy was killed in another sort of battle, at the beginning of World War I.

Many of those drawn to Péguy's shop were products of the Ecole Normale Supérieure, and most were both ardent socialists and early committed Dreyfusards. Like Herr and Jaurès, they were first intellectuals, then socialists through rational reflection, with the Affair a decisive factor for many. Their ardor for both the ideals of the Dreyfusard cause and for this "socialism of the head" was deep and persistent, a special sort of ideological commitment, which was an important legacy of the Affair in French intellectual life for decades afterward. Until his death Péguy's thought, personality, and journal provided one major focal center for what might be called the "cerebral left."

When the Ligue des Droits was established a few Catholics joined it, but the league's republican orthodoxy signified anticlericalism to most Catholics. Thus the league was not a good vehicle for addressing the Catholic faithful; Dreyfusard Catholics, led by the historian Paul Viollet, left the Ligue des Droits and in February 1899 formed the Comité Catholique pour la Défense du Droit. There were about two hundred enrolled, the rare exceptions to the rule of Catholic adherance to anti-Dreyfusard politics—although there is reason to think that the Comité's existence was unknown to some Catholics who might gladly have joined it. Many Comité members were priests, the rest being men of letters, lawyers, retired officers, engineers, and the like. They sought reconciliation based upon the facts and "free critical reasoning in politics"; denounced the evil caused by militarism, anti-Semitism, and nationalism; and swore support for the principles of 1789.

For these Catholics justice in the Affair was a profound matter of conscience, and their faith directed them to the Dreyfusard partisanship their church's hierarchy discouraged; some of them were persecuted by the Church in consequence. One priest in the Comité, the Abbé Pichot, wrote tracts on Christian conscience in the Affair, beginning one of them by repeating a remark of Leo Tolstoy on the Affair: "At last the French have a case of conscience to resolve."[16] Non-Catholic Dreyfusards usually did not speak about conscience.

While socialists were "neutral in opposition to the anti-Dreyfusards," most of the Church hierarchy assumed a corresponding but inverted position. Apart from a Papal injunction to neutrality in August 1898, the Church did not make authoritative statements about the Affair. However, the partisanship of the hierarchy was understood by all and occasionally was evident. The Comité Catholique pour la Défense du Droit was denied the episcopal sponsorship thought essential to its conciliatory efforts, which achieved little if any success. Committee members believed that Catholics confounded its "free critical reasoning in politics" with free critical reasoning in matters of faith, which the Church found intolerable. Dreyfusard Catholics and non-Catholics alike saw Protestants as being drawn to the Dreyfusard cause because they were accustomed to critical reasoning in their faith, while the opposite experience among Catholics impelled them to credulity in the Affair.

The militant anti-Dreyfusard and anti-Semitic campaign of the Assumptionists and *La Croix* was unique. Individual priests were vocal anti-Dreyfusards, but, despite the contrary belief of anticlericals, there probably was little or no other concerted action by the Catholic clergy. Nevertheless, Dreyfusard anticlericalism was aggravated by the Church's failure to stop real and imagined clerical misconduct.

In the republican tradition, anticlericalism was a central article of faith, one that those who were republicans by principle held sacred. However, much of the actual anticlerical program had been accomplished (especially in the secularization of education) or transformed into reflexively routine politics. The Dreyfus Affair changed this drastically, reviving with greater force than ever the old hatred of the Church and the drive to crusade against it. This is illustrated by the following extracts from *La Forêt noire* (*The Black Forest*), published in 1899 by Jean Ajalbert, who was on the staff of the newspaper *Les Droits de l'homme*:

THE BLACK FOREST? THE CHURCH: its deadly trees, its vegetation of poison and death, its tangled branches over the most stinking beasts in creation, over the most hideous larvae of the shadows, over the cruellest ambushes, over the slimiest slopes, the CHURCH, with its muddy caverns, its bloody thickets, its atrocious dovecotes, where there grows only wood for torture, execution pyres, and the gallows, the CHURCH, such as it has been all through history, such as it has shown itself in the *Affair*—one of those affairs that are "like the coups d'Etat of God," according to Michelet's famous expression. THE BLACK FOREST? THE CHURCH, favoring the soldier's drunken plots, the judge's evil strokes, the magistrate's villainous tricks! . . .

It is in the lasting shadow of the Cross that the Saber glitters in the fists of the forgers and the troublemakers. It is under the sorrowful eyes of Jesus that the Balances deceived and went out of kilter in the courts! Poor old Cross of Christ, I imagine that he is dumbfounded by the unanimous infamy of Christians!

And, later in the book:

> The Revolution has not been made; it is necessary to
> make it.
> The Revolution, for now, is the application of the law to
> all.
> It does not suffice to have routed the enemy; it is advisa-
> ble not to let it form again in peace.
> The victory must not be platonic.[17]

Not only did anticlericalism correspond to anti-Semitism in polemical excesses like this one, but also in its fears of occult forces, with Jesuits the principal mysterious order. Some Army officers had been educated in Jesuit schools, especially the Ecole de la Rue des Postes in Paris. A well-known Jesuit, Père Stanis- laus Du Lac, was the confessor of Boisdeffre, De Mun, and per- haps a few other officers. Du Lac may have been involved in some minor Affair intrigues. From this Dreyfusards built a myth: Most or all of the General Staff officers implicated in the Affair's crimes had been indoctrinated as youths at the "Rue des Postes" and were confessed by Père Du Lac. As a result, they were all creatures or confederates of the Jesuits. For many Dreyfusards Du Lac was a central, controlling figure in the General Staff machinations and one of the chief villains of the Affair.

Anticlericalism was probably the most important factor mak- ing possible a Dreyfusard alliance of disparate elements, who united in defense of the Republic on this basis. Moreover, anti- clerical passions greatly aggravated Dreyfusard departures from the cool rationality they prized and heightened the constant ten- sion the combatants suffered.

An incident of July 19, 1898, demonstrates how explosive was the situation, with antagonism and suspicion instantly ig- nited. Père Henri Didon gave an address, "L'Esprit militaire dans une Nation," at a school awards ceremony where the Army's commander-in-chief, General Edouard Jamont, presided. An educator and a member of the Dominican order, Didon was committed to democracy and the Republic. His political and so- cial views were much more liberal and progressive than the cler- ical norm. He had expressed them often and ardently; in consequence the Master-General of the Dominican order had once exiled him to a Corsican monastery and had banned him for years from preaching. In his school speech the good father justified militarism with eloquently lucid rationality, arguing on humanistic grounds that the formation of national communities is desirable and necessary, and that military spirit is morally, intellectually, and practically essential to each nation.

Père Didon's reasoning was quite persuasive, while his position really differed little from those taken in less agitated times by many Dreyfusards. The published text of the address includes only one oblique reference that could be construed as referring critically to Dreyfusard attacks on the Army, although provocative passages may have been excised from the printed version.

Nevertheless, Didon's speech was inevitably seen as a combative and partisan assertion that preserving the Army's integral strength took precedence over anything claimed for right and justice. Hence, the oration had to be a frontal assault upon the Dreyfusards by the militant and reactionary Church. The liberal Didon was automatically perceived only as spokesman for the Dominicans, the order identified as having chief responsibility for the Inquisition and construction of the Church's dogmatic theology. His actual words were disregarded, and the import attributed to them aroused tirades from Dreyfusard polemicists. Joseph Reinach reflected his comrades' fears when in 1904 he recalled about this incident that "the idea of a violent operation to put an end to the affair was so much in the air, and its realization seemed so close, that the Church militant, which would have gained the most from it, wanted as well to have the honor of initiating it."[18] The anticlerical reflexes of Dreyfusards were so sensitive that they could readily think such "a violent operation" was imminent, and they prepared to fend it off.

Although Père Didon's actual words were misunderstood, his advocacy of militarism reflects an attitude that was pervasive in France, encouraged by both patriotism and the system of nearly universal conscription. Not only anti-Dreyfusards but also many Dreyfusards venerated the Army. The most common Dreyfusard attitude was expressed at the Zola trial on February 15, 1898, by Edouard Grimaux, who taught would-be Army officers at the Ecole Polytechnique until his open Dreyfusard partisanship led to his dismissal:

> I am one of those patriots who runs to watch the regiments march by. And, when the flag passes, I salute it respectfully, my heart moved and beating hard . . .
> I have to say that it is in our ranks, among those who

think like me, that are found the most enlightened patriots, the ones who see the best interest of the Fatherland. The true insulters of the army are those dubious journalists who accuse a Minister of having sold himself for 30,000 francs to a supposed Jewish syndicate! These insulters of the army are those heros of fear who used to say to you at the affair's beginning: "Let the innocent suffer an undeserved torture, rather than arouse the enmity of a foreign power."

. . . The insulters of the army are those who run through the streets shouting, "Long live the army!" without shouting, "Long live the Republic!" These two cannot be separated. . . .

For, in the end, the army . . . who does not count within it a brother, a son, a parent, a friend? . . . But the army, it is the flesh of our flesh, the blood of our blood.[19]

However, Dreyfusards who had revered the Army were moved by the Affair to a much more critical view. The struggle caused many of them to think that the Army as then constituted and led was the implacable enemy of democracy and the Republic. The Army's authoritarianism, hierarchy, and discipline, and its status as a society apart made it seem incompatible with the ideals that had moved the Dreyfusard crusade. Clemenceau said at the Zola trial: "It is necessary that the universal army, the army of all, be permeated with the ideas of all, since it is composed of the universality of citizens." He warned of the danger that surrender to military servitude would preserve the native soil but abandon the ideas of justice and liberty that had given France its glory and renown among men.[20]

While old republican nationalists like Clemenceau criticized the Army reluctantly, some Dreyfusards were unreservedly hostile toward it. For anarchists and most socialists, antimilitarism was a fundamental article of faith. And then there was Urbain Gohier, a wild, unstable, paranoid, misanthropic, and anti-Semitic polemicist who used L'Aurore and the Dreyfusard crusade as vehicles to attack some of those he hated. His eloquent, vicious invective against the Army outraged many Dreyfusards. However, they felt compelled to defend him when he was prosecuted in November 1898 for attacks on the Army; to do otherwise would have been a denial of press freedom and a concession to the anti-Dreyfusards. Gohier was a substantial factor exacerbating strife in the Affair.

Socialists and anarchists damned militarism, conservative

172   MORE THAN A TRIAL
tally hostile to workers and their liberation. This can be seen in
a confrontation of February 15, 1898, at a rally organized and
addressed by leading anti-Semites, including Jules Guérin. It
was held in the town hall of Suresnes, an industrial suburb of
Paris. As reported in *Le Temps* on February 17, the hall was
packed by a hostile crowd of workers, most of them apparently
socialists. They heckled the anti-Semite speakers, laughing and
taunting when Lucien Millevoye tried to tell them a note from
the Kaiser existed that proved Dreyfus's guilt. Georges Thiébaud
thought he could appeal successfully to their desire for national
independence, which he said was menaced by the Affair. The
socialist Deputy of the district, René Chauvin, rose in response:

"Me too, I am for national independence. But independence
is liberty, and you are in contradiction with yourself, since you
claim that we can not render justice in our own house without
fearing the intervention of tyrants from near by." (*Applause*.)
Grimaux had said much the same thing at the Zola trial earlier
that same day.

"That is what you call patriotism! Our fathers were prouder
than you. Well, we are internationalists. We want to preserve
and defend the liberties and rights handed down to us. We do
not want to be kept in darkness and we do not believe the emperor of Germany involves himself in our affairs. It is not only
the Semites who have betrayed France. Bazaine [the general
thought a traitor for surrendering the main French army in 1870]
was Catholic. Anti-Semitism is a trap held out to workers in
order to divide them. You speak of the Syndicate! The most dangerous one of all is the one whose seat is in the Vatican. If the
people are repelled by the advice which proceeds from the synagogue or temple [i.e., Protestant church], they are far more repelled by the cockroaches in cassocks who lie in hiding behind
you.

"As for the citizens present, my electors, divided formerly
by Boulangism, they have come to agreement over my name. Be
at ease, Monsieur Thiébaud, they will not be divided again. You
can take your propaganda elsewhere."

Chauvin received an ovation, and a nearly unanimous vote of
the audience condemned the anti-Semitic campaign.

11

Struggle for the Republic

While the struggle went on in France, troops of French journalists made a pilgrimage to Berlin; Colonel Max von Schwartzkoppen, to whom either Dreyfus or Esterhazy had given secrets, had been transferred to command of a regiment there. Nearly every day in late 1897 and early 1898 at least one reporter arrived on the 8:00 A.M. train and presented himself at the colonel's house. Realizing that few in France would believe him, and not wanting to exacerbate the situation, Schwartzkoppen politely turned away all the visitors without commenting on the case. Each returned to Paris the same day on the 1:00 P.M. train.[1]

Although most of the public remained hostile, the Dreyfusard campaign soon began to enjoy some success. During the spring of 1898, clarification of facts and revulsion against anti-Dreyfusard excesses extended the Dreyfusards' support among those inclined toward them by political beliefs. After the May 1898 elections to the Chamber of Deputies were out of the way, support for Revision began to spread in both Chambers, especially the Senate, which was comparatively insulated from popular reaction. Even the enthusiasm of the Deputies for Cavaignac's July 7 speech "proving" Dreyfus guilty was not a real setback, for the War Minister conceded key points the Dreyfusards had been insisting upon, and—for those who would listen—they had strong arguments against his defective evidence even before Henry's exposure.

Political prejudice and expediency were not the only factors impeding conversion of the cabinet and the parliament to Revision. Significant pieces of information were kept by Ministers from the chambers, from one another, and from their successors as ministries changed. Many members of the parliament did not follow the whole controversy closely enough to be fully aware of what was happening.

This can be seen in the hearing of Cavaignac's big speech. When he spoke of the document soon to be known as the *faux Henry*, few Deputies realized that General Gabriel de Pellieux, testifying at the first Zola trial, had already revealed it, or that the Dreyfusard press had said much to cast doubt upon the document's authenticity. Former Premier Jules Méline kept silent, although he knew that the Italian ambassador had on his honor denied the authenticity of the *faux Henry*, which was supposed to be a letter from the Italian military attaché to Schwartzkoppen. Also silent were Charles Dupuy, who had been Premier when Dreyfus was condemned, and two of his Ministers, Louis Barthou and Raymond Poincaré. They knew Cavaignac's confession story had been adjudged spurious by the government when first reported at the time of alleged event.

Gabriel Hanotoux, who had been Foreign Minister for all but six months since May 1894, kept much from Théophile Delcassé, who succeeded him only nine days before Cavaignac's speech. Premier Henri Brisson was kept in the dark by Méline and Dupuy, and both he and Delcassé were much confused for some weeks.

The ferment over the Affair was extremely intense throughout the summer and fall of 1898. Besides the controversy surrounding Cavaignac's speech, there were others occasioned by the second trial of Zola, his action against Judet, preliminary examination of charges against Picquart and his attorney, Louis Leblois, and another of charges against Esterhazy and his mistress, Marguérite Pays. There was close combat over the Legion of Honor: When Zola was expelled on July 25, other Dreyfusards angrily submitted their resignations, and the Legion's council insisted that a member could not resign.

The intellectuals were disseminating a flood of propaganda, above all *Les Preuves* of Jaurès, but also many other quite powerful polemics and appeals to people's sense of morality and justice. Anti-Dreyfusards were less energetic but still very active in arousing people to repudiate forcefully both the Dreyfusard campaign and the politicians who tolerated or encouraged it. The invective in the more violent organs of the anti-Dreyfusard press seems to have been exceptionally heated that summer. The atmosphere was such as to encourage Cavaignac in his effort to have all the leading Dreyfusards arrested and prosecuted for sedition.

Ferment was especially strong in the schools, particularly the letters and science divisions of the universities. By this time high proportions of the people there were deeply engaged by the Affair. In addition to participation by faculty and students in the general struggle, there was much strife within academic halls, including both oral and physical brawls.

The case of one Dreyfusard academic, Paul Stapfer, was especially celebrated, both as part of the Affair and as a matter of academic freedom. Stapfer was dean of the division of letters at the University of Bordeaux. On July 23, 1898, he made strongly Dreyfusard remarks in his funeral oration for the division's rector, who had been much upset by the Affair. Stapfer was suspended by the Education Minister, Léon Bourgeois, and in November 1899 was turned out of office permanently by vote of the predominantly anti-Dreyfusard faculty. On August 3, 1898, another scandal was created by Ferdinand Buisson, a Sorbonne professor and a former national director of primary education. Buisson gave a Dreyfusard oration at the funeral of another Dreyfusard educator, Félix Pécaut. It did not escape the anti-Dreyfusards' attention that Stapfer, Buisson, and Pécaut were all Protestants. Incidents like these helped to keep the atmosphere in academe very hot indeed.

At the end of August a close-spaced sequence of shocks shifted the character of the conflict. Esterhazy, who so recently had been a hero invulnerable to prosecution, was brought before an Army board of inquiry, charged with a variety of misdeeds other than espionage. On August 27 the board found him guilty of habitual misconduct and recommended his dismissal from the Army; the action was finally confirmed four days later. On the thirtieth Henry confessed his forgery to Cavaignac; this news was released to the press at midnight. Henry was placed in the cell at the Mont-Valérien fortress that had been occupied before him by Picquart and would later be occupied by Cuignet, the man who discovered that the *faux Henry* was fraudulent. (Cuignet became implicated in yet another matter of misconduct in the Affair.)

On August 31 the public learned that the main evidence against Dreyfus was forged, that Dreyfus's principal accuser was responsible and in prison, that the Chief of Staff, General Boisdeffre, had resigned in shame, and that Esterhazy had been dismissed from the Army. The Cabinet met four times that day but temporized, unable to act decisively. At midnight came the official announcement that Henry had cut his throat in his cell that afternoon. Before morning Esterhazy had begun his flight to England, shaving off his large, characteristic moustache in order to avoid detection at the Belgian frontier. Small wonder that for a few hours there was nearly universal assent to Revision of the Dreyfus condemnation. Then conviction got the better of reason, and those who had been strongly anti-Dreyfusard continued to maintain that position.

However, the shocks were sufficient to change the minds of Premier Brisson and many others not compelled by prior conceptions to deny the import of Henry's exposure. The Cabinet was irresolute and beset by division, confusion, and fear of popular reaction, but most of its members no longer resisted Revision. On September 26 they finally decided upon it, and the long process of official review began. Although the Brisson government fell a month later, and its successor was far less supportive to the cause of the Dreyfusards, they no longer had to fight adamant official resistance.

Opponents in the struggle actually intensified their campaigns. With the government committed to Revision, they could concentrate more on fighting each other and mustering or holding public support. Each side increased the number of its public meetings, with the Ligue des Patriotes resurrected at the same time as Revision was decided and the Ligue de la Patrie Française to follow three months later. Fist fights at the meetings and in the streets outside were common, for tensions and animosities were more severe than ever.

In October 1898 the tensions seemed unbearable, exacerbated as they were by international and labor crises and by fears of a rightist coup d'état. It should be recalled that France then faced the danger of immediate war with England over the confrontation between their colonial expeditions at Fashoda in Africa, and Paris was teeming with large numbers of troops turned out to control workers striking over issues unrelated to the Affair.

On October 2 Déroulède and Guérin organized a large mob to break up a Dreyfusard meeting; police prevented severe violence by the adroit device of arresting the Dreyfusard speakers as soon as they appeared. Rumors circulated concerning a coup by the radical right, acting in concert with the Army. On October 16 all the socialist deputies issued a manifesto condemning the "state of seige" constituted by the massive troop movements in Paris. Three days later all socialist factions united for the first time in a "Comité de Vigilance" to fight threats to liberty and defend the Republic. Marxist leader Jules Guesde and many other socialists feared not only for the Republic's survival but still more that the bourgeoisie would use the Affair as an opportunity to suppress the workers; with the movement of troops against striking workers, this seemed already to have begun.

The Comité de Vigilance resolved to have a huge mass demonstration outside the Chamber of Deputies when it convened on October 25; this effort was attentuated, however, to avoid playing into the hands of those supposed to be plotting a coup. On October 22 provocative manifestoes were issued by both the Ligue des Patriotes and an *ad hoc* coalition of revolutionary socialists and anarchists; they promised action on the twenty-fifth. The next day the Ligue Antisémitique made its own provocative proclamation, and on the day after, October 24, the Ligue des Droits de l'Homme issued a manifesto calling for resistance to agitation.

On October 25 the Chamber of Deputies convened in the Palais Bourbon, meeting for the first time since Henry had been unmasked. The Palais was surrounded by barriers, police were out in great force, and regiments of cavalry waited nearby in the Tuileries gardens. Nevertheless, arriving Deputies had to struggle through vast, unruly crowds. Great roars resounded upon the arrival of celebrities, especially those of the right, like Cassagnac and Déroulède. Followers of Déroulède and Guérin seemed to predominate and to control the Place de la Concorde. Guérin and company tried to march upon the Palais Bourbon in an apparent attempt at a coup, but they were met by the police in a bloody confrontation. Guérin and three companions were arrested, and arrests of others in diverse disorders mounted quickly.

Tumult within the Chamber of Deputies was scarcely less frenetic than the scene outside. Premier Brisson was doomed from the start, with both the right and center determined to drive him from office. The surprise resignation of War Minister Chanoine only sealed the ministry's fate. Prolonged, extremely acrimonious debate ended with a vote of no confidence, terminating Brisson's tenure in office.

As the Deputies exited from the Palais Bourbon at 8:00 P.M. they were met by the cries of the still agitated mob, which then flooded out into nearby boulevards. Traffic in these streets became impossible, shops hastily closed up, and in places the police were overwhelmed. The passage through the crowds by Drumont and his associates was welcomed with noisy demonstrations of support, and there was much commotion centered upon the offices of *La Libre parole,* on whose lighted balcony hung flags and a banner proclaiming "Down with the Jews!" The crowds dispersed slowly, and scattered brawls lasted well into the night.[2]

More fuel for the fires was added by the decision, only four days later, of the Cour de Cassation that there were ample grounds for appeal in the Dreyfus case. While Dreyfusards rejoiced, they also stormed because Alfred Dreyfus himself was not to be informed. The anti-Dreyfusard press kept the public in ignorance of the reasons the court gave for its judgment, so that popular reaction was not tempered by recognition that the court might be impartial.

In the weeks that followed Dreyfusard agitation concentrated on the injustice of Picquart's imprisonment and prosecution. There were public meetings every night, and the atmosphere remained super-heated. It was more than a matter of the hero persecuted: If held, a court-martial would probably have convicted Picquart, seemingly reinforcing the 1894 conviction of Dreyfus while it was under review by the Cour de Cassation. The issue soon precipitated the commitment to the fray of republican politicians who until then had avoided taking either side. They now assumed positions generally regarded as Dreyfusard, although most of these figures still tried to limit their involvement.

Greatest impact resulted from the entry of two of France's most respected and influential politicians, Raymond Poincaré and René Waldeck-Rousseau. Both were rather conservative and had carefully avoided making any public remarks whatever about the Affair. Waldeck-Rousseau had been an important republican leader for two decades and would become Premier in mid-1899. Although then only thirty-eight, Poincaré had already been a Minister in four governments; between 1912 and 1929 he would be either President or Premier for thirteen and a half years.

On November 24, 1898, Picquart's court-martial on December 12 was ordered by General Emile Zurlinden, who had succeeded Cavaignac as War Minister, had resigned after only twelve days, and now was Military Governor of Paris. Quite apart from lack of substantial evidence against Picquart, there were serious legal objections to the military trial, among them Picquart's then being a civilian, since he had been dismissed from the Army.

For some days there was a storm in the two parliamentary chambers, both in the corridors and voiced by speakers at the tribunes. On November 28, a Deputy was railing against the Syndicate when Raymond Poincaré suddenly interrupted, exclaiming, "That's enough of that, in truth!" and demanded recognition to address the Chamber. He said that he spoke "because I am convinced that at this moment the continued silence of some among us would truly be cowardice." ("*Hear! Hear!*")

Poincaré strongly condemned all the actions taken against Picquart, calling them reprisals and persecution. He went on to speak of the confidential knowledge he had of the Dreyfus case, through his having been a Minister when the captain was condemned in 1894. Amidst a very agitated Chamber, Poincaré said that on this basis he had known all along that the bulk of what had been said against Dreyfus was false—and he had remained silent, which he now deeply regretted. Another important leader in the Chamber of Deputies, Louis Barthou, announced, "I associate myself with your position absolutely." Barthou had been a Minister with Poincaré in 1894; there was no direct response from Charles Dupuy, who was Premier both then and at the moment of Poincaré's revelation.

Poincaré finished by saying, "I see very well that in breaking a silence today that has weighed upon me" (*from the right: "It's too late!"*) "I expose myself to attacks, to insults, to calumnies. I do not care, and I am happy to have seized at this tribune the occasion I have so long awaited, to liberate my conscience." (*Lively applause from a great number of benches to the left and in the center.*)

Three days later came Waldeck-Rousseau's turn to intervene, this time in the Senate. Since he had been preoccupied with his practice as one of the most successful Paris barristers and had been out of office from 1889 to 1894, it was about a decade since he had actually spoken in the chambers at all. His reputation was so great, however, that his action now was all the more impressive for having broken his long silence. Waldeck-Rousseau was profoundly disturbed by much of the Affair's uproar, especially by the offense to jurisprudence involved in Picquart's prosecution. He proposed to empower the Cour de Cassation to suspend that action; the Senate passed his proposal, although Picquart's prosecution eventually was suspended by other means.

From Barthou on the right, past Poincaré and Waldeck-Rousseau, past the left-of-center Léon Bourgeois, to the very moderate socialist, Alexandre Millerand, there was now an array of important republican leaders who had departed from neutrality late and very reluctantly and who were committed despite themselves.[3] Many others were to follow: From this point on politicians loyal to the Third Republic were increasingly supportive to the Dreyfusard cause, despite the conservatism and the wish to avoid trouble that had long held many of them back.

During the remaining winter months of 1898–99 the struggle continued, with full propaganda and agitation programs by the various leagues and by socialist and anarchist groups. The press and parliament were kept busy for months by Quesnay de Beaurepaire's démarche and the subsequent debate over transferring the Dreyfus case from the Cour de Cassation's Criminal Chamber to the entire court. Waldeck-Rousseau eloquently condemned this procedure, but to no avail.

The death in February of President Faure led to much more furor, first in a dispute over who should succeed him, then over the supposed Dreyfusard partisanship of the successor named, Emile Loubet. Déroulède and company's attempt at a coup during Faure's funeral further exacerbated animosities, as did the trial of Déroulède and Habert in late May.

On March 4, 1899, Esterhazy's deposition to the Cour de Cassation was published by the *Daily Chronicle* in London and soon afterward by Paris newspapers. Esterhazy said much about his collusion with General Staff officers in various machinations and presented a portrait of the General Staff continuously plotting to prevent justice from being realized. His testimony was suspect but was reinforced by much else that came out before the high court. During April, Mathieu Dreyfus and friends surreptitiously turned over transcripts of the court's proceedings to *Le Figaro*, where they were published throughout the month. There were many astonishing revelations, which not only supported Esterhazy about General Staff officers' crimes but also clarified many points that previously had been obscure or insufficiently demonstrated by evidence. For those who cared to see, the absence of evidence against Alfred Dreyfus was all the more clear.

If revelations or propaganda produced substantial shifts in public opinion, it is difficult to perceive them. The most likely result was a deepening division, with ever more people impelled by preconceived political beliefs ever farther from any middle ground. While the Ligue de la Patrie Française grew most rapidly, popular support for the Dreyfusards also spread. In recollections written much later, and judging on the basis of enthusiastic receptions given Dreyfusard speakers, socialist Deputy Alexandre Zévaès said that by May 1899 there were Dreyfusard majorities in many large cities, including Marseille, Lyon, Lille, Saint-Etienne, and Grenoble. While his judgment was inadequately founded, it is significant that a Dreyfusard militant like Zévaès had this impression.[4]

The final sessions of the Cour de Cassation on the Dreyfus case coincided with the trial of Déroulède and Habert for attempting to overthrow the government. Premier Dupuy might have arranged this in order to balance the two predictable outcomes: reversal of Dreyfus's conviction and acquittal of the two Ligue des Patriotes leaders. The latter occurred on May 31, 1899, the former on June 3. Both occasioned much celebration and anger on the opposed sides. At the same time, the French commander at Fashoda the previous fall, Major Jean Baptiste Marchand, returned to France. Receiving a tumultuous hero's welcome in Paris on June 1, he said that France's humiliation by Britain in the Fashoda crisis had been the result of being fatally distracted and weakened by the Affair. Marchand repeated this charge many times in a speaking tour conducted on behalf of the anti-Dreyfusard campaign.

On June 4 President Loubet was assaulted at the Auteuil race course. On June 5 Zola returned to France and published an article called "Justice" in L'Aurore. On June 6 an anti-Semitic Deputy, Joseph Lasies, published an article in La Libre parole, calling upon the army to revolt. On June 9 Dreyfus and Picquart left their respective prisons, where the former had been kept for more than four years and the latter for close to one. On June 11 came the republican mass demonstration at Longchamp. And on June 12 the Dupuy government was voted out of office.

René Waldeck-Rousseau formed a new government on June 22. Minister of War was General Gaston de Galliffet, who was hated by the left as the "butcher" who had bloodily crushed the Paris Commune revolt in 1871. The Minister of Commerce and Industry was Alexandre Millerand, who was hated by the right as the first socialist Minister. And it was a scandal to socialists throughout Europe that one supposedly of their number should serve in a bourgeois government.

Despite these and other animosities, this was supposed to be a compromise "Government of Republican Defense," which would save the Third Republic by reconciling the opposed sides. That was its only program, and in the circumstances it was a courageous one.

Waldeck-Rousseau's government was the culmination of a trend that had been developing throughout the preceding year. Increasingly, republicans had come to believe—with good reason—that the survival of the Third Republic was seriously endangered. What at first had seemed to many a mere squabble fomented by a few troublemakers on each side came to be the central issue in public life for everyone. The extremity of the more violent anti-Dreyfusard polemics, the plotted coups, the urge to major constitutional revision even by moderate anti-Dreyfusards, all were gravely menacing. Belief that this was so seems to have spread from the summer of 1898 onward, with the resistance of anti-Dreyfusards to all disclosures of fact, the persecution of Picquart, the agitation over removal of the case from the Criminal Chamber, and continuing street violence all contributing to republican fears. Sooner or later, for most of them all other issues in contention were subordinated to "Republican defense." Waldeck-Rousseau, the conservative republican barrister, was the ideal person to lead the government when this attitude had matured.

Anti-Dreyfusards regarded the new regime as the instrument of the Syndicate. Rancor was extreme on June 26 at the first meeting of the Deputies after the Ministry was named; the vote of confidence there was close but positive. In the Senate the new government had overwhelming support. Meanwhile, the Ligue des Patriotes and Ligue Antisémitique prepared to remove the government with more forceful weapons than votes. They were closely observed by police spies.

Apparently Jules Guérin was planning a coup in concert with André Buffet, the principal agent of the royalist pretender, the Duc d'Orléans. It was to seize power for restoration of the Duc on the day General Mercier testified at Dreyfus's second court-martial, or on the day the verdict was rendered. The night before Mercier was to testify on August 12, 1899, police acting on Waldeck-Rousseau's orders conducted a sweep, arresting suspected plotters and radical right leaders. Thirty-seven were caught, including Buffet and Déroulède. Some escaped, including Guérin.

The Ligue Antisémitique chieftain had earlier purchased a house with Buffet's subsidies and had equipped it with arms and other supplies to withstand a seige. He called it "Fort Chabrol," after the street where it was located. Fleeing the police, Guérin and some confederates shut themselves into their fort and defied the police to take them by force. The police surrounded the house and, with Waldeck-Rousseau refusing to let them assault it, contented themselves with outlasting the men within. This frustrated Guérin's hope of inspiring support by making a heroic defense. Fort Chabrol surrendered ignominiously, its defenders split by squabbles, on September 20, the day after Dreyfus's release. That was not quite the end of Jules Guérin, however: In 1910 he died from pneumonia contracted while trying to save a drowning boy from the flooding Seine River.

A month earlier, during the Dreyfus retrial and the seige of Fort Chabrol, Paris saw its worst street combat in many years.

On Sunday, August 20, thousands of anarchists and anti-Semites met in repeated pitched battles. Focal points for conflict were the Place de la République, Fort Chabrol, and several churches, one of which was badly damaged by anarchists. Hundreds were injured and hundreds more were arrested.

On the same day, first word reached the Colonial Ministry in Paris of an extraordinarily bizarre and terrible episode that had been happening in Africa while the struggle raged in France. Crimes far more disgraceful than any attributed to Captain Dreyfus had been committed by two French captains, Voulet and Chanoine. The Army's honor was retrieved by the action of black colonial soldiers insisting that they themselves were French, at the same time the Army's honor and "alien" Jews were so much in contention in metropolitan France.

Voulet and Chanoine commanded an expedition to establish French control of territory in the African interior, now part of the Niger Republic, which until then had been largely unknown and unvisited by Europeans. On July 15, 1898, Voulet and Chanoine left Bordeaux with several subordinate white officers, going to the French colony of Senegal. After recruiting and training a force of black soldiers, they entered the Niger territory on January 3, 1899. They had six hundred black troops and about three times that number of porters, camp followers and, in time, captive women for use by the soldiers.

As this expedition moved east toward the interior, it waged a campaign of unprovoked terror. One town after another was destroyed and many thousands of people were slaughtered. Voulet and Chanoine also killed many of their own black personnel for minor infractions like using too many cartridges. Word of the carnage eventually reached French colonial authorities. While French expansion in Africa had regularly been cruel and bloody, this was excessive, and it endangered the expedition's mission. In early May 1899 Lieutenant Colonel Arsène Klobb was sent with a small force to overtake the expedition and intervene. By July 9 Klobb was close enough to announce his impending arrival to Voulet by sending couriers ahead to him.

Voulet told the couriers, "If it is because of my *galons* [insignia of rank] that the colonel is coming to shit all over me, I have no more need of my *galons*. Fuck my *galons*!" He then removed and destroyed the *galons* in a carefully prearranged ritual, which makes a nice parallel to removal of Dreyfus's insignia at his degradation four and a half years before. Voulet next said, "I'd rather die than see the colonel come in. The colonel has a father, mother, wife, children in France. Me, I have nothing, I fuck it all. Anyway, I shit upon the colonel." He sent the couriers back to Klobb with threats to receive him with gunfire.

On July 14, 1899—Bastille Day, the national holiday of the French Republic—Klobb caught up with Voulet and a part of his force. The captain had his troops shoot until all of Klobb's party had fallen or fled. Klobb was killed, and the one European with him, Lieutenant Octave Meynier, was wounded. Afterward Voulet declared to his officers, who had not been at the killings, that he was no longer French and would create a great and impregnable empire for himself in Africa, using his expeditionary force: "what I have done is only a coup d'état. If I were in Paris, I would today be master of France!" Chanoine, who had planned Klobb's killing with Voulet, immediately joined him. The other officers were placed under guard.

However, when Voulet told his black regular Army sergeants of his planned empire, they rebelled. Sergeant Souley Taraore said, "The captain has said we were no longer French. Yes! We are so!" The black soldiers killed both Voulet and Chanoine, then turned command over to the remaining white officers, who took the expedition on to complete its assigned mission.

When news of these events got back to France, it caused a major sensation. Klobb was made a hero, fallen bravely for France. *Le Figaro* collected public contributions for his widow and published lists of contributor names, as *La Libre parole* had done for Henry's widow—but this time the lists included many Jewish names, several Dreyfuses among them.

Every day more stories about the Voulet–Chanoine affair appeared on newspaper front pages all over France, right next to stories about the Dreyfus court-martial at Rennes. The first week of the sensation was one when a succession of Army officers perjured themselves in the Rennes courtroom, which also then heard the deposition of that honorable gentleman, ex-Major Esterhazy.

Neither then nor later was a connection or comparison made between these simultaneous developments, although the crimes of Voulet and Chanoine made a grotesque mockery of the defense of the Army's honor by their brother officers in Rennes. No one commented upon the fact that it was on Bastille Day that

Voulet killed Klobb and renounced France. There was no comment that Captain Chanoine was the son of the General Chanoine who as War Minister a year before had tried to block Revision. Nor was there comment when, in early October, some newspapers revealed another, comparatively minor African atrocity story in which the guilty officer had been General Mercier's son.

Many people refused to believe the stories about Voulet and Chanoine, even though the press reproduced and closely followed official Army reports. The disbelievers were anti-Dreyfusards, men no more able to tolerate the shameful truth here than truth in the Dreyfus Affair. The inability to hear the truth reflected the same attitudes in both cases.

A Deputy who had been a Dreyfusard, Paul Vigné d'Octon, conducted a campaign against French colonial atrocities, culminating in a powerful and dramatic speech in the Chamber of Deputies on November 23, 1900. This brought a prepared rejoinder from Joseph Lasies, the nationalist Deputy who on June 6, 1899, had urged the Army to rebel. Lasies denied that Voulet and Chanoine had committed the atrocities, and he simply ignored Klobb's murder and the renunciation of France by the two captains. He defended the Army's honor at length, as he had in the Dreyfus Affair, by twisting evidence in the most tortuous ways. To Lasies and a great many like him it was inconceivable that French officers of impeccable Catholic background could act as Voulet and Chanoine had—hence the captains had not really done it. The nationalists' delusions about Dreyfus and the Dreyfusards were more elaborate, and their patriotic resistance to truth much more violent and bizarre.

Anti-Dreyfusards' response to the Voulet-Chanoine affair, displayed by many and articulated eloquently by Joseph Lasies, reflects very well the determined commitment to preconceived beliefs so characteristic of the Dreyfus Affair. No Jews, no intellectuals, no known republicans were involved in the African episode. The facts were scarcely disputable and were attested to entirely by the Army itself. But if the events had really occurred, then the Army's honor might no longer be unassailable. The Army might not be a solid foundation for the nationalist ethos. Voulet and Chanoine were swiftly and conveniently forgotten, and their records disappeared from archives; one will find scant mention of them in French historical literature, and, in some places mentioned, Klobb's murder is shifted from Bastille Day to the day after. Voulet and Chanoine put a fitting period to the main struggle over Captain Dreyfus.[5]

When Dreyfus was condemned a second time, on September 9, 1899, what to do next was much disputed both in the Cabinet and among the Dreyfusard leaders. Of the ministers only the War Minister, General Galliffet, wanted the commutation of Dreyfus's sentence; the others thought the judicial process should continue. Determined to bring the struggle to a close, Gallifet got his way by threatening resignation;[6] he would later do the same to secure legislation for a general amnesty.

Most of the French were eager for relief from unending and unendurable crisis. They rejoiced in finding a chance to rest. When Galliffet sent his famous general order to the Army—"This incident is closed!"—the struggle may still not have ended, but the main crisis was over. While efforts to clear Dreyfus and Picquart continued, the elements that had made the conflict were diverted into other forms of expression. Alfred Dreyfus was no longer the principal focal point for contention, but France remained divided and at war with itself.

12

Continuing Aftershocks of the Affair

Bifurcation of French political factions into two sharply distinct camps continued after Dreyfus's release, perpetuating the alignments established in June 1899 to support or oppose Waldeck-Rousseau's Ministry of Republican Defense. To one side was the alliance of left republicans and socialists, banding together still to defend the Republic—and to exploit their unprecedented victory over their longtime opponents. To the other was a mixed bloc of rightists bound to one another by hostility to the Third Republic and its supposed disruption of organically integral nationality.

Also split in two was the large centrist group of moderate republicans that had dominated French politics during most of the two preceding decades, through opportune alliances with either the right or left, as circumstances changed. Defense of the Republic and victory over its deadly enemies were important enough to many moderates for them to adhere to the leftist bloc and maintain that adherance through much of the continuing struggle that followed. Former Premier Jules Méline led the rest of the moderates into alliance with the right in opposition to the Waldeck-Rousseau Ministry and its successors. These "Anti-Ministerial" republicans perceived that their own conservatism was more naturally and advantageously tied to that of the anti-Republican right, despite their differences.

Throughout the Affair conservatives had been driven by fear that Dreyfusard victory meant a major enhancement in the strength of the radical left, especially the socialists. Moderate republicans were socially conservative; their fear of social upheaval and even of social reform was a major factor inducing the opposition of many of them to both the Dreyfusards and the succession of primarily left republican governments beginning with that of Waldeck-Rousseau. The same fear was also potent for much of the rest of the right. It was reflected in Méline's January 22, 1898, attack in the Chamber of Deputies upon the socialists, which had precipitated Jaurès's furious rejoinder and the subsequent battle of the Deputies.

Now the governing bloc depended on socialist support for a majority and on Jaurès to marshal that support despite socialists' disinclination to sustain a bourgeois regime. Conviction that the Republic remained in peril kept the leftist bloc together for years and impelled it on a more radical course than any previous coalition had followed, although it did not in fact attempt any radical social reforms.

The bloc maintained a remarkable degree of solidarity—for a French political coalition. In time it organized a steering committee representing all participating factions and attempting to assure united action. Only this relative unity and the quirks of parliamentary and electoral politics enabled the left to prevail over the right, whose forces remained strong.

For a time the continuing power of the nationalists was evident in the massive, angry propaganda campaign that went on unabated and in their successes in the 1900 municipal and Senate elections. (General Mercier was one of those elected to the Senate then.) In the 1902 Chamber of Deputies elections the leftists strengthened their hold on power, but nationalists increased their Chamber seats also, both sides winning at the expense of the center. The total popular vote was evenly divided between the two blocs, but collaborative electoral tactics succeeded in winning more seats for the left, and a significantly more radical combination emerged in control of the Chamber. Waldeck-Rousseau retired from public life in June 1902, immediately after his coalition's election victory. He was succeeded by a left republican, Emile Combes. The bloc continued in power until January 1905, when a more centrist government was formed. Georges Clemenceau's first ministry lasted from October 1906 until July 1909 with little socialist support. Left republican Premiers (including several Dreyfusards) governed much of the time thereafter, until the Third Republic's fall in 1940. The Affair had produced a permanent shift in French politics, so that the left could have a major share in power.

As soon as Dreyfus had been released, the Ministry of Republican Defense set out to disarm the Republic's enemies. The government swiftly brought to trial those thought chiefly responsible for plotted coups d'état. Most were acquitted, but the Ligue des Patriotes chiefs, Déroulède and Habert, were condemned to exile, as was Buffet, the principal agent of the royalist pretender. Guérin of the Ligue Antisémitique and Fort Chabrol was sentenced to ten years in prison. Without their leaders, without Dreyfus, without internal coherence or effective organization, both leagues were doomed. The Ligue de la Patrie Française soon followed, but the Action Française remained to pick up its fallen banner.

Steps also were taken to bring the Army to heel. The first War Minister under Waldeck-Rousseau, General Galliffet, was no republican, but he purged the Army in order to restore it. Even more, Galliffet acted because of his disgusted contempt for the stupidity with which many officers had conducted themselves during the Affair. He transferred or retired a number of them, including some guilty of no more than indiscreet remarks. Galliffet also took steps to reduce the functions of the Statistical Section, but the remaining rump got into more mischief over the Dreyfus Affair anyway. The resulting scandal was trivial, but like so much else in the Affair it was blown up into a major confrontation between the opposed forces. The Ministry barely survived, and Galliffet resigned on May 28, 1900.

His successor was a solidly republican general, L.-J.-N. André, who was intent upon republicanizing, democratizing, and modernizing the Army. André undertook a variety of measures to accomplish all this, as well as initiating the first thorough search of Army files for evidence about the Dreyfus case. Among André's measures to transform the Army was taking into his own hands the decision of promotions and other preferments for all officers. Those preferred had to be demonstrably loyal republicans, and not practicing Catholics, whose political disloyalty was assumed. To learn the politics of officers, André sought and kept records of information from government administrators, police, and political organizations, including the Ligue des Droits and the Freemasons.

The last group was very active in finding informants and tattlers. The Masons collected and transmitted to the War Ministry some twenty-five thousand record cards. After the four years of this, one of the Masons involved sold the secret of the informant system with some of the record cards to two nationalist Deputies, Gabriel Syveton and Jean Guyot de Villeneuve.

It was a perfect scandal: satanic Freemasonry, political espionage, and cutthroat republicans combined in dishonorable machinations against the men upon whom France relied for survival! In October and November 1904 the right made the most of this *affaire des fiches* [record cards]. André had to resign and the Combes government was so damaged that it fell two months later.

Combes was saved temporarily by Jaurès and by Syveton himself. Jaurès successfully urged all good republicans to stand fast against the right's attack. His oratory would not have sufficed, however, had not Syveton outraged many by slapping General André in the Chamber of Deputies, thus winning sympathy for the general.

In April 1903 parliamentary inquiry into the propriety of Syveton's election had provided Jaurès with the opportunity he seized to reopen the Dreyfus case to a new official review. (Jaurès managed to connect a campaign poster to alleged faults in the conduct of the Rennes court-martial.) Now, the trial of Syveton for assaulting André might yield enough scandal to provide the right with the opportunity to upset the ruling leftist bloc. Syveton prevented that by killing himself the day before he was to go to court. Of course, many said it was murder, but he had ample motivation for suicide: It had just been discovered that he had embezzled large sums from the Ligue de la Patrie Française, of which he was secretary, and that he had had illicit sexual relations with his daughter-in-law.

The scandal over the political loyalty system for Army officers had graver consequences than the embarrassment of the
Combes government, which probably would not have survived
much longer anyway. It greatly aggravated the hostility between
those who believed the Army to be the vital center of the nation
and the left, which supposedly had been bent upon destroying
the Army since the Affair began. Also deepened were animosities within the officer corps between republicans and the rest.
Both inside the Army and out the enmity had been worsened as
well by the use of soldiers in inventories and seizure of Catholic
Church property, in the campaign against the Church described
below. Some officers refused to command such operations and
had resigned or been broken in consequence.

Moreover, the moral sleaziness of the secret political informant system repelled many on the left also. The scandal contributed to the growing belief of some that participants in the ruling
bloc, including Jaurès, were cynical opportunists who had
turned the noble Dreyfusard crusade into a dirty pursuit of self-
interested political gain. This judgment was much reinforced by
the bloc's simultaneous anticlerical campaign.

While most republicans wanted only to republicanize the
Army and not at all to destroy it, it was easy for the right to argue
plausibly that destruction was the real aim. Antimilitarist propaganda assaults were waged with increasing intensity by some
on the left, and the government undertook to reduce the term of
required military service from three years to two. This measure,
finally enacted after long and bitter debate in April 1905, *looked*
antimilitarist whatever the intentions of its backers.

Like other divisive issues, the continuing conflict over the
Army was not only a matter of genuine substance but also an
excuse for invective. With the Dreyfus Affair no longer an important arena for contention, the still hostile factions were eager
for occasions to do battle and for targets that seemed vulnerable
to attack.

The victory of the left republicans and their enjoyment of its
fruits added a note of desperation to the polemics of the right.
The rapid decline and demise of the Affair's rightist leagues increased the dismay of many on the right. Moreover, many conservatives found cause to fear imminent social revolution, not
only because of the left's success overall, but especially because
of real and imagined increments in socialist strength and through

fears aroused by a rapid growth in labor disturbances, strikes, and violence. This stimulated more urgent activism by the right, even as hopes for changing or replacing the Third Republic receded. In practice the ministries of the republican left remained socially conservative, but the right tended to see foretastes of social revolution in any suggestion by the left of populist words or action.

However, there was one principal factor drawing together the diverse political factions: severe anxiety over France's apparent isolation in international power politics. Russia appeared to be too weak, disinterested, and politically alien for the Franco-Russian alliance to provide any real protection. Diplomatic efforts to reduce hostility from Germany and Austria had proved futile. Relations with Great Britain were more severely strained than ever, especially with Anglo-French competition in securing African colonial territory and France's open favoring of the South African Boers in their war with Britain (1899–1902). The Spanish–American War (1898) had demonstrated the power of the United States, which had been antagonized by France's favoring Spain. Relations with Italy were also poor.

Anxiety over isolation had been a significant factor throughout the Affair, especially through fears that the Dreyfusard campaign would cause further deterioration of France's international position. The concern had aggravated reaction against criticism of the Army and had contributed to the Méline government's reluctance to allow reopening of the Dreyfus case. Nevertheless, much of the time effects of this anxiety were not readily evident, except in connection with the Fashoda crisis and in some of the exaggerated claims of anti-Dreyfusard invective.

Concern about Francophobia abroad and French isolation did become apparent with the second conviction of Dreyfus at Rennes. The trial there had been closely followed in the press all over the Western world.

> " '. . . If I was president iv this coort-martial, I'd say to Cap Dhryfuss: "Cap, get out. Ye may not be a thraitor, but ye're worse. Ye're become a bore." An' I'd give him money enough to lave th' counthry. Thin I'd sind th' gin'ral staff off to some quiet counthry village where they'd be free fr'm rumors iv war, an' have nawthin' else to do but set around in rockin'-chairs an' play with th' cat. Thin I'd cut th' cable to England; an' thin I'd gather all the journalists iv Paris together, an' I'd

say, "Gintlemen," I'd say, "th' press is th' palajeem iv our liberties," I'd say; "but our liberties no longer requires a palajeem," I'd say. "This wan, whativer it means, is frayed at th' risbands, an' th' buttonholes is broken, annyhow," I'd say. "I've bought all iv ye tickets to Johannisberg," I'd say, "an' ye'll be shipped there tonight," I'd say. "Ye'er confreres iv that gr-reat city is worn out with their exertions, an' ye'll find plenty iv wurruk to do. In fact, those iv ye that're anti-Seemites 'll niver lack imployment," I'd say. "Hinceforth Fr-rance will be free—fr'm th' likes iv ye," I'd say. An' th' nex' mornin' Paris 'd awake ca'm an' peaceful, with no newspapers, an' there 'd be more room in our own papers f'r th' base-ball news,' says I.

" 'But . . . what ye propose 'd depopylate France,' says th' prisident.

" 'If that's th' case,' says I, 'Fr-rance ought to be depopylated,' I says. 'I've been thinkin' that's th' on'y way it can be made fit to liv in f'r a man fr'm Chicago.' . . ." [Martin Dooley, commenting on the Rennes trial in the *Chicago Journal*, 1899].[1]

Dreyfus's renewed condemnation produced very wide and intense outrage, especially in Britain and the United States. In addition to newspaper attacks on France, there was extensive popular protest, including public meetings, violence against French property and persons, a flood of sympathy letters to Madame Dreyfus, and even the gesture of selecting a Jewish woman as Carnival Queen in Wichita, Kansas.[2]

Immediately there was much sentiment abroad for a boycott of the Paris Exposition of 1900. This huge display, which in fact became the grandest world's fair ever held, had been in preparation for years, and the French had much staked upon it. A boycott would have been regarded as a terrible disaster, not least because it would have seemed to be final proof of how utterly isolated and vulnerable France had become. Moreover, the French were too proud of their nation's supposed world cultural leadership to endure a failure of the Exposition. Fear of the boycott added to the pressure on the Cabinet and President Loubet to free Dreyfus and to terminate the Affair through amnesty legislation.

Three days after Dreyfus was condemned, Judet wrote in *Le Petit journal* that there should be silence about the Affair thenceforth, to save the Exposition and restore French international prestige. A similar position was taken by many others on both sides of the struggle, and in the next year there was frequent talk of "the Exposition's truce." Conflict between opponents in the Affair was attenuated, and the feared boycott was avoided. The Exposition and concern about France's international position could not really change the divisions within the country, but they did serve to restrain many from aggravating enmity.

Nevertheless, this moderating force was counteracted and nearly overwhelmed by the concerted anticlerical campaign initiated by the leftist bloc as the main element in its program of Republican Defense. On November 11, 1899, police seized officers of *La Croix* across the country, and action was undertaken to dissolve the Assumptionist order, whose very existence had never been legally authorized. The government could no longer tolerate the propaganda of *La Croix* and the extensive aid, including large sums of money, given to anti-Republican political figures by the order.

In January 1900 a judicial decree dissolved the Assumptionists, dispersing the order's priests abroad or to assignment as secular clergy. Several prelates and other clerics who openly expressed sympathy with the order were punished by suspension of their salaries, which ordinarily were paid by the state. However, *La Croix* continued publication, because timely Papal intervention had secured the transfer to laymen of its ownership and operation.

All other Catholic religious orders were also immediately the objects of action by the Ministry of Republican Defense. The orders and their members, both male and female, were very numerous and played most important roles serving both the Church and French society. They were subject to control by a complex of poorly enforced laws, according to which the actual existence in France of most of the orders was illegal. The Jesuits had been expelled from the country in 1880 and by 1898 were back in full force, to become in anticlerical eyes the most formidable of enemies, villains still worse than the Assumptionists.

On November 14, 1899, three days after police seized *La Croix*'s offices, Waldeck-Rousseau introduced legislation in the Chamber of Deputies that was intended to curb the religious orders. He claimed that the proposed bill was necessary for the Republic's "self-preservation." In his conception, the law would have provided for dissolution of genuinely threatening religious orders and the systematic, determined regulation of the rest, according to legal principles long established but not usually enforced for these orders.

As the legislation moved along a very tortuous road to enactment and then enforcement, its character shifted. It became an act for exorcising devils and punishing evil, past and present, real and mythical. It was almost two years before enactment of the legislation was fully accomplished, on July 1, 1901. Much of the rancor of the Dreyfus Affair was carried over to the contest over passage and application of this law.

Thus, with the Affair still festering, there was ample occasion in current controversy for expression of the same opposed attitudes and ideologies that had made the struggle over Dreyfus so intense. The anticlerical campaign occasioned the most acrimonious conflict, which was further aggravated by disputes over the Army and by conservative fear and fury about the power of the left republican bloc and rising socialism. Anti-Dreyfusards' fears about threats to the nation's vital foundations, the Church and the Army, seemed to have found all too dreadful realization, while most Dreyfusards were determined to crush the forces of reaction and obscurantism that stood in the way of progress.

Initially, the new law regulating religious orders was applied by Waldeck-Rousseau firmly but with some restraint. While many of the orders were dissolved and dispersed, he conducted the process slowly and provoked only limited active resistance. However, when he resigned eleven months later, the new Premier, Emile Combes, was determined to apply the law with urgent and unrelenting rigor. Every effort was made to suppress teaching and preaching orders, while charitable and nursing orders were often tolerated. Catholic schools relying for teachers upon religious orders were closed. Protesting clerics suffered punitive actions, especially removal of their state salaries. The Combes government's anticlerical policy was not altogether draconian, but it did provoke extensive outrage. There were even anticlerical republicans who thought the policy excessively vindictive, displaying the worst passions that discredited republican politics.

Official efforts against the Church developed progressively as additional measures were taken or advocated. The campaign was met by increasingly intransigent resistance from the Vatican, especially after the election of Pope Pius X in August 1903. A century-old concordat guaranteed Catholicism in France the extensive privileges of a state church but also subjected it extensively to secular authority. Now the State's claims of authority over the Church in France conflicted sharply with those of the Vatican. This conflict intensified through provocative actions by both sides, drawing them toward a conclusion that few on either side had originally sought. The French government terminated all relations with the Vatican in August 1904. By then movement toward separation of Church and State was well under way, with a momentum unaltered by Combes being forced from office. In December 1905 the new government enacted legislation ending Catholicism's status as the State Church.

Dissolution of religious orders and the separation law had a highly visible impact in every corner of France. Catholic institutions were closed by the thousands. Priests, nuns, and brothers were dispersed by the tens of thousands, going abroad or at least away from the lay communities where they were known and often esteemed. Catholic schools disappeared in many places. Much valuable property was confiscated. State-conducted inventories of the rest were alarming and provocative to the faithful.

When, as often happened, these actions were physically resisted by lay persons, monks, or nuns, then the State enforced its will with the police and the Army. Both law and administrative regulations provided for alternatives to closed schools and State financial support of the Church—but acceptance of these substitutes was bitterly resisted.

All of this greatly reinforced the antagonism between the Republic and the many who thought the Church vital to the French nation. In the long run the Church benefited immeasurably from its forced independence, which compelled it to restore and reform its own internal resources. The anticlerical laws proved to be a priceless boon to French Catholicism, but comparatively few could see that this might be the outcome. The animosities released and concentrated in the Affair bore fruit in the 1899–1905 anticlerical campaign, leaving a long persistent ground for continuing severe conflict.

At the same time, political anti-Semitism in France declined with startling suddenness. Animosity toward Jews did not disappear, but it ceased to play an important part in political discourse and action. Those who continued to make anti-Semitism the center of their political activity lost nearly all their influence.

Most organizations and publications that had exploited anti-Semitism in this way vanished. *La Libre parole* survived, but with few readers. Edouard Drumont became as obscure as he had once been notorious, and his associates slipped away. After reaching peak intensity in 1898–99, political anti-Semitism collapsed; by 1906 it was essentially finished as a distinct species of politics.

Anti-Semitism in French politics continued only as a subordinate accessory to the dominant themes of polemic by some on the right and as a casual expression of enduring prejudice. Candidates for elected office no longer campaigned successfully as anti-Semites. Of the many publications, organizations, and individuals that had heavily stressed anti-Semitism during the Affair, the surviving ones and the successors to those that failed generally shifted away from that emphasis.

Frenchmen admiring and collaborating with the Nazis revived political anti-Semitism in the 1930s and 1940s. They proved ready enough to treat Jews cruelly and to contribute to their slaughter. The grounds for hatred of Jews had not disappeared after 1899, but anti-Semitism could no longer sustain rightist politics until the Nazis added new dimensions to the political picture in France.

During the 1880s and 1890s political anti-Semitism in France had paralleled that in Central and Eastern Europe; although the French version was less potent, in the Dreyfus Affair it temporarily found comparable or greater intensity. Yet east of the Rhine, anti-Semitism retained much of its force in politics long after its sudden collapse in France, a contrast constituting a puzzle for which solutions offered must be partly speculative.[3]

Political anti-Semitism has varied in extent, intensity, and impact because it involves a conjunction of elements that occur in very different combinations according to time and place. Fundamental have been the fears, rage, and dread of anti-Semites about themselves and about perceived threats and losses, with which the despised Jews have had little if anything to do. Much of this has involved defensive reactions against modernity, although the circumstances for this varied greatly from those already described for France to those which prevailed in contemporary Russia or in territories in between.

Anti-Semitic reaction has taken its specific forms according to distinct conditions of social and political reality, in which many factors including the actual presence and roles of Jews have had determining parts. Substantial political anti-Semitism entails organized action, usually appealing effectively to substantial segments of the population, although in imperial Russia it was more a matter of official manipulation of a largely inchoate polity. In this it was important that French Jews were so few, because there was scarcely anything in social reality to bolster the political efforts of organized anti-Semitism. In particular, with no Jews at all in most of the French countryside, it proved too difficult to establish the enduring agrarian base that supported political anti-Semitism to the east. Potent though they were for the French, the myths of Drumont and the counter-Revolutionary priests were not a substitute for the lightning rods of enmity offered by local Jewish merchants, money-lenders, and communities in Germany and the Austro-Hungarian and Russian Empires.

French anti-Semitic organizations were incompetently led and failed to exploit very effectively the opportunities given them when the Dreyfus Affair aroused extraordinary passion. One can thus ascribe anti-Semitism's quick decline in part to accidents like Guérin's corruption and Drumont's shortcomings as a leader. However, with more favorable conditions of political and social reality, anti-Semites would have found able leaders or would have flourished without them.

While anti-Semitic propaganda flourished in France for about a decade and a half, other organized anti-Semitism succeeded only briefly, while the Affair sustained it. There emerged no larger movement incorporating anti-Semitism as one of several core theses, although experience in Central Europe suggests that this was essential to the enduring organizational success of anti-Semitism itself. There were perceptible reasons for this, in addition to the lack of a social base where an actual Jewish presence could be widely felt.

France did have the semblance of a liberal order, however unevenly established, which could accommodate diverse interests more readily than could most other regimes and societies. Antagonisms could thus be more quickly attenuated and contained, or even left behind because grievances had been redressed or outgrown. This did happen with some of the enmity in the Dreyfus Affair, even though substantial portions of it persisted.

Moreover, universalist humanism was well established among the country's compelling traditions, even though not all of the French were equally compelled by it. France was enough of a liberal, and thus tolerant, order that the mentality and political positions most common among public men did not accommodate extreme anti-Semitism readily, however common comparatively mild prejudice may have been. It is difficult to imagine a contemporary German right without anti-Semitism, yet much of the French right displayed rather little of it before or after the 1890s. Likewise, liberal efforts to condemn anti-Semitism as altogether contemptible made an especially profound impact upon many of the French, in part because the Affair's trauma moved them as rhetoric alone could not.

Perhaps the cleavage between friends and enemies of the liberal, parliamentary Third Republic did not leave much room for anti-Semitism. The terms of struggle that division engendered may not have been ones to which anti-Semitism could be closely linked, except temporarily and in special circumstances like those of the Affair. At the least, it is clear that one part of this cleavage, the opposition between anticlericals and clericals, provided a way of displacing animosities that might otherwise have gone into anti-Semitism. Moreover, there were alternatives to anti-Semitism in anti-Masonism and anti-Protestantism, which did have some genuine basis in political reality, since anticlericalism found much of its strength among Masons and Protestants. Catholic hostility to the Republic continued to be associated with anti-Masonic and, to a lesser degree, anti-Protestant demonology.

The Dreyfus Affair has been accorded a central place in retrospective views of anti-Semitism; although it probably merits some such position, the role played in the Affair by anti-Semitism has been misunderstood. Alfred Dreyfus was not persecuted because he was Jewish: The decisive factors in actions by officials against him would have been little if any altered had he been a Gentile. They had motivations that were more compelling than any prejudice in determining their conduct: The need of Army officers to be right and to protect themselves and the Army, the desire of Ministers to avoid both domestic and international political losses.

The struggle over Captain Dreyfus did acquire much of its character from anti-Semitic furor and reaction to it. Yet the furor

and reaction were the exterior expression of a fundamenta
position of attitudes and ideas in which Jews were really u
portant. That opposition could have found alternative expression
in bitter struggle had Dreyfus been a Gentile, especially if he
were not a practicing Catholic. Anti-Semitism gave the struggle
an intensity and viciousness that probably would not have been
approached otherwise: The heat and cruelty of passion against
Jews far exceeded that against substitutes available to the French.
Nevertheless, in political terms Jews were just convenient symbols, for whom there were functional equivalents, and not the
essential vehicles for developing the ideas and attitudes that
were expressed through anti-Semitism.

To say this is not to diminish the significance of the Affair's
anti-Semitism but rather to modify understanding of how and
why it was effective. Moreover, it remains important still to recognize how potent anti-Semitism could be in a comparatively
liberal political order, in a society where enmity against Jews had
been subdued and relatively innocuous. Terrible rancor was not
confined to Slavs and Germans or to repressive regimes under
which freedom and toleration had not taken root.

France was supposed to lead the world in establishing liberty; if Jews could not be accepted even there, then how could
they hope to live as a minority among Gentiles anywhere? Anguish over this question resulted in the Dreyfus Affair's giving
twentieth-century Zionism its single most powerful impetus before the advent of the Third Reich. Theodor Herzl and others
who reshaped Zionism into the form it assumed after 1900 had
been profoundly impressed by the Affair's anti-Semitism. In
1894 Herzl was in Paris as a correspondent for the *Neue Freie
Presse* of Vienna. He covered the Dreyfus Affair in its early period and was much moved by the cruelty of the ritual degradation of January 5, 1895, and by the apparently innocent conduct
of Dreyfus there. The experience stimulated him to complete his
transition from assimilated Jewish intellectual to visionary leading his people to Zion. In 1896 he published Zionism's principal
manifesto, *Der Judenstaat*. When Dreyfus was condemned again
at Rennes, Herzl saw in his tragedy poignant support for the new
Zionism's inspiration: Assimilation was a hopeless strategy for
Jews, since none had tried harder to assimilate nor experienced
greater disaster in the attempt than did Alfred Dreyfus.[4]

The Dreyfus Affair provided much of the impulse giving

new vigor and direction to a pre-existing movement, Zionism, where a singular intellect, Herzl's, played the decisive role in rendering the old into new form. Much the same can be said for a very different movement, the Action Française, which transformed the French right with a new structure conceived above all by another singular intellect, that of Charles Maurras.

This movement began in the spring of 1898 with the formation of an initially insignificant committee by two young men of letters, Maurice Pujo and Henri Vaugeois, reacting against the Dreyfusard campaign. A year later the Action Française began to gather force, with the addition of Maurras and other men of letters. They believed the Ligue de la Patrie Française to be too faint-hearted and uncertain a vehicle to carry the nation's banner in contention against the Dreyfusard intellectuals.

Although the other early adherants of the Action Française had not before been royalists, Maurras managed nevertheless to convert them and to make the movement's explicit primary purpose the restoration of monarchy. In place of the old, sometimes blindly reflexive loyalties that had long motivated royalists, Maurras and the Action Française employed coldly reasoned logic, which led them to the conclusion that a stable national order had to rest upon foundations of hereditary monarchy and the Catholic Church. The Action Française proclaimed itself ready to undertake revolutionary action to realize this goal. The movement was more radical in its pretensions than in its deeds, but it was nevertheless a sharp departure from the conservatism of more traditional royalists.

Maurras fashioned a systematic and compelling ideology from a combination of valid and fallacious logic. Like many another anti-Dreyfusard, he often took unfounded propositions and provided impressive but specious arguments to rationalize them. He was a master of sophistry, but his theory had more substantial strengths as well.

This ideology provide a solid, extensively elaborated, and well-integrated basis for renewal of the nationalist right of the 1890s, including many of its radical populist elements, and for traditional royalism. Only the latter had had a well-formed ideology, and that was ill-adapted to the twentieth century.

What Maurras and his associates really did was isolate most of the elements that had given anti-Dreyfusard thought and attitudes their main force, and build for them a new structure independent of the incidents and controversy peculiar to the Dreyfus case itself. In this revised form the ideology achieved a coherence and adaptability to changing circumstances that had been lacking before.

Although the Action Française never got anywhere close to securing control of the State itself, it was the French right's fountainhead of thought until its entire approach was discredited along with the Vichy regime in 1944. Many rightists who did not accept Maurrasian royalism or the movement's extremism found in the Action Française the principal genius of their political vision. And men of ideas drawn to fascism in France began with the Action Française, moving away from it only because they did not find it revolutionary enough.

In January 1945, after Vichy's collapse, the new regime put Charles Maurras on trial for criminal "intelligence with the enemy." The charge, its lack of genuine substance, the conduct of the trial, and the sentence all resembled those in the Dreyfus case. When condemned to degradation and life imprisonment, the seventy-six-year-old Maurras exclaimed, "It's the revenge of Dreyfus!" There was also a campaign for revision of this condemnation, with Maurras finally released in 1952 and dying later that year. Given these parallels and his earlier role, one might say that the Affair itself died at last only when he did.

Maurrasian ideology and continuing conflict over anticlericalism and other issues helped to keep many conservatives hostile to most of what they thought the Third Republic represented. However, outside the immediate orbit of the Action Française, the right increasingly became inured to accepting the Republic without substantial constitutional revision, as inevitably the system within which political struggle would continue.

In the 1890s monarchist politicians had muted their advocacy of restoration, many of them ceasing to identify themselves as monarchists; both Papal injunction and their resignation to the inevitable induced the change. At the same time, however, radical right nationalists had energetically demanded constitutional revisions toward more authoritarian government. Typically these "revisionists" were also strident anti-Semites, with their antiplutocratic populism closely tied to antiparliamentarism and antiliberalism.

During the upheaval of the Dreyfus Affair, much of this radical, anti-Republican nationalism (and its anti-Semitism) had

captured the sometime monarchists and many conservative republicans, including most of the members of the Ligue de la
Patrie Française. In the aftermath of the Affair, the drive of radical nationalism to overturn or transform the Third Republic no
longer made much sense. The left republican bloc was too strong,
and such immediate needs as fighting the anticlerical and anti-
military campaigns were too urgent. The frenetic nationalism
animating the rightist leagues declined, while the leagues themselves disappeared. Although the Action Française conserved
much of that type of nationalism in revised form, years passed
before the new organization gained much influence. Not before
the mid-1930s did dissatisfaction with the Republic again put it
in jeopardy.

The anti-Republican nationalism of militant anti-Dreyfusards declined for much the same reasons as did the anti-
Semitism associated with it: lack of a continuing basis in political
and social reality, displacement by competing factors in political
conflict, and the genuine power of liberal traditions in French
political culture. However, a reconstituted and more broadly
based nationalism developed gradually in France from 1905 onward. It resulted especially from a growing fear of war, war in
dangerously disadvantageous circumstances.

Fear of social revolution also contributed to nationalist sentiment; this fear was intensified by labor's and socialism's growing challenges, and it strengthened desires for the stable and
authoritative order sought by conservative nationalists. Even left
republicans were moved by this reconstituted nationalism. Enjoyment of power made them more cautious and less sympathetic
to the "dangerous" masses they had sometimes championed,
thus making them more concerned with order and authority also.
Besides, most left republicans had been ardent nationalists of an
older type, until the radical right had temporarily made the label
"nationalist" its exclusive property.[5]

The final exoneration of Alfred Dreyfus in 1906 coincided
approximately and fortuitously with the end of an era resulting
from the Affair. Beginning with Waldeck-Rousseau's moves in
the fall of 1899 against supposed plotters and clerical orders, "Republican Defense" had quickly become a drive by left republicans taking advantage of their victory to secure their own power
as well as the Republic. By 1906 such defense of the Republic no
longer seemed necessary. The Church, the anti-Semites, and the

nationalist demogogues had been beaten, and defense again foreign enemies and social revolution were the more urgent tasks. Georges Clemenceau became Premier, but without depending upon coalition with the socialists, whose constituents he subjected to ruthless suppression in antistrike actions. Georges Picquart became War Minister, but his tenure had scarcely more than incidental and perhaps misleading symbolic significance.

Between 1898 and 1906 the character of French politics had been transformed. The much-increased power of the left secured the Third Republic and the forms of liberal democracy as they had never been secured before. In parliamentary politics, the complex of partisan divisions had shifted, with the ever mobile center fluctuating around a new point well to the left of earlier fulcrums. While the attitudes of the still deeply divided French changed much more slowly, these attitudes found political expression now in circumstances that had changed so quickly and profoundly that some spoke of the "Dreyfus Revolution."

However, great as these changes were, they were not what mattered most fundamentally to those who had been intensely engaged by the Affair, especially the intellectuals. They had been aroused by a contest over their basic convictions, which had been challenged by their opponents. Contestants on each side had hoped to see their most sacred beliefs emerge from the conflict as the principles that really directed French social and political life. These challenges and hopes created the Affair's intense excitement and occasional desperation, and they made engagement on either side a crusade. For many, and above all for intellectuals who were not professional politicians, ideological upheaval and crusade seemed to have amounted to a revolutionary transformation, a much more profound revolution than the changes wrought in practical partisan politics.

Indeed, the practical victories of the left distressed many Dreyfusards nearly as much as they did anti-Dreyfusards. The intellectuals' crusade for principle seemed debased by the policies of the leftist parliamentary bloc and Ministries, and by the virulence with which many on the left continued to attack their opponents to the right. This distress of the intellectuals found its most powerful and celebrated expression in the writing of that pivotal figure of the "cerebral left," Charles Péguy, and of two of his intimates, Daniel Halévy and Georges Sorel. However, it was

often expressed elsewhere as well, even by some moderate, prag-
matic persons like Joseph Reinach.[6]

Exaltation of their efforts and hopes into something holy was
typified by Péguy's later emphasis upon *"our* mystique" and
"their politics"—the vindictive and opportunistic policies of the
left in parliament and the press. He wrote in 1910 of "the contam-
ination, the degeneration, the dishonor, the diversion, the degradation of our mystique into politics." Péguy was especially
hurt and outraged by those who sought to "play the double
game," to "take advantage together of their politics and our mystique, to play together the temporal and the eternal." Emphasizing especially but not solely the demogogic and persecutory
anticlericalism of the past decade, he wrote:

> It must never be forgotten that Combism [the spirit of Premier
> Emile Combes's policy], the Combist system, the Comb-
> ist tyranny, from which come all these evils, has been an
> invention of Jaurès, that it is Jaurès who, by this detestable
> political force, by his oratorical force, by his parliamentary
> force, has imposed this invention, this tyranny on the coun-
> try.[7]

Jean Jaurès was the chief villain because he had been their
cherished leader, exemplar of the best in intellectual socialism.
During the Affair's heroic hours he had frequented and dominated gatherings of the "cerebral left" at Péguy's shop and the
Ecole Normale Supérieure. Then it had been grand that Jaurès
sought as always to put ideals into practice, but now it was
betrayal. The Affair's struggle had left no room for compromise,
but more ordinary political practice demanded it, degrading the
mystique.

Péguy's lament and rage remain very moving, but he was
wrong in thinking there had been a gulf between noble idealism
and cynical opportunism in the Affair and its aftermath. (Halévy
was more sensitive to the ambiguity of the differences, but Sorel
and other disillusioned intellectuals were even more harshly reactive than Péguy.) In the Affair the demands of ideals could for
a time coincide with the most urgent demands of immediate
political practice. Jaurès and Reinach, Clemenceau and Herr,
Péguy and Scheurer-Kestner: Such men were fitted by neither
intellect nor political partisanship to make common cause in or-

dinary times, but in the struggle both intellect and partisanship drove them to fight side by side. Much the same can be said for the likes of Brunetière, De Mun, Barrès, and even, with qualifications, Rochefort, Drumont, and Déroulède.

The struggle had been fought simultaneously and without distinction at several levels, with debate over evidence and law important mainly as the basis for fighting over greater issues. For all parties except the anarchists, the object of most immediate importance was control of the government of France. Dreyfusards wanted to prevent the right from subverting the Republic and to remove obstacles to republicanism offered by entrenched powers, especially the Army and the Church. Whether actively anti-Dreyfusard or not, conservatives wanted to prevent increased strength and even domination by the left, especially the socialists. Anti-Dreyfusards wanted to restore and enhance the strength of those institutions they thought essential to national life, especially the Army and the Church, and to reduce or eliminate the strength of all that sapped national vitality, especially the forces represented by the "diabolical trinity." Many wanted also to alter the Republic's basic identity, so that republicanism really was in jeopardy, even if conspirators plotting coups did not themselves pose a grave threat.

In all of this personal self-interest was often involved, whether in calculating one's chances in the next election, in quests for ego-satisfying celebrity, in long-term benefits hoped for from the success of one's faction, or even in gratification derived from injuring one's enemies. Yet many risked more than they stood to gain, or engaged themselves more deeply than called for by self-interest. More important, it is quite clear from their words and deeds that most thought the stakes to be much greater than those of personal advantage. Even the exploitation of victory so much condemned by Péguy and others was more an effort to secure the Republic in regular practice than to secure the power of individual victors and their factions. Jaurès was no different when condemned by Péguy in 1910 from the Jaurès of 1898 who fought for an unpopular cause, though it probably assured the election defeat he suffered that year.

Dreyfusards *knew* they were fighting for more than parliamentary majority and putting Jesuits and aristocratic officers in their proper places. As Clemenceau put it in a passage already quoted:

And, in this frightful combat of all the tyrannies on earth against the creature in distress, what recourse for the weakness of one man alone come to grips with the vastness of the sovereign powers? Nothing but ideas, abstractions. . . . Ideas, words, but magical words all the same. . . .

Justice, a little word indeed! The greatest of all. . . . A fine word . . . which man cannot hear without finding himself larger, without feeling himself better. . . . Word stronger than force, by means of hope.

With this word for our entire armament, we have joined battle.[8]

Ideas mattered because through them personal attitudes and self-interest were transcended and positions were assumed for joint action. Ideas mattered because cultivated people had learned to prize them, play with them, joust with them, define and illuminate their compelling traditions with them. Dreyfusards were men of ideas, except for some of the plebeian socialists and anarchists who, though employing ideas, did not live by and for them so fully.

"Justice" subsumed all other ideas Dreyfusards thought to be at issue in the Affair. At other times differences over social and economic policy would establish substantial disparities in visions of justice held by collaborators in this cause; Jaurès, Clemenceau, and Reinach had been opponents before and would be again. Yet, despite differences, they all believed that every citizen had to be guaranteed rights and fair treatment, that government should exist primarily to establish those guarantees, and that the Third Republic was the best means yet for providing such government.

This vision of justice demanded that it be universal, rational, lawful, and never subordinated to other political considerations. When Dreyfus was denied justice because he was Jewish, then universality was lost, and any citizen might also be denied justice because he was not the right sort of person. When the overwhelming weight of evidence was rejected, then justice's rationality was denied. When for Dreyfus the law was ignored, then justice's lawfulness was denied. When it was claimed that Dreyfus's fate mattered less than the superior needs of the State or Army, then justice as the supreme purpose of government was denied, and all citizens would be at the mercy of the authorities established at the moment.

The anti-Semitic furor, the general retailing of calumny and fallacy in the face of incontrovertibly demonstrated truth, the obdurate refusal of the Méline government to allow reopening of the Dreyfus case, the submersion of Dreyfus's claims beneath those made irrationally for Army and Nation—all of these aroused Dreyfusards to holy war, a war to save justice from its deadly enemies. The real and imagined machinations of General Staff officers, clerical orders, secret conspiracies, and the anti-Dreyfusard leagues seemed to be especially dangerous threats, making the struggle all the more desperate. The most ardent Dreyfusards had little doubt that the whole future of France and even of humanity would be determined by the struggle.

All this aroused extraordinary exaltation and commitment, and among many intellectuals it led to something more. Engaged by politics as never before, they found the Republic too weak and uncertain a guarantee of justice. They discovered in the social conservatism of most republicans, even Dreyfusards, too little concern for rendering justice to the poor and weak, too little disposition to correct the iniquities of maldistributed wealth. To an extent never before seen in France, bourgeois intellectuals became socialists, following the example of the few like Jaurès and Herr who had earlier come to the same perspective.

For such socialist intellectuals the Dreyfus Affair became a stage in crusading for socialism. It was not enough to preserve the Republic: They had to transcend it. Many thus began a life-long devotion to socialism, establishing a tradition in France of intellectuals associated with socialism and, later, communism. Often they remained outside any party, and their attachment was frequently too cerebral for them to be effective militants in plebeian movements, but they lent themselves to the cause as best they could. In the immediate aftermath of the Affair many turned to formation of "Universités Populaires" and other projects for popular education and indoctrination, as well as to using their talents in a more general war of words.

Beginning this transcendence was the real Dreyfus Revolution for these socialist intellectuals. Jean Jaurès and other moderate socialist politicians concentrated upon securing whatever gains could be won within the existing political system. Transcendence demanded something more, though perhaps not immediate overthrow of the existing order. Thus Jaurès had betrayed those he had done so much to arouse. Some of them turned away permanently from reformist socialism, to the revolutionary syndicalism then on the rise or to other substitutes for the mystique they had found in the Affair's heroic years, from the autumn of 1897 to the autumn of 1899.

Few anti-Dreyfusards were consumed by such intense engagement. Although clearly the struggle mattered greatly to them as well, they gave less of themselves to it and were less likely to find that it had transformed their lives. One often has the impression that their expressed fury was more a matter of pose and artifice than was that of their opponents. Perhaps the passion of mobs in the Affair was more profound, but even in that there can be some question. The rare photographs of mobs show people standing around waiting for something to happen rather than displaying agitation—although this may show only the limited ability of the photographers to capture action.[9]

However, noting the limits upon engagement by anti-Dreyfusards is like admitting self-interest to the motivations of Dreyfusard crusaders. Once noted, we must go on to recognize that deep conviction was decisive for anti-Dreyfusards also.

With "right" and "left" ordinarily just relative terms, referring to vaguely identified segments along a continuum, it can be difficult to comprehend the absolute cleavage between sides in the Affair. The situation becomes more clear when we compare decisive convictions.

"Justice" was not part of the political lexicon of anti-Dreyfusards. In their discourse they employed the word mainly to attack their opponents for making justice an idol. They knew other moral imperatives, like honor and courage; other political imperatives, like order and national power; other social imperatives, like natural relationship and integral cohesion.

For them the Jew Dreyfus was an alien, and thus he had little claim upon the guarantees the French government gave its citizens. Evidence could not decide the conflict, because reason only called upon evidence to the extent useful to support preconceived judgments. Judgments relied upon intuitive insight more than reason, which was itself more a useful instrument for justifying decisions than the essential means of making them. Law could be a convenient tool also, but it would have to defer to higher requirements when they conflicted. The requirements of the State acting in the national interest had to prevail over the interests of any individual.

In criticizing the General Staff, Dreyfusards attacked honor of the entire Army, undermined its leaders' stature in eyes of their men, and gravely weakened the Army's capacit function. The Army was the nation's moral heart and backbone, its protector against foreign aggressors (who were even then menacing) and domestic rebels, and its hope for recovery of honor and territory lost to archenemy Germany. No one must threaten the Army, and any who did were traitors just through posing the threat. Guilty or not, Dreyfus was nothing beside the importance of the Army.

Next to be saved from the Dreyfusards was the Church. Revolution and republic had been doing their best to destroy the Church for more than a century, and the Church was as necessary to the nation as the Army. Dreyfusards were anticlericals using Dreyfus as an excuse to wage war on the Church as well as on the Army, and they had to be stopped.

The Republic as then constituted was an artificial contrivance ill adapted to the real nature of the French people, culture, and traditions. The men controlling the Republic were corrupt and concerned only with advancing their own interests, not those of the nation. The system was ineffectual and completely unable to act with the resolute strength necessary to protect the vital interests of the nation. In their every move, their every word the Dreyfusards demonstrated and deepened the fatal flaws of the Third Republic. They had to be driven from the scene if the nation was to survive.

The French nation was a natural entity that had to be inspired and led by ideas and acts appropriate to its essential nature. For more than a century France had been too much directed by the false and unnatural products of abstract reasoning. Dreyfusards perfectly demonstrated this devastating process. Organic society and sacred faith had already almost been lost. France's remaining soul would be lost if the process were not arrested and reversed quickly.

The preceding litany is too exactly stated to fit the minds of all anti-Dreyfusards equally well, especially since few attempted to define all their convictions with complete precision. Yet few would have departed far from many of these particulars.

This ideology and that of the Dreyfusards had nothing at all in common except, sometimes, elements of patriotism and animosity toward old rivals abroad. The positions taken by the two

sides were entirely incompatible. Neither side could comprehend the other or discover a basis for approaching it. Each felt it
had far too much at stake to consider concessions. Consequently,
few anti-Dreyfusards could ever tolerate the thought that Dreyfus
might really be innocent, or the evidence against him absurdly
inadequate.

Dreyfusards won the contest at last because so many republicans felt compelled to rally in defense of the Republic and to
form a coalition in which normally irreconcilable differences
were subordinated. They did not have greater forces, but they
marshaled them better. With each increment of strength, more of
those who had not before openly taken sides joined the victors,
until the rehabilitation of Dreyfus found comparatively ready
acceptance. At Rennes in 1899, General Mercier dominated the
proceedings with his vocal opposition to acquitting Dreyfus. In
1906 Mercier spoke in the Senate to oppose restoring Dreyfus
and Picquart to the Army but was repeatedly shouted down by
Senators impatient with what by then seemed obnoxious nonsense.

In 1898 and 1899 anti-Dreyfusard beliefs and sentiments resonated widely throughout France. Anti-Dreyfusard militants
did not have the skills or the unity to translate that into political
dominance. When the crisis faded, so too did the opportunity to
make the kinds of changes they envisioned for the political system.

Nevertheless, neither defeat nor fading crisis could alter the
deep convictions just described. Details and emphasis might
change with the circumstances, but in general form these beliefs
were remarkably persistent, and the anti-Dreyfusards found
their revenge through the like-minded Vichy regime of 1940–44.
For anti-Dreyfusard men of letters and ideas, conviction and crusade composed a sacred mystique comparable to that discovered
by many intellectuals on the other side. Where the intellectuals
sought to relocate their mystique in some form of socialism,
anti-Dreyfusards found their mystique conserved and revitalized
in the ideology of Charles Maurras and the Action Française.
While neither socialism nor neoroyalism prevailed in France,
they provided the inspiration whereby the cleavage of the Dreyfus Affair was perpetuated.

At the end of the nineteenth century France, like much of

the rest of Western civilization, prospered with such vigor
self-assurance that it was easy to regard it as a country a
whose elements moved coherently in the same direction. Its
splendid high culture was not monolithic, but neither were the
obvious variations very great. Such divisions as could be recognized seemed like residues from the past or the epiphenomena
of recent developments; in either case, one might expect them to
diminish and disappear.

This appearance of cohesion and uniformity was an illusion.
Because few probably believed the appearance to be altogether
real, perhaps it is best called a shroud obscuring the real differences and divisions within the country.

Creation of a modern civilization involved sharp departures
from the premodern. In France the process had been going on for
so long that it was possible to think it fully a modern civilization
as the twentieth century began. The 1900 Paris Exposition was
intended to celebrate that achievement. Nevertheless, many of
the French still had not accepted the habits of thought and action
essential to modern Western civilization, even if they were
pleased with the new era's motor cars, electric lights, sanitation,
and repeating rifles.

They might react against whatever they disliked or dreaded
in modernity, but ordinarily it was difficult to find satisfactory
ways of doing so. Often they could not clearly conceptualize
what bothered them. Where it was possible to do so, it was
difficult to make protests as weighty as the discontent that provoked them. Literary vehicles for such criticism were common
and were taken seriously by some, but they could change very
little. Parliamentary government might have provided an effective forum and a means for accomplishing the changes needed,
but it was nearly always occupied with mundane, immediate
concerns.

The Dreyfus Affair provided the opportunity that usually
was lacking. Those repelled by much of the modern world could
attempt to reverse the tide. Those who had embraced the modern
could attempt to end insidious assaults on public principles and
institutions they thought essential to sustaining modern culture
and modern man.

The struggle was fought on legal and political grounds, but
it embraced much more. Just as the political ideologies on the

two sides were mutually incomprehensible, so too were their entire perspectives upon the world. Thus the cleavage of the Affair was absolute and enduring.

Crisis can reveal the fundamental nature of a culture as nothing else can. The Dreyfus Affair is important because it reveals so much of what France has been. And, because France is so close and so important to the rest of Western civilization, illuminating the French experience serves to reveal much of what that entire civilization has been.

Notes

Chapter 1: Crimes and Cover-up

1. The real author of the *bordereau* almost surely was a French major named Esterhazy. A 1972 book offered an intriguing but incredible thesis: that the *bordereau* was actually forged by German intelligence to discover whether secrets sold it by Esterhazy were genuine, the Germans expecting that French discovery of the document would lead to the major's arrest—if he had been selling genuine material. Esterhazy is supposed to have been selling false information as a personal agent of General Saussier, the commander-in-chief of the French Army. Michel de Lombarès, *L'Affaire Dreyfus, la clef du mystère* (Paris: Laffont, 1972). This thesis became the basis of Jacques Charrier and Jean Chérasse's 1974 motion picture, *Dreyfus, ou l'intolérable vérité;* see the book of the same title by Chérasse and Patrice Boussel (Paris: Pygmalion, 1975).

2. Major Hubert Henry, a central figure in the Affair, has been identified as the source of this leak, but the evidence on the point is contradictory, and the leak's source remains yet another mystery.

3. Then and later the German government made repeated official denials that there had ever been any relations whatever between Dreyfus and its representatives or agents. The German and Italian military attachés in Paris, both supposedly involved in the espionage, repeatedly and confidentially communicated to the French through intermediaries that they had known nothing of Dreyfus before he had been publicly accused. All the denials were completely discounted by the French, who expected these attachés and their governments to deny any of their involvement in espionage.

4. Alfred Dreyfus, *Lettres d'un innocent* (Paris: Stock, 1898), first published in a newspaper, *Le Siècle*, beginning January 19, 1898—a critical moment in the Affair. His *Cinq années de ma vie, 1894–1899* (Paris: Fasquelle, 1901, 1962) contains a selection of these letters, a journal, and other revealing material; the 1962 edition is especially

helpful. Both books were translated into many languages, including
English.

5. Mathieu Dreyfus, *L'Affaire telle que je l'ai vécue* (Paris: Grasset, 1978),
pp. 74–75. This is the first published edition of these memoirs, although the typed manuscript has been available in the Bibliothèque
Nationale, and some excerpts appeared with other previously une-
dited texts in Robert Gauthier, ed., *Dreyfusards!* (Paris: Julliard,
1965).

6. Schwartzkoppen had written his account around 1903 and died in
1917; as he lay dying he cried out to his wife that Dreyfus was
innocent. Max von Schwartzkoppen, *Die Wahrheit über Dreyfus* (Berlin: Verlag für Kulturpolitik, 1930); a French translation was also
published in 1930. Spectral analysis found that Dreyfus could not
have written the *bordereau* and Esterhazy may have. Jean-Marc Four-
nier, "Analyzing Handwriting with Optical Computing Methods,"
CNRS Research, No. 4 (1976), pp. 30–37.

7. The probable complicity of these men with Henry is one of the
revelations made by Marcel Thomas, whose book is the best on
evidence in the Dreyfus case: *L'Affaire sans Dreyfus* (Paris: Fayard,
1961), pp. 337–45.

Chapter 2: The Affair Explodes

1. The first close study of them is Stephen Wilson, "The Antisemitic
Riots of 1898 in France," *The Historical Journal,* XVI, No. 4 (December
1973): 789–806.

2. One chronology of the Affair includes at least thirty-two duels,
nearly all of them between men prominent in the conflict; presumably there were many more. Paul Desachy, *Répertoire de l'affaire
Dreyfus,* 2d, enlarged edition (n.p. [1905]).

3. Paraphrase of Reinach in his *Histoire de l'affaire Dreyfus* (Paris: La
Revue blanche and Fasquelle, 1901–11), V: 566.

4. The political controversy over this interpretation and the legal issues
involved are discussed at length in Albert Chenevier, "L'Article 445
et la Cour de Cassation," *Pages libres,* Nos. 411, 412 (Nov. 14 and 21,
1908), pp. 527–48, 563–75.

Chapter 3: Dreyfus, the Man

1. *The Letters of Captain Dreyfus to His Wife,* trans. L. G. Moreau (New
York and London: Harper, 1899), pp. 1, 2–3, 7, 8, 31, 44–45, 124,
150, 211.

2. G. W. Steevens, *The Tragedy of Dreyfus* (London and New York: Harper, 1899, pp. 42–43.

3. Alfred Dreyfus, *Cinq années de ma vie* (Paris: Fasquelle, 1962), p. 219.

Chapter 4: A Country Divided

1. Portions of my treatment of regional differences and their partial transformation are derived from Eugen Weber's exceptionally important book, *Peasants into Frenchmen* (Stanford, Calif.: Stanford University Press, 1976).

2. This is an important finding of a thorough study of strikes in this period. See Edward Shorter and Charles Tilly, *Strikes in France, 1830–1968* (London: Cambridge University Press, 1974).

3. The State's measures to avert proletarian upheaval are closely examined in Arthur Fryar Calhoun, "The Politics of Internal Order: French Government and Revolutionary Labor, 1898–1914," Ph.D. dissertation, Department of History, Princeton University, 1973.

4. An official census of the 1870s listed about 600,000 Protestants, 50,000 Jews, and 80,000 freethinkers; the rest of the 36,000,000 in France were supposedly Catholic—including more priests (55,369) than Jews. Weber, *Peasants into Frenchmen*, p. 339.

5. Napoléon III had died in 1873, and his only son was killed in 1879 fighting Zulus with the British army; Bonapartists could not then rally with ardor to any surviving Bonaparte, and their party declined to virtual insignificance. In 1883 the Legitimist pretender, the would-be Henri V, died without issue, leaving most monarchists to adhere to the Orleanist dynasty. Its head, the Comte de Paris, died just before the Dreyfus Affair began, on September 8, 1894. His son and heir, the Duc d'Orléans, was politically incompetent and badly fumbled his part in the machinations undertaken during the Affair to put him on a restored throne.

6. This differentiation was revealed by André Siegfried's penetrating book, *Tableau politique de la France de l'Ouest sous la IIIe République* (Paris: Colin, 1913, 1964), which has been extremely influential. Later refinements of his work have shown still greater complexity than even Siegfried imagined.

7. Ernest Psichari, quoted in John McManners, *Church and State in France, 1870–1914* (New York: Harper & Row, 1973), p. 124. Ernest Psichari died fighting in the Army in 1914; his father, Jean, was a prominent intellectual who had been actively involved as a Dreyfusard, against the Army.

8. "Chanson," from *Nouveaux chants du soldat* (1875), in Paul Déroulède, *Chants du Soldat* (Paris: Calmann Lévy, 1888), pp. 139–40.

Chapter 5: Diabolical Trinity: Jews, Masons, and Protestants

1. Edouard Drumont, *La France Juive*, New, 115th edition (Paris: Marpon & Flammarion, n.d.), I: 9–10.

2. An 1897 census by the Consistoire Central (the Jewish community's administrative agency) is said to be unreliable by Michael R. Marrus, *The Politics of Assimilation: A Study of the French Jewish Community at the Time of the Dreyfus Affair* (Oxford: Clarendon, 1971), p. 29. Much of my information on assimilation comes from this book, the best on French Jews and anti-Semitism at the time of the Affair. Robert F. Byrnes, *Antisemitism in Modern France. Vol. I: Prologue to the Dreyfus Affair* (New Brunswick: Rutgers University Press, 1950), is the standard work, but Byrnes did not complete his planned second volume on anti-Semitism during the Affair itself.

3. My treatment of the crash's consequences for anti-Semitism is partly based upon Jeannine Verdès-Leroux, *Scandale financier et antisémitisme catholique: Le Krach de l'Union Générale* ([Paris]: Le Centurion [1969]).

4. Much of my treatment of *La Croix* is based upon Pierre Sorlin, *"La Croix" et les Juifs (1880–1899)* (Paris: Grasset, 1967).

5. "La Trio de la haine," *La Croix*, November 13, 1896; quoted in Sorlin, *"La Croix" et les Juifs*, p. 117.

6. My account of Taxil and his hoaxes is based upon Byrnes, *Antisemitism in Modern France*, pp. 304–19. A fuller treatment with excellent insights into the Vaughan story's significance is Eugen Weber, *Satan franc-maçon: la mystification de Léo Taxil* (Paris: Julliard, 1964).

Chapter 6: Credulity and Conviction in the Affair

1. Reprinted in Finley Peter Dunne, *Mr. Dooley in Peace and in War* (Boston: Small, Maynard, 1898), pp. 234–37. Dunne's fictional "Mr. Dooley" often commented on the Dreyfus Affair in the *Chicago Journal*. His remarks frequently seem more perceptive as well as funnier than what Paris journalists were then writing.

2. Mathieu's odyssey in seeking help is described in his memoirs, *L'Affaire telle que je l'ai vécue* (Paris: Grasset, 1978), pp. 58–59, and in Joseph Reinach, *Histoire de l'affaire Dreyfus* (Paris: *La Revue blanche* and Fasquelle, 1901–11), II: 167–71.

3. Georges Clemenceau, Preface, dated January 15, 1899, to *L'Inquité!* (Paris: Stock, 1899), pp. i–iv. This is a collection of Clemenceau's almost daily *L'Aurore* articles on the Affair; six more volumes of his Dreyfusard writing followed.

Chapter 7: The Crusaders for Dreyfus

1. "Unus" (pseudonym of Charles Vogel), *Le Syndicat de trahison* (Paris: Stock, 1898), p. 29; this is a volume of pen portraits of forty-two Dreyfusards.

2. These numbers are computed from Table One in Robert Fox, "The Savant Confronts His Peers: Scientific Societies in France, 1815–1914," in Robert Fox and George Weisz, eds., *The Organization of Science and Technology in France 1808–1914,* to be published by the Cambridge University Press in 1980.

3. For the French press much of my information, though not my judgments, is derived from Pierre Albert, "La Presse française de 1871 à 1940," in Claude Bellanger *et al.,* eds., *Histoire générale de la presse française* (Paris: Presses Universitaires de France, 1972), III: 135–622, and Janine Ponty, "La Presse quotidienne et l'Affaire Dreyfus en 1898–1899," *Revue d'histoire moderne et contemporaine,* XXI (1974): 193–220. Numbers given are actually of copies printed, not of those sold, and are approximations that vary considerably within short periods.

4. I have to use the words "academe" and "academics" to refer to all teachers in secular higher and secondary education. They generally had the same level of training. Secondary teachers moved to universities if successful, and there were important institutions of advanced learning besides the universities.

5. Most of the preceding account of Blum and Herr is taken, with some paraphrasing and the quotations indicated, from Léon Blum, "Souvenirs sur 'L'Affaire,' " *L'Oeuvre de Léon Blum* (Paris: Albin Michel, 1954–65), IV, pt. ii: 517–23; the whole memoir (pp. 511–78) first appeared as seven articles in a weekly, *Marianne,* from July 24 to September 7, 1935.

6. "Le 'syndicat' grandit," *L'Aurore,* January 18, 1898.

7. This paragraph is based upon the standard Jaurès biography, Harvey Goldberg, *The Life of Jean Jaurès* (Madison: University of Wisconsin Press, 1962), pp. 217–25.

8. While Reinach, Lazare, and Mathieu Dreyfus were the only Jews playing major roles in the Affair, some of the most revealing memoirs of the struggle were written by Jewish participants. Halévy's principal one is "Apologie pour notre passé," composed 1907 to 1910 and published in Peguy's organ, *Cahiers de la Quinzaine,* Series XI, No. 10 (1910), and in Halévy's *Luttes et problèmes* (Paris: Rivière, 1911), pp. 13–123. I have also been guided by Alain Silvera, *Daniel Halévy and His Times* (Ithaca, N.Y.: Cornell University Press, 1966). Silvera had access to Halévy's unpublished daily journal of the Affair years.

9. Proust recreated in altered forms the society and people he and Halévy knew together at the time of the Affair, in his novels *A la Recherche du temps perdu* and *Jean Santeuil*. In the latter, Daniel Halévy is presented as Jean's friend, Henri Durrieux. Daniel's cousin Geneviève Straus was the principal model for the Duchesse de Guermantes in *A la Recherche du temps perdu*.

10. Halévy, "Apologie pour notre passé," *Luttes et problèmes*, pp. 29–30, 42–45, 47.

Chapter 8: Combat Joined

1. Quoted in Jean France, *Souvenirs de la Sûreté Générale: Autour de l'Affaire Dreyfus* (Paris: Rieder, 1936), p. 7. Painlevé was one of the great minds of his age, a mathematician whose engagement as a Dreyfusard began for him a second distinguished career as a politician and statesman.

2. This account of the Chamber melee is based, with some paraphrasing and the indicated quotations, upon reports in several newspapers, including *Le Journal officiel*, the government gazette. Remarks quoted here and later from parliamentary debates can be found in *Le Journal officiel* in the section devoted to the *Compte-rendu* in extenso *des séances de la Chambre de deputés* (or *du Sénat*).

3. The importance of the imaginary documents to the anti-Dreyfusards is discussed above in Chapter Six; their role in obtaining Dreyfus's final exoneration is mentioned in Chapter Two.

4. Despite his Hungarian name, Esterhazy was quite French, born and educated in Paris and the son of a French general. He had no legitimate claim either to the title of Comte that he used or to the name of the Esterhazys, the greatest noble family in Hungary. His anti-French remarks were simply the outbursts of a very frustrated and angry man.

5. Joseph Reinach, *Histoire de l'affaire Dreyfus* (Paris: La Revue blanche and Fasquelle, 1901–11), III: 141. This volume was published in 1903.

6. *Le Siècle* was the only Dreyfusard newspaper not well to the left in its general political identity; it was rather conservative for a republican journal.

7. Duclaux testified at the Zola trial, on February 19, 1898, and this letter was introduced as evidence then, although, like much the Zola defense brought forth, it had no direct relevance. Dreyfus's prosecutors were not alone in emphasizing irrelevant evidence.

8. Reinach, *Histoire de l'affaire Dreyfus*, III: 167.

9. First written in his "M. Scheurer-Kestner," *Le Figaro*, November 15, 1897, and repeated in his pamphlet of January 6, 1898, "Lettre à la France." Zola's published collection of his Dreyfusard pieces (1901) was called *Truth on the March*; in his *Oeuvres complètes* (Paris: Cercle de livre précieux, 1966–70), XIV: 858–1104.

10. *La Libre parole*, February 10, 1898. The phrase "conscience of humanity" is from the oration of Anatole France at Zola's funeral in 1902.

11. "King of the Pigs" is No. 4 of V. Lenepveu's *Le Musée des horreurs*, a strikingly bizarre series of fifty-two color lithograph posters, each of them a caricature showing a celebrated Dreyfusard as some beast. One poster was issued each week, probably in 1899 and 1900. Lenepveu also produced five of a series showing anti-Dreyfusard heroes, *Le Musée des patriotes*. That chamber pots were called *zolas* is the recollection of François Mauriac, "L'Affaire Dreyfus vue par un enfant," in Alfred Dreyfus, *Cinq années de ma vie, 1894–1899* (Paris: Fasquelle, 1962), p. 15. The term could also have been inspired by Zola's fiction, which offended many with its raw portrayal of how people really live.

12. I know of no serious effort to make a balanced assessment of foreign opinion about the Dreyfus Affair; it would be very difficult to accomplish. What historians have said of non-French views generally reflects Dreyfusard biases. However, see note 2, Chapter Twelve, for citation of Foreign Ministry dispatches and foreign newspaper clippings on the Affair.

13. "Souvenirs sur 'L'Affaire,' " *L'Oeuvre de Léon Blum* (Paris: Albin Michel, 1954–65), IV, pt. ii: 515–16.

14. Jean Jaurès, Jules Guesde, and Gérault-Richard. In February 1899 a by-election added a forty-third socialist to the Chamber.

15. On the Saint-Mandé Program, see Aaron Noland, *The Founding of the French Socialist Party, 1893–1905* (Cambridge, Mass.: Harvard University Press, 1956), pp. 48–51, and Claude Willard, *Les Guesdistes* (Paris: Editions Sociales, 1965), pp. 405–9. Some of my other information about the socialists is drawn from these two books, while for the anarchists I have been helped by Jean Maitron, *Le Mouvement anarchiste en France* (Paris: Maspero, 1975), I: 331–42. Although for simplicity's sake I make the usual distinction between socialists and anarchists, I think anarchism is better considered a variety of socialism.

16. Sebastien Faure, "Les Anarchistes et l'affaire Dreyfus," (n.p.: Lafont, 1898), apparently published in January. Faure declared Dreyfus innocent and deserving of sympathy, in *Le Libertaire*, August 7–13, 1898. He suspended *Le Libertaire* in favor of an anarchist Drey-

fusard daily newspaper, *Le Journal du peuple,* which he operated from February 6 to December 3, 1899.

17. Paul Desachy, *Repertoire de l'affaire Dreyfus, 1894–1899,* 2d, enlarged edition (n.p. [1905]), pp. 134–48. Houghton Library has a copy of the page proofs of this; the book seems not to have actually been published, however.

18. Anatole France, *L'Anneau d'améthyste* (Paris: Calmann-Lévy, 1899), pp. 21–22, 65. This novel and its sequel, *Monsieur Bergeret à Paris* (1900), are part of France's *L'Histoire contemporaine;* they were serialized in a newspaper during the Affair. Details of this are in Chapter Ten. The Affair is also satirized in France's *Crainquebille* (1901) and *L'Ile des pingouins* (1908).

Chapter 9: The Rage Against Things Modern

1. F. Brunetière, "La Nation et l'Armée," *Discours de Combat,* 1st series (Paris: Perrin, 1900), pp. 229–30; originally a speech delivered in Paris by Brunetière on April 26, 1899, for the Ligue de la Patrie Française. A. de Mun, "Lettre adressée à Lord Russell of Killowen, Lord Chief Justice d'Angleterre, au sujet de l'Affaire Dreyfus, le 29 janvier 1899," *Discours* (Paris: Poussielgue, 1895–1904), VII: 4–5, refused by *The Times,* to which it was sent as a reply to Russell's letter published there on January 17, 1899. M. Barrès, "Les Intellectuels, ou logiciens de l'absolut," *Scènes et doctrines du nationalisme* (Paris: Juven [1902]), p. 44; italics in the original; article first published earlier in the Affair, date and place not stated here. H. Rochefort, "La Trahison obligatoire," *L'Intransigeant,* February 21, 1899.

2. Maurice Barrès, "L'Etat de la question," *Scènes et doctrines du nationalisme,* 34, first published in *Le Journal,* on October 4, 1898, just after the Cour de Cassation accepted the Dreyfus case for review.

3. Alphonse Aulard, "La Statue de Taine," *Polémique et histoire* (Paris: Cornély [1904]), pp. 41–43, first published in a daily newspaper, *L'Action,* July 19, 1903. Aulard was a Dreyfusard, but he seems not to have been active in the cause.

4. Julien Benda, *Dialogues à Byzance* (Paris: La Revue blanche, 1900), pp. 3–6, first published as a series in *La Revue blanche* in 1899.

5. Emile Duclaux, "Avant le procès" (Paris: Stock, 1898), pp. 12–34; first published in the *Revue du palais,* May 1, 1898, as a rejoinder to F. Brunetière, *Après le procès. Réponse à quelques intellectuels* (Paris: Perrin, 1898), which itself was first published in the *Revue des Deux mondes,* March 15, 1898. Another intellectual's rejoinder was Al-

phonse Darlu's *M. Brunetière et l'individualisme* (Paris: Colin, 1898), first published in the *Revue de métaphysique et de morale*, May 1898.

6. Maurice Barrès, "La Réplique aux intellectuels: le sens du relatif," *Scènes et doctrines du nationalisme*, pp. 82, 85; date of original article and the place published not stated.

7. Janine Ponty, "La Presse quotidienne et l'affaire Dreyfus en 1898–1899," *Revue d'histoire moderne et contemporaine*, XXI (1974): 193–220.

8. Information about nationalists in Paris and the observation about lack of party and union organization are from D. R. Watson, "The Nationalist Movement in Paris, 1900–1906," in David Shapiro, ed., *The Right in France, 1890–1919* (London: Chatto & Windus, 1962), pp. 49–84. The sources of support for the Ligue Antisémitique are only partly known; available information is examined in Stephen Wilson, "The Ligue Antisémitique Française," *Wiener Library Bulletin*, XXV, No. 3/4 (1972): 33–39, and Zeev Sternhell, *La Droite révolutionaire, 1885–1914* (Paris: Editions du Seuil, 1978), pp. 221–44.

9. An adequate picture might be formed by thorough study of police and administrative archives, since government agents did watch and report most such events. The only study of this type I know is Stephen Wilson, "The Antisemitic Riots of 1898 in France," *Historical Journal*, XVI, No. 4 (1973): 789–806. This examines riots in January and February 1898—sixty-six in metropolitan France, plus those in Algeria. In a variety of other published sources, I have noted sixty-five violent events at other times in the Affair, about evenly divided between Paris and the provinces. My published sources reported only twelve of the sixty-six riots Wilson found in archival records; at that ratio the sixty-five other riots I found would represent more than 350 that actually occurred from March 1898 through September 1899.

10. Here I use another of Stephen Wilson's invaluable studies, "Le Monument Henry: La structure de l'antisémitisme en France 1898–1899," *Annales: Economies, Sociétés, Civilisations*, XXXII, No. 2 (1977): 265–91, and a Dreyfusard's elaborate analytic classification of the contributor lists that *La Libre parole* published: Pierre Quillard, *Le Monument Henry* (Paris: Stock, 1899). Wilson began with Quillard's analysis, then went far beyond it.

11. This is an approximation based only on my comparison between Wilson's map of the distribution of contributors (p. 268) and maps showing distributions of Deputies elected from the right and left in successive elections, in François Goguel, *Géographie des Elections*

françaises sous la troisième et la quatrième Républiques (Paris: Colin, 1970), pp. 32–41.

12. Jean-Pierre Rioux, *Nationalisme et conservatisme: la Ligue de la Patrie Française, 1899–1904* (Paris: Beauchesne, 1977), pp. 20–30. Though detailed, this analysis does not go as far as does Wilson's treatment of the Monument Henry. Here the list is taken from newspapers, where publication was cut short by the death of President Félix Faure on February 16, 1899; the Ligue's records have been lost. Some of the numbers I cite are not Rioux's but are calculated from his.

13. The signatures on behalf of Picquart were collected by Dreyfusard newspapers and published together with a dozen fine lithographs as the *Hommage des artistes* [i.e., these lithographers] *à Picquart* (Paris: Société libre d'édition des gens de lettres, 1899). Other lists are included in the *Livre d'hommage des Lettres françaises à Emile Zola* (Paris and Brussels: Société libre d'édition des gens de lettres and Georges Balat, 1898). In addition to these lists I have referred to two recent studies employing them: Christophe Charle, "Champ littéraire et champ du pouvoir: Les écrivains et l'Affaire Dreyfus," *Annales: Economies, Sociétés, Civilisations*, XXXII (1977): 240–64; and Madeleine Rebérioux, "Histoire, historiens et dreyfusisme," *Revue historique*, CCLV, No. 2 (1976): 407–32.

14. Forain did contribute to *L'Assiette au beurre*, an important satirical cartoon weekly established in 1901. It was usually *anarchisant* but not connected to any political faction; instead, it was a widely read commercial publication.

15. Reprinted in de Mun, *Discours* (note 1 above), VI: 381.

Chapter 10: "Aux Armes, Citoyens!"

1. Repeated by Reinach in his *Histoire de l'affaire Dreyfus*, IV: 19, with the note, "Thus spoke the *syndicataire* Pascal (XIIe Lettre à un Provincial, *in fine*)."

2. Ernest Judet, "Zola père et fils," *Le Petit journal*, May 23, 1898; for Emile Zola's reply, see "Mon père," *L'Aurore*, May 28, 1898. There had been an embezzlement, for which another officer was convicted; his court-martial absolved Zola *père* of any complicity. Judet prosecuted Emile Zola for calumny in the same affair, obtaining a token judgment. In the "J'Accuse!" defamation case, furnishings in Zola's home were seized for sale in lieu of payment of his fine; an anonymous admirer (said to be the publisher, Fasquelle) paid 30,000 francs for one rather ordinary table, ten times the amount of the fine.

3. *Psst . . . !:* eighty-five issues, February 5, 1898, to September 16, 1899. *Le Sifflet:* twenty issues, February 17, 1898, to June 16, 1899. *Le Musée des Horreurs:* described above, Chapter Eight, note 11. *La Feuille,* written by Zo d'Axa, cartoons by Steinlen and others: twenty-five issues, October 6, 1897, to March 28, 1899. Postcard catalog: Xavier Granoux, *L'Affaire Dreyfus* (Paris: Daragon, 1903). There were many contemporary collections of Affair cartoons and other pictures. One that included foreign cartoons is John Grand-Carteret, *L'Affaire Dreyfus et l'image* (Paris: Flammarion [1898]). The various kinds of material described here are included in the collection of the Houghton Library at Harvard University.

4. For the 1974 film *Dreyfus, ou l'Intolérable Vérité,* see above, Chapter One, note 1. Romain Rolland, *Les Loups* (performed in 1898 under the title *Morituri*) (Paris: Georges Bellais, 1898). Hans J. Rehfisch and Wilhelm Herzog, with French version by Jacques Richepin, *L'Affaire Dreyfus* (Paris: Albin Michel [1931]).

5. Jean Lemazurier, "Catéchisme dreyfusard" (Paris: Stock, 1898), pp. 1–2, 5.

6. *La Libre parole,* September 22, 1898. Guyot and Pressensé were prominent Dreyfusard leaders; Brisson was Premier; and Bourgeois, a former Premier, was the Minister of Education.

7. Brunetière reiterated his "incompetence" both before and after Henry's exposure, in twelve letters published in *Le Siècle* from August 13 to September 9, 1898, and reprinted as "A propos de 'l'Affaire,' " in his *Lettres du Combat* (Paris: Perrin, 1912), pp. 13–104. In January 1899 De Mun laid out his position fully in two letters addressed to *The Times* (one of which is quoted at the beginning of Chapter Nine) and printed in his *Discours* (Paris: Poussielgues, 1895–1904), VI: 419–36 and VII: 1–12.

8. For the Ligue Antisémitique, in addition to the Wilson and Sternhell studies cited in Chapter Nine, I have used several memoirs by anti-Semites. Especially valuable is one by a close associate of Guérin who turned against him: Charles Spiard, *Les Coulisses du Fort-Chabrol* (Paris: Spiard [1899]).

9. Much of my information here is drawn from Peter M. Rutkoff, "The Ligue des Patriotes: The Nature of the Radical Right and the Dreyfus Affair," *French Historical Studies,* VIII (1974): 584–603. He suggests that the Ligue was mainly lower middle class in composition, well-organized, and the most important agency of rightist agitation; I have reservations about each of these points.

10. J.-P. Rioux, *Nationalisme et conservatisme* (see note 12, Chapter 9), pp. 40n., 58.

11. Jules Lemaître, "L'Oeuvre de la Patrie Française" (Paris: *La Patrie*

française, 1899), p. 27. The preceding analysis is drawn from a number of Ligue publications, especially another catechism, the "Manuel du bon citoyen" (Paris: *La Patrie française*, 1902), and a collection of speeches, Jules Lemaître and Godefroy Cavaignac, *La Campagne nationaliste* (Paris: Michaud, 1902).

12. Most of this paragraph paraphrases a history of the league by one of its first members: Henri Sée, *Histoire de la Ligue des Droits de l'Homme* (*1898–1926*) (Paris: Ligue des Droits de l'Homme, 1927), pp. 12–14. Much of my information on the league comes from this book.

13. Preface dated August 29, 1898, to Paul Brulat, *Violence et raison* (Paris: Stock, 1898), p. xxv.

14. I identified Masons by cross-comparison of two sources, neither of them very reliable for the purpose: Pierre Chevallier, *Histoire de la franc-maçonnerie française* (Paris: Fayard, 1975), Vol. III; and Henry Coston, *La Franc-maçonnerie sous la IIIe République* (Paris: Editions C.A.D. [1943]). The latter is an anti-Masonic tract that includes what purports to be a full list of Masons who were Ministers, Deputies, or Senators in the Third Republic.

15. Ernest Renauld, *Le Péril protestant* (Paris: Tolra, 1899), pp. 206, 166, and Pierre Froment, *La Trahison protestante* (Paris: Pierret, 1899).

16. L. Pichot, "La Conscience chrétienne et l'affaire Dreyfus" (Paris: Société d'éditions littéraires, 1899), p. 5. The main text of this pamphlet is a long letter to the editor of *La Croix*, dated August 28, 1898. My description of this Comité Catholique is based primarily on the book of a member, Henri de Saint-Poli (pseudonym of Abbé Joseph Brugerette), *L'Affaire Dreyfus et la mentalité catholique en France* (Paris: Storck, 1904), and on the Comité's "Declaration de principes" (Paris: Stock, 1899).

17. Jean Ajalbert, *La Forêt noire* (Paris: Société libre d'édition des gens de lettres, 1899), pp. i–ii, 20. The first passage is from a preface dated August 3, 1899.

18. Joseph Reinach, *Histoire de l'affaire Dreyfus*, IV: 51. The speech was published as a pamphlet in 1898; historians have often discussed this incident as if Dreyfusard reports of what Didon said were accurate, so that one wonders if any have actually read the text. Didon's democratic outlook is more clearly evident in other compositions, for example his *L'Education présente* (Paris: Plon, Nourrit, 1898).

19. Testimony excerpted in Louis Leblois, *L'Affaire Dreyfus* (Paris: Quillet, 1929), pp. 672–73.

20. Georges Clemenceau, *L'Inquité* (Paris: Stock 1899), p. 204.

Chapter 11: Struggle for the Republic

1. Visits discussed by Schwartzkoppen with Princess Marie Radziwill, who wrote about them in letters of February 27–28, 1898, and January 6–7, 1899, in her *Lettres de la princesse Radziwill au Général du Robilant, 1889–1914* (Bologna: Zanichelli, 1933), II: 124, 174.

2. Description of street scenes based mainly on a report in *Le Matin* the next morning.

3. This point originates with Pierre Sorlin, *Waldeck-Rousseau* (Paris: Colin, 1966), p. 395.

4. Alexandre Zévaès, "L'Affaire Dreyfus: Quelques souvenirs personnels," *La Nouvelle revue*, CXXXXI (1936): 207–8; his entire memoir appeared January–March 1936, CXXXXI: 197–208, 287–96, and CXXXXII: 45–53, 96–104.

5. "Atrocity in Africa and the Dreyfus Affair," my article giving a full account of the Voulet–Chanoine episode (scheduled for September 1980 publication by *Harvard Magazine*), is based upon reports by participants in the events. Of these the most valuable are Paul Joalland, *Le Drame de Dankori* (Paris: Nouvelles Editions Argo, [1930]), and Emilie Klobb, ed., *A la recherche de Voulet* (Paris: Nouvelles Editions Argo, [1931]). The only frank and substantial historical account I know is Jean Suret-Canale, *Afrique noire occidentale et centrale* (Paris: Editions Sociales, 1968), I: 296–304. The author's strong anti-colonialism removed inhibitions that may have kept other French historians from writing of this remarkable affair. Suret-Canale tells (p. 296 n.) of efforts to suppress the story, notably the apparent removal of records from the archives of French West Africa's colonial administration.

6. Discussed by Galliffet with Princess Marie Radziwill, and reported by her in a letter of October 27, 1899, in *Lettres de la princesse Radziwill . . .*, II: 222.

Chapter 12: Continuing Aftershocks of the Affair

1. Reprinted in Finley Peter Dunne, *Mr. Dooley in the Hearts of His Countrymen* (Boston: Small, Maynard, 1899), pp. 282–84. Johannesburg was the main center of conflict between the Boers and the British, with the war between them beginning shortly after this piece was written.

2. Details on protests are in Richard D. Mandell, *Paris 1900* (Toronto: University of Toronto Press, 1967), pp. 93–96. Mandell drew his information from seven volumes of Foreign Ministry dispatches and newspaper clippings on the Affair, in the French national archives

under the heading: Ministère des affaires étrangères, Correspond-
ance politique, Allemagne, Relations avec la France, *Affaire Dreyfus*
(his citation, p. 158, n. 14). My next two paragraphs are partly based
on Mandell's book, pp. 96–103.

3. Some of the ideas in the following analysis were first suggested to
   me by Dan White, a specialist in modern German social history, in
   the course of a discussion where we sought solutions to this "puzzle."

4. Theodor Herzl, "L'Affaire Dreyfus," newspaper articles translated
   by Léon Vogel (Paris: Impr. des Deux Artisans, 1958), pp. 19–20, 32.

5. While the analysis I offer here differs from Eugen Weber's, my understanding of the Action Française and of nationalism after the
   Affair owes much to his *Action Française* (Stanford, Calif.: Stanford
   University Press, 1962) and *The Nationalist Revival in France, 1905–
   1914* (Berkeley and Los Angeles: University of California Press,
   1968).

6. For Péguy the most important piece is *Notre jeunesse*, first published
   in his *Cahiers de la quinzaine*, XI, No. 12 (1910), as a rejoinder to
   Halévy's *Apologie pour notre passe*, in the *Cahiers de la quinzaine*, XI,
   No. 10 (1910). Georges Sorel, *La Révolution dreyfusienne* (Paris: Rivière, 1909); the second edition (1911) includes a preface responding
   to Halévy's *Apologie*. Volume VI of Reinach's *Histoire de l'affaire
   Dreyfus* appeared in 1908 and reflected his disillusionment and distress, though he was by then once more part of the ruling order in
   the Chamber of Deputies. Volume VII (1911) contains only errata
   and an index, and thus shows no further development of his attitude.

7. Péguy, *Notre jeunesse*, in his *Oeuvres en prose, 1909–1914* (Paris: Gal-
   limard, 1961), p. 586.

8. Georges Clemenceau, *L'Inquité!* (Paris: Stock, 1899), pp. ii–iv.

9. Dreyfus Affair photographs in the press and elsewhere almost never
   showed scenes where action was involved; typically they portrayed
   individuals in the news posing or attending some orderly event like
   a trial. A singular exception is a collection of photographs of anti-
   Semitic riots in Algiers, found in a scrapbook compiled for Drumont
   and now in Houghton Library at Harvard, under the title
   "L'Antisémitisme en images, 1898," Vol. I.

Bibliography

Suggestions for further reading

REINACH, JOSEPH. *Histoire de l'affaire Dreyfus.* 7 vols. Paris: *La Revue blanche* (Vol. I) and Fasquelle, 1901–11. A brilliant historical work by any standard. Reinach rose far above his prejudices, which are easily recognized; both his knowledge of the Affair and his literary skills make the effort of reading his 4,100 pages richly rewarding.

THOMAS, MARCEL. *L'Affaire sans Dreyfus.* Paris: Fayard, 1961. The best study of evidence in the Dreyfus case, effectively resolving many disputed points. Does not discuss the wider struggle over Dreyfus or most developments occurring after 1897.

Other French histories of the Affair have most often been too biased, shallow, or—with surprising frequency—obsessed with "proving" a novel but highly unlikely theory of what *really* happened. For a general history of the Affair, one can not do better than the Chapman and Johnson books cited next. Chapman's is more detailed, while Johnson's examines the overall French situation more fully.

CHAPMAN, GUY. *The Dreyfus Case.* London: Rupert Hart-Davis, 1955; New York: Reynal, 1956. Chapman's *The Dreyfus Trials* (1972) is an abridgement of this, with some minor updating.

JOHNSON, DOUGLAS. *France and the Dreyfus Affair* (London: Blandford, 1966).

TUCHMAN, BARBARA. "Give Me Combat!," chapter 4 of *The Proud Tower.* New York: Macmillan, 1966. A fine, vivid re-creation of the Dreyfus struggle from a perspective different from mine.

Fiction, verse, and drama about the Affair have been very abundant. Most of such material suffers from distorted vision or poor literary quality; some better works give only brief or narrowly perceived glimpses of the Affair. I find Anatole France's satires the best of this literature, especially *L'Anneau d'amethyste, Monsieur Bergeret à Paris,* and *L'Ile des Pingouins* (Paris: Calmann-Lévy, 1899, 1900, 1908); all three have been translated into English.

Research collections and tools

The major library collections
Bibliothèque Historique de la Ville de Paris. Includes the Collection Ochs on the Affair, plus a large collection of Affair periodical materials.

Houghton Library, Harvard University (augmented by materials in other Harvard libraries). Very rich collection, described in the Preface to this book.

Archives and court records
  Archival collections concerning the Affair are very extensive; there is a convenient bibliography of much of this in Pierre Sorlin, *Waldeck-Rousseau* (Paris: Colin, 1966), pp. 497–527. Probably most important are police records in the Archives Nationales, Series F^7, especially F^7 12464–73 (the Dreyfus Affair), and the court records in Series BB^{19}.

  Transcripts of many court inquiries and trials were published, mainly by Dreyfusards. These are described as items 49–72 in the Lipschutz bibliography cited next.

Bibliographies
LIPSCHUTZ, LÉON. *Bibliographie thématique et analytique de l'affaire Dreyfus*. Paris: Société Littéraire des Amis d'Emile Zola and Editions Fasquelle, 1970. First published in *Les Cahiers naturalistes* (1968–69): No. 35, pp. 83–115; No. 36, pp. 189–211; No. 37, pp. 91–101; and No. 38, pp. 191–220. Thorough analytic bibliography, with extensive comments on many items. Excludes virtually all periodical and non-French publications, but includes most other significant items. His information was based in large part upon his own collection, which is now in Harvard's Houghton Library.

DESACHY, PAUL. *Bibliographie de l'affaire Dreyfus*. Paris: Vaugirard, 1905. Checklist of 728 items, including some omitted by Lipschutz.

HOUGHTON LIBRARY, HARVARD UNIVERSITY. Unpublished shelf list for Dreyfus Affair collection, shelf number prefix * FC9.D8262 (card file available in Houghton Reading Room). Includes much that is not in the Lipschutz or Desachy bibliographies.

Other

DESACHY, PAUL. *Répertoire de l'affaire Dreyfus.* N.p. (1899). 2d, much enlarged, edition: n.p. (1905), 338 pp. The Houghton Library has a copy of the enlarged version's page proofs, but the edition appears not actually to have been published. This second edition is a very detailed day-by-day chronology, with press excerpts, and I found it most valuable for perceiving the full dimensions of the Dreyfus struggle.

MARIN, PAUL. *Histoire documentaire de l'affaire Dreyfus.* 11 vols. Paris: Librairie Illustrée (Vol. I) and Stock, 1898–1902. Series discontinued after giving June 1899 decision annulling the first Dreyfus conviction. Nearly 5,000 pages of newspaper articles and transcripts of parliamentary and court proceedings. Emphasizes Drumont and Rochefort articles, although Marin was Dreyfusard.

REINACH, JOSEPH. *Histoire de l'affaire Dreyfus* (cited in full above). Reinach's wealth of detailed and firsthand knowledge makes this work essential for further research. He used all available resources, including private papers besides his own. The index (Vol. VII) identifies most of the individuals named, and thus constitutes the best "who's who" of the Affair.

Selected works not included in Lipschutz or Desachy bibliographies

Omitted here are pieces, such as broadsides and newspaper articles, that I found illuminating when seen together but not individually noteworthy. Also omitted are many recent works that I think do not add substantially to understanding of issues emphasized in this book.

BENDA, JULIEN. "L'Affaire Dreyfus et le Principe d'autorité," *Revue blanche,* XX (1899): 190–206.

BLUM, ANTOINETTE. "Romain Rolland, *Les Loups* et l'Affaire Dreyfus." Ph.D. dissertation, Romance literature, Yale University, 1977.

BOURDREL, PHILIPPE. *Histoire des juifs en France.* Paris: Albin Michel, 1974, pp. 205–300.

BRUNETIÈRE, FERDINAND. "A propos de 'l'Affaire,' " *Lettres de combat.* Paris: Perrin, 1912, pp. 13–104.

———. "La Nation et l'armée," *Discours de combat,* 1st series. Paris: Perrin, 1900, pp. 213–48.

BUSI, FREDERICK. "Bibliographical Overview of the Dreyfus Affair," *Jewish Social Studies,* XL, No. 1 (1978): 25–40.

————. "The Dreyfus Affair and the French Cinema," *Wiener Library Bulletin*, XXIX, No. 39/40 (1976): 56–59.

CAGNIARD, GASTON. "Les 'Intellectuels' et l'Affaire Dreyfus," and "Les 'Intellectuels' de la Patrie Française," *La Revue socialiste*, XXIX (April and June 1899): 471–87, 714–37.

CAZENAVE, ELIZABETH. "L'Affaire Dreyfus et l'opinion bordelaise," *Annales du Midi*, LXXXIV, No. 106 (1972): 63–76.

CHARLE, CHRISTOPHE. "Champ littéraire et champ du pouvoir: les écrivains et l'affaire Dreyfus," *Annales: Economies, Sociétés, Civilisations*, XXXII (1977): 240–64.

CHARRIER, JACQUES and JEAN CHÉRASSE. *Dreyfus ou l'intolérable vérité.* Feature-length motion picture, 1974.

COSER, LEWIS. *Men of Ideas*. New York: Free Press, 1965, pp. 215–226.

DREYFUS, MATHIEU. *L'Affaire telle que je l'ai vécue.* Paris: Grasset, 1978.

DREYFUS, PIERRE, ed. *Capitaine Alfred Dreyfus: Souvenirs et Correpondence.* Paris: Grasset, 1936.

DURKHEIM, EMILE. "L'Individualisme et les intellectuels," *La Revue bleue*, XXXV (July 2, 1898): 7–13.

GAUTHIER, ROBERT. "Les Alsaciens et l'Affaire Dreyfus," *Saisons d'Alsace*, No. 17 (1966), pp. 56–80.

————, ed. *Dreyfusards! Souvenirs de Mathieu Dreyfus et autres inédits.* Paris: Julliard, 1965.

GOGUEL, FRANÇOIS. *La Politique des partis sous la IIIe République.* Paris: Editions du Seuil (1958), pp. 86–109.

GREEN, NANCY L. "The Dreyfus Affair and Ruling Class Cohesion," *Science and Society*, XLIII (1979): 29–50.

GYP DE BLIDAH (pseudonym of Comtesse de Martel de Janville). "Chansons anti-juives." Blidah: Grand-Coudurier, 1898.

HALASZ, NICHOLAS. *Captain Dreyfus*. New York: Simon & Schuster, 1955.

HALÉVY, DANIEL. *Apologie pour notre passé*, in his *Luttes et problèmes.* Paris: Riviere, 1911, pp. 13–123, and *Cahiers de la Quinzaine*, Sér. XI, No. 10 (1910).

HERR, LUCIEN. "Lettre à Maurice Barrès," *Choix d'écrits.* Paris, 1932, I: 39–50. First published in *La Revue blanche*, February 15, 1898.

HERZOG, WILHELM. *From Dreyfus to Petain*. New York: Creative Age Press, 1947.

————, ed. *Der Kampf einer Republik: Die Affäre Dreyfus*. Zürich: Europa-Verlag, 1933.

HERZL, THEODOR. "L'Affaire Dreyfus: reportages et réflexions traduits par Léon Vogel." Paris: Imp. des Deux Artisans, 1958.

Hubert, Renée Riese. *The Dreyfus Affair and the French Novel*. Cambridge, Mass.: n.p. 1951.

Huch, R. K. "British Reactions to the Dreyfus Affair," *Social Science*, L, No. 1 (1975): 22–28.

Jussem-Wilson, Nelly. "L'Affaire Jeanne d'Arc et l'Affaire Dreyfus: Péguy et 'Notre Jeunesse,' " *Revue d'histoire littéraire de la France*, LXII (1962): 400–415.

———. "Péguy et l'Affaire Dreyfus." Thesis, Sorbonne, 1958.

———. See also Wilson, Nelly.

Kedward, H. Roderick. *The Dreyfus Affair*. New York: Harper & Row, 1965.

Kohler, Max J. "Some New Light on the Dreyfus Case." Vienna: n.p., 1929.

Lacroix, Sigismond. "Récit rétrospectif," *Le Radical*, June 15, 1901, p. 1. Recalls panic over possible coup in October 1898.

Lagardelle, Hubert. "Le Socialisme et l'Affaire Dreyfus," *Mouvement socialiste*, I, Nos. 3, 5 (February 15, March 15, 1899): 155–66, 285–99.

Lanoux, Armand. "Accusé Zola, levez-vous!" In Gilbert Guilleminault, ed. *Le Roman vrai de la Troisième République*. Paris: Denoël, 1956, I: 111–215.

Larkin, Maurice. *Church and State After the Dreyfus Affair*. New York: Harper & Row, 1974.

Launay, Michel. "Jaurès, la Sorbonne et l'affaire Dreyfus," *Bulletin de la Société d'études jaurèsiennes*, VIII, No. 26 (1967): 14–19.

Lecanuet, Edouard. *L'Eglise de France sous la IIIe République*. Vol. III: *Les Signes avant-coureurs de la Séparation*. Paris: Alcan, 1930, pp. 132–97.

Lewis, David L. *Prisoners of Honor: The Dreyfus Affair*. New York: Morrow, 1973.

Librairie Antisémite (Paris). "Catalogue des ouvrages antisémites, antimaçonniques et nationalistes que l'on trouve à la Librairie antisémite." (Paris, 1900).

Lorenzi, Stellio. and Arnand Lanoux. *Zola ou la conscience humaine*. Four-part French television dramatization, c. 1978.

Louzon, Robert. "La faillité du dreyfusisme ou le Triomphe du parti juif," *Mouvement socialiste*, VIII, No. 176 (July 1906): 193–99.

Maitron, Jean. *Le Mouvement anarchiste en France*. Paris: Maspero, 1975, Vol. I.

Mandell, Richard D. "The Affair and the Fair: Some Observations on the Closing Stages of the Dreyfus Case," *Journal of Modern History* XXXIX, No. 3 (1967): 253–65.

————. *Paris 1900: The Great World's Fair*. Toronto: University of Toronto Press, 1967.

MARRUS, MICHAEL R. "Le comité de Defense contre l'Antisémitisme," in Shlomo Simonsohn and Joseph Shatzmiller, eds. *Michael IV*. Tel Aviv: Diaspora Research Institute, 1976, pp. 163–75.

————. *The Politics of Assimilation: A Study of the French Jewish Community at the Time of the Dreyfus Affair*. Oxford: Clarendon Press, 1971.

MAURIAC, FRANÇOIS. "L'Affaire Dreyfus vue par un enfant," *Revue de Paris* (1962). Also in Alfred Dreyfus. *Cinq années de ma vie*. Paris: Fasquelle, 1962, pp. 11–21.

MAURRAS, CHARLES. *Au signe de Flore: Souvenirs de vie politique, Affaire Dreyfus, la fondation de l'Action Française, 1898–1900*. Paris: Les Oeuvres Représentatives, 1931.

MITCHELL, ALLAN. "The Xenophobic Style: French Counterespionage and the Emergence of the Dreyfus Affair," to be published in *The Journal of Modern History*, 1980.

MOODY, JOSEPH N. "Dreyfus and After." In John M. Oesterreicher, ed. *Bridge II*. New York: Pantheon, 1956, pp. 160–87.

MUN, ALBERT DE. Letters to *The Times*, January 11 and 29, 1899. In Albert de Mun. *Discours*. Paris: Poussielgue, 1895–1904, VI: 419–36 and VII: 1–12.

————. Speeches in the Chamber of Deputies on the Affair, December 4, 1897; January 13, 1898; and October 25, 1898. In de Mun. *Discours*, VI: 337–49, 395–409.

PARTIN, MALCOLM O. *Waldeck-Rousseau, Combes and the Church, 1899–1905*. Durham, N.C.: Duke University Press, 1969.

PÉGUY, CHARLES. "Notes politiques et sociales," *Les Cahiers de l'Amitié Charles Péguy*, No. 11 (February 2, 1957). Eleven 1899 articles about the Affair from *La Revue blanche*.

PETER, JEAN-PIERRE. "Dimensions de l'Affaire Dreyfus," *Annales: Economies, Sociétés, Civilisations*, XVI, No. 6 (November–December 1961): 1141–67.

PIART, ROBERT. "La Presse régionale au sommet de l'Affaire Dreyfus." Thesis, Diplome des Etudes Supérieures, Lille, 1959.

PIERRARD, PIERRE. *Juifs et catholiques français: De Drumont à Jules Isaac (1886–1945)*. Paris: (Fayard, 1970).

PONTY, JANINE. "La France devant l'affaire Dreyfus: Contribution à une étude sociale d'opinion publique." Thesis, 3d cycle, Ecole Pratique des Hautes Etudes, 1971.

————. "*Le Petit Journal* et l'affaire Dreyfus (1897–1899): analyse de contenu," *Revue d'histoire moderne et contemporaine*, XXIV (1977): 641–56.

———. "La Presse quotidienne et l'affaire Dreyfus en 1898–1899: Essai de typologie," *Revue d'histoire moderne et contemporaine*, XXI (1974): 193–220.

RADZIWILL, PRINCESS MARIE. *Lettres de la princesse Radziwill au Général du Robilant, 1889–1914*. Bologna: Zanichelli, 1933, Vol. II.

RANC, ARTHUR. "M. Cavaignac," *Le Radical*, May 15, 1903, p. 1. Recalls embattled band of Dreyfusards and Cavaignac's effort to arrest them.

———. *Souvenirs—correspondence, 1831–1908*. Paris: Cornély, 1913.

REBÉRIOUX, MADELEINE. *La République radicale? 1898–1914*. Paris: Editions du Seuil (1975), pp. 3–41, 157–89.

———. "Histoire, historiens et dreyfusisme," *Revue historique*, CCLV, No. 2 (1976): 407–32.

RIOUX, J.-P. *Nationalisme et conservatisme: La Ligue de la patrie française, 1899–1904*. Paris: Editions Beauschesne, 1977.

RUTKOFF, PETER M. "The Ligue des Patriotes: The Nature of the Radical Right and the Dreyfus Affair," *French Historical Studies*, VIII (1974): 584–603.

SÉE, HENRI. *Histoire de la Ligue des droits de l'homme (1898–1926)*. Paris: Ligue des droits de l'homme, 1927.

SILVERA, ALAIN. *Daniel Halévy and His Times*. Ithaca, N.Y.: Cornell University Press, 1966.

SMITH, ROBERT J. "L'Atmosphère politique à l'Ecole normale supérieure à la fin du XIXe siècle," *Revue d'histoire moderne et contemporaine*, XX (1973): 248–68.

———. "The Ecole Normale Supérieure in the Third Republic: A Study of the Classes of 1890–1904." Ph.D. dissertation, history, University of Pennsylvania, 1967.

SNYDER, LOUIS, ed. *The Dreyfus Case: A Documentary History*. New Brunswick, N.J.: Rutgers University Press (1973).

SORLIN, PIERRE. *"La Croix" et les Juifs (1880–1899)*. Paris: Grasset, 1967.

———. *Waldeck-Rousseau*. Paris: Colin, 1966.

STEEVENS, GEORGE WARRINGTON. *The Tragedy of Dreyfus*. New York and London: Harper, 1899.

STERNHELL, ZEEV. *La Droite révolutionnaire 1885–1914*. Paris: Editions du Seuil, 1978.

THALHEIMER, SIEGRIED. *Macht und Gerichtigkeit: Ein Beitrag zur Geschichte des Falles Dreyfus*. Munich: Beck, 1958.

THIBAUDET, ALBERT. "Réflexions," *Nouvelle revue française*, XXXV (1930): 871–78, XXXVI (1931): 580–92, XXXIX (1932): 265–72. Recalls combat in the Affair.

VIAU, RAPHAËL. *Vingt ans d'antisémitisme*. Paris: Fasquelle, 1910.

WATSON, D. R. "The Nationalist Movement in Paris, 1900–1906." In David Shapiro, ed. *The Right in France, 1890–1919*. London: Chatto & Windus, 1962, pp. 49–84.

WEBER, EUGEN. "Jews, Antisemitism, and the Origins of the Holocaust," *Historical Reflections*, V, No. 1 (1978): 1–17.

———. "The Secret World of Jean Barois." In John Weiss, ed. *The Origins of Modern Consciousness*. Detroit: Wayne State University Press, 1965, pp. 79–109.

WEINER, ROBERT I. "Paul Cambon and the Dreyfus Affair, A Case Study," *Proceedings, Western Society for French History*, II (1974): 227–43.

WESSELING, H. L. "Engagement tegen wil en dank: Franse intellectuelen en Dreyfus-affaire," *Tijdschrift voor Geschiedenis*, Vol. LXXXVII (1974).

WILLARD, CLAUDE. "Le P. O. F., l'affaire Dreyfus et l'entente socialiste." In Claude Willard. *Les Guesdistes*. Paris: Editions Sociales, 1965, pp. 410–21.

WILSON, NELLY. *Bernard-Lazare: Antisemitism and the Problem of Jewish Identity in Late Nineteenth Century France*. Cambridge: Cambridge University Press, 1978. See also Jussem-Wilson, Nelly.

WILSON, STEPHEN. "The Antisemitic Riots of 1898 in France," *Historical Journal*, XVI (1973): 789–806.

———. "Antisemitism and Jewish Response in France During the Dreyfus Affair," *European Studies Review*, VI, No. 2 (1976): 225–48.

———. "Catholic Populism in France at the Time of the Dreyfus Affair: The *Union Nationale*," *Journal of Contemporary History*, X (1975): 667–706.

———. "The Ligue Antisémitique Française," *Wiener Library Bulletin*, XXV, No. 3/4 (1972): 33–39.

———. "Le Monument Henry: La Structure de l'antisémitisme en France 1898–1899," *Annales: Economies, Sociétés, Civilisations*, XXXII, No. 2 (1977): 265–91.

———. "Proust's 'A la recherche du temps perdu' as a Document of Social History," *Journal of European Studies*, I (1971): 213–43.

WISTRICH, ROBERT S. "French Socialism and the Dreyfus Affair," *Wiener Library Bulletin*, XXVII, No. 35/36 (1975): 9–20.

ZEVAÈS, ALEXANDRE. "L'Affaire Dreyfus: Quelques souvenirs personnels," *La Nouvelle revue*, Series 4 (1936), CXLI: 197–208, 287–96; CXLII: 45–53, 96–104.

Index

237

DATE DUE